Natural Ventilation in the Urban Environment

Assessment and Design

BUILDINGS | ENERGY | SOLAR TECHNOLOGY

Natural Ventilation in the Urban Environment

Assessment and Design

Edited by Cristian Ghiaus and Francis Allard

Series Editor M. Santamouris

London • Sterling, VA

First published by Earthscan in the UK and USA in 2005

ISBN: 1-84407-129-4 hardback

Typesetting by MapSet Ltd, Gateshead, UK
Printed and bound in the UK by Bath Press, Bath
Cover design by Paul Cooper

For a full list of publications please contact:

Earthscan
8–12 Camden High Street
London, NW1 0JH, UK
Tel: +44 (0)20 7387 8558
Fax: +44 (0)20 7387 8998
Email: earthinfo@earthscan.co.uk
Web: **www.earthscan.co.uk**

22883 Quicksilver Drive, Sterling, VA 20166-2012, USA

Earthscan is an imprint of James and James (Science Publishers) Ltd and publishes in
association with the International Institute for Environment and Development

A catalogue record for this book is available from the British Library

Library of Congress Cataloging-in-Publication Data has been applied for

This book is printed on elemental chlorine free paper

Contents

List of Figures and Tables

FIGURES

TABLES

List of Contributors and Reviewers

CONTRIBUTORS

Francis Allard (LEPTAB, Université de La Rochelle)

Manuela Almeida (IDMEC, University of Porto)

Patrice Blondeau (LEPTAB, Université de La Rochelle)

Chrissa Georgakis (University of Athens)

Mario Germano (LESO-PB, École Polytechnique Fédérale de Lausanne)

Cristian Ghiaus (LEPTAB, Université de La Rochelle)

Gérard Guarracino (Ecole Nationale des Travaux Publics de l'Etat ENTPE, URA CNRS)

Vlad Iordache (LEPTAB, Université de La Rochelle)

Eduardo Maldonado (IDMEC, University of Porto)

Fergus Nicol (LEARN, School of Architecture, London Metropolitan University)

Liam Roche (Building Research Establishment)

Claude-Alain Roulet (LESO-PB, Ecole Polytechnique Fédérale de Lausanne)

Mateos Santamouris (University of Athens)

John Shelton (LEARN, School of Architecture, London Metropolitan University)

John Solomon (LEARN, School of Architecture, London Metropolitan University)

Michael Wilson (LEARN, School of Architecture, London Metropolitan University)

REVIEWERS

Nicolas Heijmans (Belgian Building Research Institute) (Chapters 2, 7, 8, 10)

Liam Roche (Building Research Establishment) (Chapters 1, 2, 10)

Frank Tillemkamp (Axima AG Axima Lab) (Chapters 3, 4, 5, 6, 9, 10, 11)

Foreword

This book is the work of the teams involved in the European project 'URBVENT: Natural Ventilation in the Urban Environment', which has been carried out as part of the Fifth Research and Development Programme of the Directorate for Science, Research and Development of the European Commission. This project was coordinated by Francis Allard and Cristian Ghiaus from the University of La Rochelle, France. The assistance of Dr George Deschamps, the manager of the programme, and Professor Mordechai Sokolov, external expert of the European Commission, is highly appreciated.

The URBVENT project aimed to create a methodology, embedded in software, to assess the potential and feasibility of, and to design optimal openings for, natural ventilation in the urban environment, accessible to architects, designers and decision-makers. The methodology and the tools have been tested in three stages by the developers, the end-users and the project integrator. This book provides knowledge, tools and information on the efficient use of natural ventilation in urban buildings in order to decrease energy consumption for cooling purposes, increase indoor thermal comfort and improve indoor air quality.

The book includes contributions from the whole URBVENT consortium. The writing of each chapter followed the same philosophy as the project as a whole: drafting, reviewing and editing. The people involved in each process were different and each of their contributions are important.

The first chapter is an introduction, drafted by Mat Santamouris and reviewed by Liam Roche, presenting the importance of natural ventilation technologies for urban buildings in order to prove that, although it is not an energy 'machine', natural ventilation is an effective engine for progress and development.

Chapter 2, drafted by Claude-Alain Roulet and reviewed by Liam Roche and Nicholas Heijmans, describes the role of natural ventilation in indoor air quality, reduction of energy consumption and comfort.

Chapter 3, which was written by Cristian Ghiaus and Francis Allard, introduces the reader to the physics of natural ventilation. It is organized into three main sections: the basics of fluid dynamics, the atmospheric boundary layer and the modelling of air flows in buildings.

Chapters 4, 5 and 6 address the relationship between urban environment and natural ventilation. Reduced wind velocity, higher temperatures due to heat island effect, noise and pollution are considered as barriers to the application of natural ventilation in the urban environment. Models based on first-hand experience acquired within the URBVENT project and in a related project financed by the French government (the PRIMEQUAL programme) are presented.

Chapter 4, drafted by Chrissa Georgakis and Mat Santamouris and reviewed by Frank Tillenkamp, presents the wind and temperature in street canyons. It is based on experiments achieved in Athens.

Chapter 5 was written by Michael Wilson, Fergus Nicol, John Solomon and John Shelton and was reviewed by Frank Tillenkamp. The chapter explores the problem of noise reduction in street canyons. The results are derived from experiments carried out in the same streets as the wind and temperature measurements.

Chapter 6 provides information about outdoor–indoor pollution transfer as a function of building permeability and outdoor pollutant concentration. It was authored by Cristian Ghiaus, Vlad Iordache, Francis Allard and Patrice Blondeau, and Frank Tillenkamp carried out a review.

Chapter 7, drafted by Cristian Ghiaus and Claude-Alain Roulet and reviewed by Nicholas Heijmans, presents the strategies for natural ventilation and gives the order of magnitude for pressure difference and airflow rate.

Chapter 8 describes specific devices for the use of natural ventilation. Examples of the various technologies and some examples of their application are given: from operable windows to stacks, self-regulating vents and fan-assisted natural ventilation. Claude-Alain Roulet and Cristian Ghiaus are the authors of this chapter, and Nicholas Heijmans reviewed their work.

Chapter 9 was drafted by Manuela Almeida, Eduardo Maldonado, Mateo Santamouris and Gérard Guarracino, and describes the methodology used to obtain a database of airflow and air change rates as a function of ventilation strategy used (single-sided or stack-induced) and the position, form and dimensions of the openings. This database can be used as it is for finding the optimal opening for a known flow rate. Alternatively, a neuro-fuzzy model was developed to find the optimal opening when the ventilation strategy and airflow rate are given.

Chapter 10 introduces an original method for evaluating natural ventilation potential, which was developed as part of the URBVENT project by Mario Germano, Cristian Ghiaus and Claude-Alain Roulet. A review of the method and of the chapter was carried out by Frank Tillenkamp, Nicholas Heijmans and Liam Roche. The natural ventilation potential (NVP) is expressed by the probability of ensuring an acceptable indoor air quality using only natural ventilation. Ensuring an acceptable indoor air quality or cooling down the building structure using natural ventilation depends upon the site (outdoor air quality, temperature, wind, moisture and noise, urban structure, etc.) and upon the building (indoor pollutant, heat sources and stored heat, position and size of ventilation openings, orientation of building, internal air path distribution, etc.). The NVP cannot, therefore, be expressed as a single number. It is a multiple attribute variable – that is, a list of quantitative and qualitative characteristics of the site and of the building, based on available input data. It is, nevertheless, possible to decide, on the basis of these characteristics combined with the requirements, if a given building – or a room in a building – is likely to be sufficiently ventilated or not when natural ventilation is used. The method is based on two paradigm shifts. The first, applied to the site, is a qualitative comparison of existing experience representing the quantification and formalization of qualitative thinking. The second, applied to the building, is based on the concept of free-running temperature and uses a modifiable database to estimate the potential for cooling by ventilation and the possible role of stack-driven ventilation.

Chapter 11, drafted by Cristian Ghiaus and Liam Roche, presents an analysis of the whole-life costs of ventilation options.

This book is the result of common effort and contributions of the consortium of the URBVENT project. The participants in this project were:

- Francis Allard and Cristian Ghiaus, LEPTAB (Building Physics Laboratory), University of de La Rochelle, France;
- Mat Santamouris and Chrissa Georgakis, Group of Building Environmental Physics, University of Athens, Greece;
- Claude-Alain Roulet and Mario Germano, École Polytechnique Fédérale de Lausanne, Switzerland;
- Frank Tillenkamp and Joachim Borth, Axima Lab, Switzerland;
- Nicholas Heijmans, Belgian Building Research Institute, Belgium;
- Fergus Nicol and Michael Wilson, London Metropolitan University, UK;
- Eduardo Maldonado and Manuela Almeida, IDMEC, University of Porto, Portugal;
- Gérard Guarracino, CNRS/LASH-ENTPE, France;
- Liam Roche, Philippa Westbury and Paul Littlefair, Building Research Establishment, UK.

We would also like to acknowledge the contribution of James Axley from Yale University, US, who provided comments and suggestions during his sabbatical year spent at the University of La Rochelle, France.

Cristian Ghiaus and Francis Allard
March 2005

List of Acronyms and Abbreviations

°C	degrees Celsius
ACH	air changes per hour
AR	aspect ratio
BBRI	Belgian Building Research Institute
BRE	Building Research Establishment (UK)
CFD	computational fluid dynamics
clo	Unit for the thermal resistance of clothing; 1 clo = 0.15 m^2K/W
cm	centimetre
CO	carbon monoxide
CO_2	carbon dioxide
Cal PX	California Power Exchange
CSTB	Centre Scientifique et Technique de Bâtiment
dB	decibel
DT	temperature difference between the outside and inside environment
ESDU	Engineering Sciences Data Unit
ETI	Hungarian Institute of Building Science
FAR	frontal aspect ratio
GNP	gross national product
GW	gigawatt
ha	hectare
HOPE	Health Optimization Protocol for Energy-Efficient Buildings project
HVAC	heating, ventilation and air conditioning
I/O	indoor–outdoor pollutant ratio
IAQ	indoor air quality
ISO	International Organization for Standardization
J	joule, unit of energy
K	Kelvin, unit of temperature
kg	kilogram
km	kilometre
km/h	kilometres per hour
LDC	less developed country
LM	Lokal-Modell
LPE	Swiss environment protection law
m	metre
m/s	metres per second

m^2	square metres
m^3	cubic metres
m^3/h	cubic metres per hour
met	unit of metabolism, 1 met = 58 W/m^2 body area
MeteoSwiss	Swiss Federal Office of Meteorology and Climatology
mm	millimetre
MW	megawatt
MWh	megawatt hour
NO_2	nitrogen dioxide
NPL	neutral pressure level
NVP	natural ventilation potential
O_3	ozone
OECD	Organisation for Economic Co-operation and Development
Pa	Pascal, unit of pressure
PAD	plan area density
PCP	passive cooling potential
PDEC	passive downdraught evaporative cooling
PM	particle matter
PMV	predicted mean vote
ppb	parts per billion
ppm	parts per million
RH	relative humidity
RbH	relative building height
s	second
SAR	side aspect ratio
SCATS	Smart Controls and Thermal Comfort
SO_2	sulphur dioxide
TWh	terawatt hour
toe	tonnes of oil equivalent
UK	United Kingdom
URBVENT	Natural Ventilation in the Urban Environment
US	United States
VOC	volatile organic component
W	Watt, unit of power
W/m^2	watt per square metre. For thermal comfort, the area is the body area
WHO	World Health Organization

1

Energy in the Urban Built Environment: The Role of Natural Ventilation

Mat Santamouris

INTRODUCTION

During the second half of the last century, the world's urban population has increased tremendously. In the 1950s, there were no more than 200 million urban residents; but by the end of the century their total number was close to 3 billion and it is expected to increase to approximately 5 billion by 2025 (UNFPA, 1998). Migration to cities has primarily occurred, and will continue to happen, in the so-called less developed countries as the result of increased economic and social opportunities offered in urban areas and the degradation of rural economies and societies.

The growth rate of the urban population is much faster than that of the rural one. It is reported that almost 80 per cent of the world's population growth between 1990 and 2010 will be in cities, and most probably in Africa, Asia and Latin America (UN, 1998). Put simply, 60 million urban citizens are added to the population every year, which, as mentioned by UNEPTIE (1991), 'is the equivalent of adding another Paris, Beijing or Cairo every other month'.

The extremely rapid urbanization has resulted in the dramatic increase in size of urban agglomerations. According to the United Nations (UNCHS, 2001), our planet hosts 19 cities with 10 million or more people, 22 cities with 5–10 million people, 370 cities with 1–5 million people and 433 cities with 0.5–1 million people. This has led to extremely serious environmental, social, political, economic, institutional, demographic and cultural problems. A detailed discussion of the problems is given in Santamouris (2003). In developed countries, the more important problems include over-consumption of resources, particularly energy; increased air pollution, primarily from motor vehicles; heat island and increase in ambient temperature because of the positive heat balance in cities; noise pollution; and solid waste management. On the other hand, poverty, environmental degradation, lack of sanitation and other urban services, and lack of access to land and adequate shelters are among the more serious issues in developing countries.

Energy consumption defines the quality of urban life and the global environmental quality of cities. Energy is linked with all aspects of development and has a tremendous impact on the well-being of urban citizens: on health, education, productivity, economic opportunities and so on. Unfortunately, the current situation regarding energy supply and consumption is extremely unfair, and wide disparities exist between the developed and the developing world. Almost one third of the world's population has no access to electricity, with another third having only very limited access (WEHAB Working Group, 2002). Although 75 million people gain access to electricity annually, the total number of people lacking electricity does not change (Albouy and Nadifi, 1999). People in the rich parts of the world consume almost 25 times more energy per person than those living in the poorest areas (Albouy and Nadifi, 1999).

Energy is the most important engine to improve quality of life and fight poverty. Given that by 2020 almost 70 per cent of the world's population will be living in cities, and 60 per cent will be below the poverty line, it is estimated by the World Bank (Serageldim and Brown, 1995) that many of the population will be energy poor. Thus, for the next decades, thousands of megawatts of new electrical capacity have to be added. Estimates (Serageldim and Brown, 1995) show that the cost of the new power generation plants over the next 30 years will amount to over US$2 trillion. However, developing countries already pay too much for energy. Citizens in these countries spend 12 per cent of their income on energy services, five times more than the average in Organisation for Economic Co-operation and Development (OECD) countries (Construction Confederation of International Contractors Association, 2002). In parallel, energy imports are one of the major sources of foreign debt. As reported during the Johannesburg summit in 2002 (Saghir, 2002), 'in over 30 countries, energy imports exceed 10 per cent of the value of all exports', while 'in about 20 countries, payments for oil imports exceed those for debt servicing'.

It is thus evident that alternative energy patterns have to be used. The use of renewable sources in combination with energy-efficient technologies could provide the necessary energy supply to the 'energy-poor' proportion of the world's population to improve their quality of life, and could make a significant contribution to reducing over-consumption of resources in the developed countries. A recent study by Lawrence Berkeley Laboratory (Der Petrossian, 1999) shows that developing countries could avoid having to spend US$1.7 trillion on oil refineries, coal mines and new power plants by spending US$10 billion annually for the next 30 years to improve energy efficiency and conservation. Another estimate by the US Office of Technology Assessment shows that developing counties have the potential to halve their electricity production if energy is used more effectively.

Ventilation and, in particular, natural ventilation is one of these technologies. Natural ventilation should not be seen just as an alternative to air conditioning. This is a very arrogant approach as it is true for only a tiny part of the world population. Natural ventilation is a more effective instrument to improve indoor air quality in urban areas, to protect health, to provide thermal comfort and to reduce unnecessary energy consumption.

This chapter aims to present, in a global way, the importance of natural ventilation technologies for urban buildings. An attempt is made to document its impact on energy, indoor air quality and thermal comfort, and to prove that natural ventilation, although not an energy 'machine', is an effective engine for progress and development.

ENERGY AND URBAN BUILDINGS

The impact of the construction sector

Construction is one of the most important economic sectors by far. It is estimated that the total world annual output for construction is close to US$3000 billion, which constitutes almost one tenth of the global economy (Leitman, 1991). About 30 per cent of this capital is from Europe, 22 per cent from the US, 21 per cent from Japan, 23 per cent from developing countries and 4 per cent from the rest of the developed countries.

Construction represents more than 50 per cent of national capital investment and, with more than 111 million employees, it accounts for almost 7 per cent of total global employment and 28 per cent of global industrial employment. However, given that every job in the construction sector generates two new jobs in the global economy, it can be said that the construction sector is directly or indirectly linked to almost 20 per cent of global employment (Leitman, 1991).

In parallel, almost one sixth of the world's major resources are consumed by the construction sector (Bitan, 1992). Buildings consume almost 40 per cent of the world's energy, 16 per cent of the world's freshwater and 25 per cent of forest timber (LRC, 1993), while they are responsible for almost 70 per cent of sulphur oxide and 50 per cent of carbon dioxide emissions (Bitan, 1992).

Energy and urbanization

Recent urbanization has put the emphasis on urban buildings. Urban buildings differ from rural buildings with regard to economy, society, energy and environment. In particular (ICLEI, 1993):

- There are many specific environmental problems in cities of both developed and less developed countries that do not occur in non-urban areas.
- The energy consumption per capita in cities is higher than in rural areas.

- Cities have a serious environmental, economic and social impact on suburban and rural areas.
- As the economic growth rate in cities is much higher than in rural areas, the demand for energy is increasing and environmental problems are accelerating.

Urbanization has a dramatic effect on energy consumption. As reported by IBGE (1993), a 1 per cent increase in the per capita gross national product (GNP) leads to an almost equal (1.03 per cent) increase in energy consumption. However, an increase of 1 per cent in the urban population increases energy consumption by 2.2 per cent (i.e. the rate of change in energy use is twice the rate of change in urbanization).

Comparison of the energy consumption per capita for the inner and outer parts of selected cities shows that the consumption in the inner part is considerably higher. For example, inner London presents 30 per cent higher energy consumption per capita than the outer part of the city (WEC, 1993). There are also many examples from developing countries showing that urban citizens consume more. For example, urban dwellers in five principle cities of Senegal consume 265kg of oil equivalent per person annually, compared with 110kg for rural dwellers (ICLEI, 1993).

Buildings are the largest energy consumers in cities. Data on the energy consumption of various European cities (Bose, 1990; WEC, 1993; Stanners and Bourdeau, 1995) show that the end-use energy consumption of the residential sector varies from 48 per cent in Copenhagen to 28 per cent in Hanover. At the same time, buildings in the commercial sector account for between 20 and 30 per cent of the final energy consumption of the cities.

Data from developing countries show almost the same tendency. Although detailed data on energy consumption for buildings are not available, reports from eight major developing countries, representing a very high percentage of the total energy consumption, show that the building sector accounts for almost 21 per cent of energy needs without taking into account electricity (Rees, 2001a). Another study for Delhi indicates that the housing sector is by far the most important consumer of fuel and accounts alone for over 60 per cent of gross energy use (Rees, 2001b)

Energy characteristics of urban buildings in developed countries

Energy and environmental problems have completely different characteristics in cities of the developed nations compared with those of less developed nations. The main problems of cities in the developed world are the consumption of energy and resources that exceed their natural production, and the production of degraded energy, wastes and pollution at levels greater than the assimilative capacity of the ecosphere can cope with. By contrast, poverty and the lack of the necessary infrastructures to ensure the health and well-being of all citizens are the main problems in cities of less developed countries.

Over-consumption of resources is a major problem for cities in the developed world. It is characteristic that an average European city with 1 million inhabitants consumes 11,500 tonnes of fossil fuels, 320,000 tonnes of water and 2000 tonnes of food every day. It also produces 300,000 tonnes of wastewater, 25,000 tonnes of carbon dioxide and 1600 tonnes of waste (Wackernagel et al, 1997). A very good index to demonstrate the level of consumption in cities is the so-called 'ecological footprint'. The ecological footprint of a population group 'is the area of land and water required to produce the resources consumed, and to assimilate the wastes generated by the population on a continuous basis, wherever on Earth that land is located' (Wackernagel et al, 1999). Although there are only 1.5ha of ecologically productive land and about 0.5ha of truly productive ocean for every person on Earth (CEC, 1995), the ecological footprint of wealthy countries is up to 10ha per capita, while people in the less developed countries have footprints of less than 1ha (Adnot, 2001; ESS, 2001).

Buildings in cities of the developed world use energy for heating, cooling, lighting and electrical equipment. In Europe, most of the energy spent in the building sector is for space heating – 70 per cent of the total energy consumption for domestic buildings and 55 per cent for commercial and office buildings – followed by electrical appliances and hot water production (Besant-Jones and Tenenbaum, 2001). However, important discrepancies are observed from country to country as a function of the existing living standards. For example, very important differences in housing floor space per person exist in Europe because of the social and economic differences. Moscow has 11.6 square metres net living space per person, while Paris has 28.2, Oslo 47.2 and Zurich 50.6 square metres per person (Wackernagel et al, 1997).

Although energy consumption for heating purposes has been stabilized during the last years as a result of intensive energy conservation measures, the specific energy needs for cooling have increased in a dramatic way. The increase of family income in developed countries has made the use of these systems highly popular. In Europe the main market for cooling and air conditioning systems is, for the moment, in the commercial sector with a total turnover of 8000 million Euros. Almost 6 per cent of office, commercial and industry buildings are cooled, which gives a total volume of about 20 million cubed metres (Boardman, 1991). According to estimates, by 2010 the volume of air conditioned buildings could even be four times larger.

In the US, the penetration of air conditioning is extremely high. More than 3.5 billion square metres of commercial buildings are cooled. The total cooling energy consumption for the commercial sector is close to 250 terawatt hours (TWh) per year, while the necessary peak power demand for summer cooling of commercial buildings is close to 109 gigawatts (GW).

The impact of air conditioners' usage on electricity demand is a serious problem for almost all countries. Peak electricity loads oblige utilities to build additional plants in order to satisfy the demand, thus increasing the average cost of electricity. In Europe, southern countries face a very important increase in their peak electricity load mainly because of the very rapid penetration of

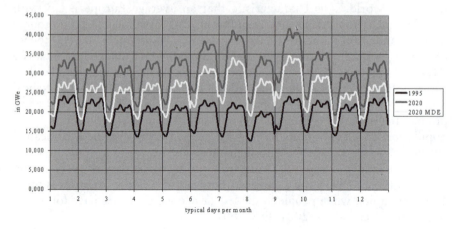

Source: Jacobs, 1996

Figure 1.1 *Load curves for 1995 and 2020 in Spain*

air conditioning. Italy faced very serious electricity problems during the summer of 2003 because of the high electricity demand of air conditioners. Actual load curves as well as the foreseen evolution of the peak electricity load in Spain are shown in Figure 1.1. As depicted, an extremely high increase in the peak load is expected, which may necessitate doubling of the installed power.

The extremely high peak demand for air conditioning was also one of the main reasons that the California energy system collapsed in 2002. As mentioned in UNCHS (1997), the demand for electricity in the summer months of 2002 was increased by air conditioning loads because of the highest temperatures recorded for 106 years. As a result of the heat wave and the corresponding increase in the electricity demand, the supply started to fall below demand. This caused the electricity prices in California to rocket. While for 1998–1999 and the first months of 2000 the market clearing price in the day-ahead California Power Exchange (Cal PX) was between US$25 and US$50 per megawatt hour (MWh), it increased to US$150/MWh during the summer months of 2000 (UNCHS, 1997).

Future projections on the energy consumption of buildings in developed nations foresee a small increase. This is mainly due to predicted increases in the quality of life that permit lower revenue classes to spend more energy, to the rapid penetration of air conditioning and to an increase in the number of buildings and the amount of space allocated per person. It has been said that in the UK alone, there are at least 8 million homes that are inadequately heated, most being the dwellings of poor households (Cairncross, 1990; IEA, 2001). In addition, it is estimated that the number of households in Europe will increase from 262.5 million in 1990 to 328.2 million in 2025 (Cairncross, 1990).

Energy characteristics of urban buildings in less developed countries

The tremendous increase in the world's population and in urbanization is the main source for the continuous increase of energy demand in the less developed countries (LDCs). Although the current consumption of LDCs represents almost one third of that of the OECD countries, it is expected to reach the same figures by 2015 (ICLEI, 1993). However, in absolute terms the energy consumption per capita remains very low compared to rich countries. Since almost 2.5 billion people live on less than US$2 a day, most of them (2.3 billion) rely mainly on biomass to satisfy their energy needs, while roughly one quarter of the world's population do not have electricity (Serageldim et al, 1995).

The buildings sector is the major consumer of energy in less developed countries. The share of at least the residential sector has increased from 22.2 per cent to 34.4 per cent during 1987–1997 (Nordberg, 1999). Construction activities in LDCs amount to approximately US$400 billion annually (Bitan, 1992) and increases by about US$20 billion every year. The estimated percentage of less developed countries in the activities of world construction has increased considerably during recent years, from about 10 per cent in 1965 to about 29 per cent in 1998.

Despite the increase of the budget devoted to construction, as estimated by the United Nations (Birol, 2002), more than 1 billion urban citizens live in inadequate housing – primarily in squatted and slum settlements – while in most LDC cities, between one third and two-thirds of the population live in poor-quality and overcrowded housing (World Bank, 2001), with insufficient water supply, inadequate or no sanitation, inappropriate waste collection, no electricity and energy networks, and housing under the risk of flooding and other environmental phenomena (Barnes and Halpern, 2002).

Construction in less developed countries has to deal with the specific economic situation. Since compliance with existing building codes makes construction expensive and, thus, not affordable for the majority of people, official building permits are rarely obtained and it is estimated that only rich households, which represent 10 per cent of the population, can afford houses that meet local building codes (Barnes and Halpern, 2002).

Absolute energy consumption, as well as the type of fuels used by urban households in LDCs, is a strong function of their economic status. Poor people consume less costly and less convenient fuels; as income rises, more expensive and highly convenient types of energy are used. This is known as the 'energy ladder'. Studies have shown that households are able to switch over to modern fuels when their incomes reach US$1000–$1500 (UNCED, 1992). A recent study in 45 cities of some less developed countries (World Bank, 1995) showed that lower-income households consume less energy, while they make use of less convenient energy sources such as wood and charcoal (see Table 1.1).

In many countries, important economic barriers make access to modern fuels very difficult. Almost US$600 has to be paid as a connection fee to the

Table 1.1 *Fuel use in 45 cities as a function of ease of access to electricity*

Access to electricity in city	Average monthly household income (US$)	Average population (thousands)	Wood	Charcoal	Kerosene	LPG	Electricity
Percentage of households using fuel							
Very difficult	33	23	56.4	73.4	57.6	26.6	21.1
Difficult	67	124	72.3	33.5	65.2	21.8	42.8
Easy	62	514	24.1	62.7	50.4	21.6	47.7
Very easy	77	1153	22.1	34.5	42.6	47.8	90.5
Fuel use (kg of oil equivalent per capita per month)							
Very difficult	33	23	1.31	10.09	0.35	1.49	0.24
Difficult	67	174	7.27	2.54	0.46	0.91	1.24
Easy	62	514	2.83	7.20	1.10	0.50	2.00
Very easy	77	1.153	1.71	1.75	1.75	2.00	2.79

Source: World Bank, 1995

electricity grid, which is far beyond the means of the urban poor (World Bank, 1995). This has a serious impact on household expenditures and income, quality of life and health. It is estimated that the necessary investments to bring clean energy technologies to the urban areas of LDCs amount to almost US$40 billion annually (1992 values) (Lampietti and Meyer, 2002).

The cost of energy, as well as its share in total expenditures, varies as a function of economic status. The poorest 20 per cent of households spend almost 15 to 22 per cent of their monthly income on energy. As shown in Figure 1.2, the lower the income, the higher the share of energy expenditures.

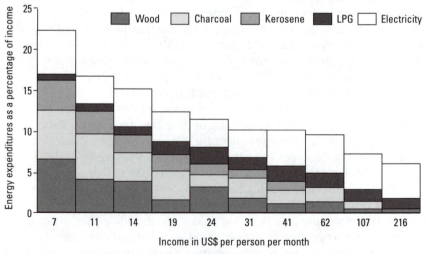

Source: Wallace, 1987; Sherman and Matson, 2003

Figure 1.2 *Energy expenditure as a percentage of income*

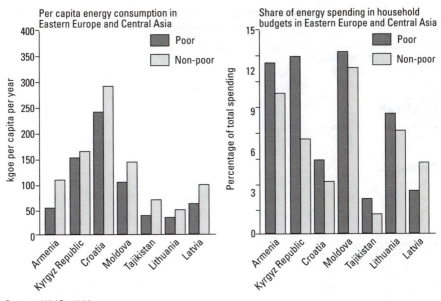

Source: WHO, 1999

Figure 1.3 *Per capita energy consumption and share of energy spending in household budgets in Eastern Europe and Central Asia*

A similar situation also exists in economies in transition (see Figure 1.3), and in some countries of the developed world such as the UK, where the lowest quintile of the population spends almost 6.6 per cent of the monthly income for energy, while the corresponding percentage for the highest quintile is close to 2 per cent.

It is evident that the specific energy situation in LDCs has a very serious impact on quality of life, comfort and the global environment. The following section discusses aspects related to energy, indoor air and health.

INDOOR AIR POLLUTION IN URBAN BUILDINGS: A REAL THREAT FOR MOST OF THE WORLD'S POPULATION

The indoor environmental quality of urban buildings is seriously affected by the concentration of harmful pollutants in the indoor environment. The sources of indoor pollutants are human activity, outdoor pollution and the presence of products and materials that emit a large variety of compounds. In developed countries, concentrations of indoor pollutants are very similar to those outdoors, with the ratio of indoor to outdoor concentration falling in the range of 0.7–1.3. However, the concentration of indoor pollutants may be two to five times higher than outdoor pollutants (WHO, 1999). According to United Nations Centre for Human Settlements, indoor air quality is inadequate in 30 per cent of the buildings around the world (LRC, 1993).

Table 1.2 *Particle concentrations and exposures in the eight major global microenvironments*

Region	Concentrations Indoor ($\mu g/m^3$)[1]	Outdoor ($\mu g/m^3$)	Exposures Indoor (per cent)	Outdoor (per cent)	Total (per cent)
Developed					
Urban	100	70	7	1	7
Rural	80	40	2	0	2
Developing					
Urban	250	280	25	9	34
Rural	400	70	52	5	57
		Total (per cent) =	86	14	100

Note: 1 microgram per cubic metre ($\mu g/m3$)
Source: Smith, 1994

Three basic strategies that may be used separately or in combination are proposed in order to reduce occupant exposure to indoor contaminants:

1   building air-tightening and pressure management;
2   ventilation and air filtration; and
3   contaminant removal (World Bank, 2000a and b).

Because of high outdoor pollution and the nature of human activities, indoor air quality problems in the urban buildings of developed countries are much more significant than in rural areas. Smith (1994) reports that exposure in the indoor environment to particulate matter is seven times higher in the indoor than in the outdoor environment, while it is 3.5 times higher in urban than in rural areas (see Table 1.2). The higher concentration of pollutants in the rural areas of developing countries is due to the use of biomass as a fuel for cooking and heating.

Indoor air quality (IAQ) in developing countries is an extremely serious problem. While in developed countries IAQ problems arise from low ventilation rates and the emission of building products and materials, the inhabitants of LDCs face problems related to pollutants generated by human activities, particularly as a result of combustion processes through the use of ovens and braziers with imperfect kitchen and stove designs. As reported by Smith (1994): 'Today about half the population of the world continues to rely for cooking and associated space heating on simple household stoves using unprocessed solid fuels that have high emission factors for a range of health-damaging air pollutants.' Compared to modern fuels such as gas, solid fuels produce 10 to 100 times more breathable particulate matter per meal (Smith, 1994). Measurements made in kitchens of homes in India showed particulate levels to be 35 times the 1-hour standard and nearly 100 times the 24-hour standard recommended in industrialized countries (IBGE, 1993).

In parallel, other pollutants, such as carbon monoxide, formaldehyde, polycyclic aromatic hydrocarbons, benzene, and 1,3-butadiene, also reach high concentrations. As reported by the World Health Organization (WHO), in some areas of China and India, the use of coal in houses leads to high indoor concentrations of fluorine and arsenic with consequent health effects (Smith, 1994).

High indoor concentration of pollutants poses a tremendous health threat to the population of the less developed countries. Worldwide, close to 2 million deaths per year are attributable to indoor air pollution from cooking fires (Serageldim et al, 1995). Recent studies by the WHO have shown that 30 to 40 per cent of 760 million cases of respiratory diseases worldwide are caused by particulate air pollution alone. 'Mostly, these health effects are caused by indoor air pollution due to open stove cooking and heating in developing countries' (WHO, 1997). Studies in Latin America, Asia and Africa have shown that indoor air pollution is also responsible for pregnancy-related problems, such as stillbirths and low birth weight. It has also been associated with blindness (attributed to 18 per cent of cases in India) and immune system depression (Schwela, 1996).

In particular, in India, it is estimated that 500,000 women and children die each year due to indoor air pollution-related causes since almost 75 per cent of the population relies upon traditional biomass fuels (Schwela, 1996). This is close to 25 per cent of the deaths worldwide attributed to indoor air pollution problems.

Other studies increase the number of premature deaths in India because of indoor air pollution problems to 3.3 million per year. Table 1.3 summarizes most of the recent estimates on premature mortality in India due to indoor air pollution problems. The severity of the problem is shown by studies that estimate the burden of disease in India for selected major risk factors and diseases. As shown in Figure 1.4, mortality due to indoor air pollution problems is very high.

It is evident that proper ventilation of urban buildings in these countries, as well as in the developed world, can contribute significantly to reducing the concentration of indoor pollutants and to protecting public health. Given that indoor pollution problems in LDCs primarily affect the poorest sector of the population, the use of advanced ventilation and filtration techniques is not

Table 1.3 *Estimate of annual premature mortality from air pollution in India (thousands of deaths)*

Outdoor exposure (thousands)	Indoor exposure (thousands)	Reference
50–300	850–3300	(IBGE, 1993)
84	590	(Bose, 1990; WEC, 1993)
200	2000	(Stanners and Bordeau, 1995)

Source: adapted from Saksena and Dayal, 1997

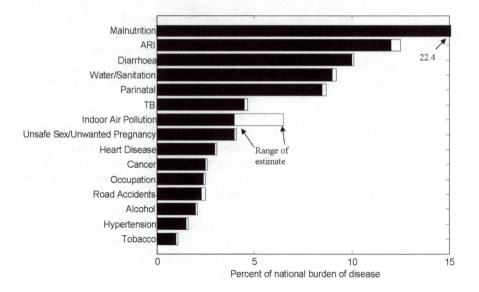

Source: Santamouris and Asimakopoulos, 1987; Saksena and Dayal, 1997; Geros et al, 1999; Geros, 2000; Santamouris, 2001

Figure 1.4 *Estimated burden of disease (DALYs) in India for selected major risk factors and diseases compared with major risk factors from indoor air pollution*

feasible at all. Thus, natural ventilation may be an effective solution if outdoor air quality is less polluted than indoor air quality. The development of appropriate strategies and techniques to enhance natural ventilation in urban buildings may save million of lives in developing countries.

HOW NATURAL VENTILATION CAN IMPROVE THE ENVIRONMENTAL QUALITY OF URBAN BUILDINGS

Natural ventilation is a very important and simple technique that, when appropriately used, may:

- Contribute to fight problems of indoor air quality by decreasing the concentration of indoor pollutants.
- Improve thermal comfort conditions in indoor spaces.
- Decrease the energy consumption of air conditioned buildings.

Conditions that are necessary to achieve these benefits are:

- The concentration of outdoor pollutants is lower than that of indoor pollutants.

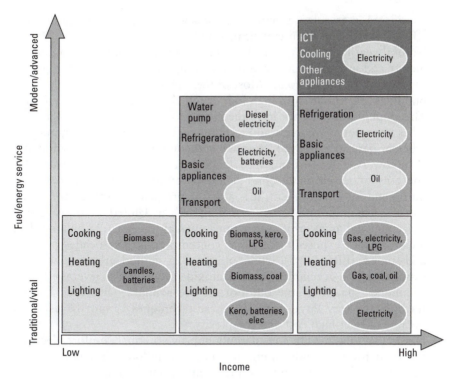

Source: adapted from Serageldim et al, 1995

Figure 1.5 *Household fuel transition and possible contribution of natural ventilation*

- The outdoor temperature is within 'comfort' limits or, in the worst case scenario, does not result in thermal stress of people.
- Natural ventilation does not cause other environmental and social problems (noise, privacy, etc.).

The contribution that natural ventilation can make to the well-being of a building's inhabitants is a function of people's life standards. The quality of the building, as well as the type of energy, services and systems used define what natural ventilation may offer (see Figure 1.5). Thus, three main clusters of possible uses/contributions may be defined as a function of income and of the corresponding energy use:

1 Natural ventilation can contribute significantly to decreasing indoor air pollution caused by combustion processes in very poor households. It is estimated that almost 2 billion people live in substandard conditions, with no access to electricity and modern fuels. The efficient and cheap design of components to enhance ventilation in these settlements is a very simple task, involving low or negligible cost. Nevertheless, this has to be

considered in association with other policies, such as the design of more efficient stoves and the use of cleaner fuels.

2   Natural ventilation may contribute significantly to improving indoor air quality and indoor thermal conditions for approximately 3 billion people of low and medium income. Most of these people live in poorly designed buildings and suffer from high indoor temperatures during the summer. This population does not have the means to use cooling equipment and relies upon natural systems and techniques. The design and integration of efficient natural ventilation systems and components, such as wind and solar towers, can assist in improving indoor thermal comfort. Since this concerns indoor air quality, and high outdoor air pollution and its impact on the indoor environment, it is a major problem for this sector of the world's urban population. According to the United Nations global environmental monitoring system, an annual average of 1.25 billion urban inhabitants are exposed to very high concentrations of suspended particles and smoke, (LRC 1993), while another 625 million urban citizens are exposed to non-acceptable sulphur dioxide (SO_2) levels. Several efficient techniques that filter the outdoor air are available; however, besides filtration of very large particles, these techniques cannot be used yet because of their high cost and complexity.

3   Natural ventilation can considerably improve thermal comfort, decrease the need for air conditioning and improve indoor air quality in the developed world. Daytime ventilation in mild climates and night ventilation in hot climates have been proven to be very effective techniques (OECD, 1991). Experimental studies (Santamouris and Assimakopoulos, 1987) have shown that effective night ventilation in office buildings may halve overheating hours (see Figure 1.6) and reduce the cooling load by at least 55 per cent (see Figure 1.7).

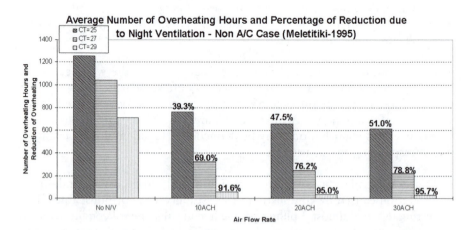

Source: Santamouris and Assimakopoulos, 1987

Figure 1.6 *Average number of overheating hours and reduction percentage due to night ventilation for three different set-point temperatures*

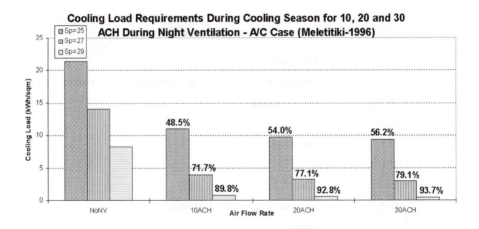

Source: Santamouris and Asimakopoulos, 1987

Figure 1.7 *Average cooling load and reduction percentage due to night ventilation for three different set-point temperatures*

A serious limitation to applying natural and night ventilation in dense urban environments has to do with the serious reduction of the wind speed in urban canyons (Geros et al, 1999). Experimental evaluation of reducing the air flow rate in single-sided and cross-ventilated buildings in ten urban canyons in Athens (Santamouris, 2001) has shown that air flow rate may reduce by 90 per cent (see Figure 1.8). Thus, efficient integration of natural and night ventilation techniques in dense urban areas requires full knowledge of wind characteristics, as well as adaptation of ventilation components to local conditions.

Outdoor pollution is a serious limitation for natural ventilation in urban areas. As reported by Wackernagel et al (1999), it is estimated that in 70 to 80 per cent of European cities with more than 500,000 inhabitants, the levels of air pollution, regarding one or more pollutants, exceed WHO standards at least once in a typical year. Filtration and air cleaning is possible only when flow-controlled natural ventilation components are used.

Noise is a second serious limitation for natural ventilation in the urban environment. As stated by Wackernagel et al (1999), unacceptable noise levels of more than 65 dB(A) affect between 10 to 20 per cent of urban inhabitants in most European cities. The same authors report that in cities included in the Dobris Assessment, unacceptable levels of noise affect between 10 to 50 per cent of urban residences. The OECD (Geros, 2000) has calculated that 130 million people in OECD countries are exposed to noise levels that are unacceptable.

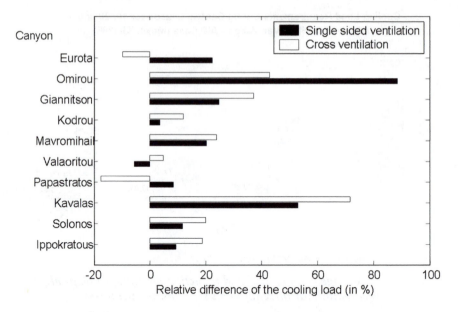

Source: Santamouris, 2001

Figure 1.8 *Reduction of air change rate for single-sided and cross-ventilated buildings in ten urban canyons*

CONCLUSIONS

Extreme urbanization during the last years has resulted in important economic, social, energy and environmental problems. Over-consumption of resources and environmental pollution are among the major problems in cities of the developed world, while poverty and lack of infrastructures comprise the main problems in the cities of the less developed world.

Urbanization increases the energy consumption and production of pollutants. Important peak electricity problems have occurred during the last years in developed countries because of the extensive use of air conditioners. In parallel, poverty obliges almost 2 billion people to use biomass for fuel, resulting in substantial indoor pollution problems.

Natural ventilation can be a significant solution to these problems by improving the environmental quality of urban buildings worldwide. Appropriate simple or sophisticated components of natural ventilation equally address the different nature of people's requirements in the urban environment and contribute significantly to decreasing indoor pollution, improving indoor air quality, enhancing thermal comfort and reducing the use of mechanical cooling.

REFERENCES

Adnot, J. (2001) *Final Report of the EERAC Study*, SAVE Programme, European Commission, Directorate General for Energy and Transports, Brussels

Albouy, Y. and Nadifi, N. (1999) *Impact of Power Sector Reform on the Poor: A Review of Issues and the Literature*, World Bank, Energy, Mining and Telecommunications Department, Washington, D.C.

Barnes, D. F., Dowd, J., Qian, L., Krutilla, K. and Hyde, W. (1994) *Urban Energy Transitions, Poverty and the Environment: Understanding the Role of Urban Household Energy in Developing Countries*, Draft Report, Industry and Energy Department, World Bank, Washington, D.C.

Barnes, D. F. and Halpern, J. (2002) *The Role of Energy Subsidies*, World Bank, Washington, D.C.

Besant-Jones, J. and Tenenbaum, B. (2001) *The California Power Crisis: Lessons for Developing Countries*, Energy and Mining Sector, Board Discussion Paper Series, Paper No 1, April, World Bank, Washington, D.C.

Birol, F. (2002) 'Energy and Poverty, World Outlook 2002', Energy Forum, 4–5 June, World Bank, Washington, D.C.

Bitan, A. (1992) 'The high climatic quality of city of the future', *Atmospheric Environment*, vol 26B, pp313–329

Boardman, B. (1991) *Fuel Property: From Cold Homes to Affordable Warmth*, Belhaven/Wiley, London

Bose, R. K. (1990) *A Linear Programming Model for Urban Energy Environment Interaction in the City of Delhi*, PhD thesis, April, Indian Institute of Technology, Delhi

Cairncross, S. (1990) 'Water supply and the urban poor', in Hardoy, J. E., Cairncross, S. and Satterthwaite, D. (eds) *The Poor Die Young: Housing and Health in Third World Cities*, Earthscan Publications, London

CECA-CE-CEEA (1995) 'For a European Union Energy Policy – Green Paper', CECA-CE_CEEA, Brussels

CICA (Confederation of International Contractors Association) (2000) 'Industry as a partner for sustainable development: Construction', CICA, Paris

Der Petrossian (1999) 'Conflicts between the construction industry and the environment', *Habitat Debate*, Sixth Sharjah Urban Planning Symposium, April, vol 5, no 2, p5

ESS (European Statistical System) (2001) *Air Conditioning Market*, CEC, Luxembourg

Geros, V. (2000) *Ventilation Nocturne: Contribution à la Reponse Thermique des Batiments*, PhD thesis, INSA, Lyon

Geros, V., Santamouris, M., Tsangrassoulis, A. and Guarracino, G. (1999) 'Experimental Evaluation of Night Ventilation Phenomena', Journal of Energy and Buildings, vol 29, pp141–154

Hardy, J. E., Mitlin, D. and Satterthwaite, D. (2001) *Environmental Problems in an Urbanizing World*, Earthscan, London

IBGE (Institut Bruxellois pour la Gestion de l'Environment) (1993) 'Constitution d'un systeme d'eco-geo-information urbain pour la region Bruxelloise integrant l'energie et l'air', Convention Institut Wallon et Mens en Ruimte, Institut Bruxellois pour la Gestion de l' Environment, Brussels, Belgium

ICLEI (International Council for Local Environmental Initiatives) (1993) *Draft Local Action Plans of the Municipalities in the Urban CO_2 reduction Project*, ICLEI, Toronto, Canada

IEA (International Energy Agency) (2001) *Energy Consumption by Economic Sector*, IEA, Paris

Jacobs, M. (1996) *The Politics of the Real World*, Earthscan, London

Lampietti, J. A., Meyer, A. S. and the World Bank (2002*) Coping with the Cold Heating Strategies for Eastern Europe and Central Asia's Urban Poor*, World Bank, Washington, DC

Leitman, J. (1991) *Energy Environment Linkages in the Urban Sector*, April, UNDP, Discussion Paper

LRC (London Research Centre) (1993) *London Energy Study Report*, LRC, London

Nordberg, R. (1999) 'Building sustainable cities', *Habitat Debate*, vol 5, no 2, p1

OECD (Organisation for Economic Co-operation and Development) (1991) *Fighting Noise in the 1990s*, OECD, Paris

Rees, W. (2001a) 'The conundrum of urban sustainability', in Devuyst, D., Hens, L. and de Lannoy, W. (eds) *How Green is the City*, Columbia University Press, New York, USA

Rees, W. (2001b) 'Global change, ecological footprints and urban sustainability' in Devuyst, D., Hens, L. and de Lannoy, W. (eds) *How Green Is the City*, Columbia University Press, New York, USA

Saghir, J. (2002) 'Multilateral Financing of Sustainable Energy', German Parallel Event on North–South Cooperation for a Sustainable Energy Future, WSSD Summit, German Stand, 3 September, Ubuntu Village, Johannesburg

Saksena, S. and Dayal, V. (1997) 'Total exposure as a basis for the economic valuation of air pollution in India', *Energy Environment Monitor*, vol 13, pp93–102

Santamouris, M. (2001) *Energy in the Urban Built Environment*, James and James Science Publishers, London

Santamouris, M. (2003) 'Solar and energy efficiency as an option for sustainable urban built environments', in Santamouris, M. (ed) *Thermal Solar Technologies for Buildings: The State of the Art*, James and James Science Publishers, London

Santamouris, M. and Asimakopoulos, D. (1987) *Passive Cooling of Buildings*, James and James Science Publishers, London

Schwela, D. (1996) 'Exposure to Environmental Chemicals relevant for respiratory hypersensitivity: Global aspects', Toxicol. Lett, vol 86, pp131–142

Serageldim, I., Martin-Brown, J. and Barrett, R. (eds) (1995) *The Business of Sustainable Cities, Environmentally Sustainable Development Proceedings*, Series No 7, World Bank, Washington, D.C.

Sherman, M. H. and Matson, N. E. (2003) *Reducing Indoor Residential Exposures to Outdoor Pollutants*, Lawrence Berkeley Laboratory Report LBNL-53776

Smith, K. R. (1994) *Workshop on the Energy-Environment Nexus: Indian Issues and Global Impacts*, Center for the Advanced Study of India, University of Pennsylvania, Philadelphia

Smith, K. R. (2000) 'National burden of disease in India from indoor air pollution', *PNAS*, 21 November, vol 97, no 24, 13286–13293

Stanners, D. and Bourdeau, P. (eds) (1995) *Europe's Environment – The Dobris Assessment*, European Environmental Agency, Denmark

UN (United Nations) (1998) *World Urbanisation Prospects: The 1996 Revision, Population Division*, United Nations, New York

UNCED (United Nations Conference on Environment and Development) (1992) *Agenda 21*, Section G, Chapter 7, UN, New York, USA

UNCHS (United Nations Council for Human Settlements) (1993) Development of National Technological Capacity for Environmental Sound Construction, HS/293/93/E, UNCHS, Nairobi

UNCHS (1997) 'Europe – Demography, Tools and Statistics Unit', UNCHS, Nairobi

UNCHS (2001) *The State of the World's Cities, 2001*, UNCHS, Nairobi

UNEPTIE (United Nations Environment Programme: Technology, Industry and Economics) (1991): 'Tomorrow's Market: Global Trends and their Implications for Business. 2002.1. Josef Leitman: Energy Environment Linkages in the Urban Sector,' Discussion Paper, UNDP, New York

UNFPA (United Nations Population Fund) (1998) *The State of World Population 1998*, UNFPA, New York

Wackernagel, M., Onisto, L., Bello, P., Linares, A. C., Falfan, I. S. L., Garcia, J. M., Guerrero, A. I. S. and Guerrero, M. G. S. (1999) 'National natural capital accounting with the ecological footprint concept', *Ecological Economics*, vol 29, pp375–390

Wackernagel, M., Onisto, L., Linares, A. C., Falfan, I. S. L., Garcia, J. M., Guerrero, A. I. S. and Guerrero, M. G. S. (1997) *Ecological Footprints of Nations*, Report to the Earth Council, Costa Rica

Waddams Price, C. (2001) 'Better Energy Services, Better Energy Sectors and Links with the Poor', World Bank, Washington, D.C.

Wallace, L. A. (1987) *The Total Exposure Assessment Methodology (TEAM) Study: Project Summary*, September, US Environmental Protection Agency, EPA/600/S6-87/002

WEC (World Energy Council) (1993) *Energy for Tomorrow World*, St. Martin's Press, London

WEHAB Working Group (2002) 'A Framework for Action on Energy', World Summit on Sustainable Development, New York

WHO (World Health Organization) (1997) *Health and Environment in Sustainable Development*, WHO, Geneva

WHO (1999) *Air Quality Guidelines*, WHO, Geneva

World Bank (1995) *Energy Issues: Consequences of Energy Policies for the Urban Poor*, World Bank, Washington, D.C.

World Bank (2000a) *Indoor Air Pollution Newsletter, Energy and Health for the Poor*, no 2, December

World Bank (2000b) *Indoor Air Pollution: Fighting a Massive Health Threat in India*, World Bank, Washington, D.C.

World Bank (2001) *Indoor Air Pollution Newsletter, Energy and Health for the Poor*, no 4, May

2

The Role of Ventilation

Claude-Alain Roulet

INTRODUCTION

The ventilation of buildings is used to maintain indoor air quality and thermal comfort. In order to attain these objectives, airflow rate should be controlled. The minimal airflow rate is determined by indoor air quality requirements so that the maximal concentration for every pollutant is lower than the maximum admitted. By changing the airflow, comfort may also be controlled. Thermal comfort is influenced by air parameters (e.g. temperature, humidity, velocity and turbulence) and surface temperatures (of walls, windows, etc.), but also by the type of human activity and clothing. Recent studies show that in naturally ventilated buildings, occupants adapt themselves to the indoor climate, accepting a wider range of indoor temperatures as comfortable.

INDOOR AIR QUALITY

Reasons for ventilation

Without ventilation, a building's occupants will first be troubled by odours and other possible contaminants and heat. Humidity will rise, thus enhancing moisture hazards (e.g. mould growth and condensation). Oxygen will not be missed until much later. The purpose of ventilation is to eliminate airborne contaminants, which are generated both by human activity and by the building itself. These are:

- bad odours, to which people entering the room are very sensitive;
- moisture, which increases the risk of mould growth;
- carbon dioxide gas, which may induce lethargy in high concentrations;

- dust, aerosols and toxic gases resulting from human activity, as well as from the materials of the building (in principle, 'clean' materials should be chosen for internal use, but this is not always possible);
- excessive heat (see 'Thermal comfort' in this chapter).

Required airflow rate

The airflow rate required to ensure good indoor air quality depends upon the contaminant sources' strengths and on their maximum acceptable concentration; as a result, it is not possible to give a fixed value.

In a homogeneous zone, the contaminant concentration, C, depends upon the intensity of the contaminant source, I, and on the outdoor airflow rate, $\dot{V}$. Writing the contaminant mass conservation, we get:

$$\rho_i V \frac{dC}{dt} = 1 - \rho_e \dot{V} (C - C_e) \tag{2.1}$$

where C_e is the outdoor air contaminant concentration, ρ_e is the external contaminant density and ρ_i is the internal contaminant density. At steady state, the right hand term is zero and:

$$I = \rho_e \dot{V} (C - C_e) \tag{2.2}$$

We can deduce from this the concentration resulting from a contaminant source of intensity I in a room ventilated with an outdoor airflow rate $\dot{V}$:

$$(C - C_e) = \frac{I}{\rho_e \dot{V}} \tag{2.3}$$

The required airflow rate $\dot{V}$ to limit the concentration below the accepted limit, C_{lim}, is given by:

$$\dot{V} = \frac{I}{\rho_e (C_{\mathrm{lim}} - C_e)} \tag{2.4}$$

The required airflow rate $\dot{V}$ is the ratio of the contaminant source rate I by the difference between accepted concentration C_{lim}, and outdoor air concentration C_e.

This equation can easily be adapted to calculate the airflow rate for cooling by considering the net heat source Q (in watts) as a contaminant and the temperature as a measure of the contaminant concentration:

$$\dot{V} = \frac{Q}{C_p \rho_e (\theta_{\mathrm{lim}} - \theta_e)} \tag{2.5}$$

where c_p is the heat capacity of the air at constant pressure. The value of Q should take account of all heat sources (e.g. occupants, appliances and solar gains) and sinks (e.g. cooling devices and transmission heat loss).

If there are several contaminants, the calculation is performed for each contaminant. The airflow rate corresponds to the largest calculated value.

Since, at a given airflow rate, the indoor pollutant concentration is proportional to pollutant source intensity, indoor air quality can be greatly improved at low cost by avoiding or reducing indoor air pollution sources.

In well-designed buildings, during the heating season the occupants are the main source of contaminants (mostly odours and water vapour). The airflow rate should then be between 22 cubic metres per hour (m^3/h) per person, which limits the carbon dioxide (CO_2) concentration to about 1000 parts per million (ppm) above the outdoor concentration, and 54m^3/h per person, which limits the CO_2 concentration to about 400 ppm above the outdoor concentration – meaning that less than 10 per cent of people entering the room will be dissatisfied by the odour (prEN 13779, 2004). Airflow rates should be much larger in poorly insulated buildings (where there is a risk of mould growth and water vapour condensation) or in spaces where there is a particular source of contamination, including spaces where smoking is allowed.

During the summer, the minimum airflow rate may be much larger than the hygienic airflow rate in order to evacuate heat or provide cooling draughts. However, when the outdoor temperature exceeds the indoor temperatures, it may be wise to decrease the ventilation rate, only allowing high levels of ventilation at night when the outdoor temperature is low (see Chapter 7, 'Passive cooling').

THERMAL COMFORT

Buildings and climate

In most cases, buildings are erected to protect their occupants from the external environment (e.g. extreme temperatures, wind, rain, noise, radiation, etc.) and, therefore, to provide them with a good indoor environment. A building that is well adapted to its climate protects its occupants against the extreme conditions observed outdoors without creating uncomfortable internal conditions. According to Pierre Lavigne (Chatelet et al, 1998), the internal climate in a free-running building (that is, without any heating or cooling system running) should be at least as comfortable as the outdoor climate. This strategy is explained below and in Figure 2.1.

Because of changes in their clothing, occupants require different temperatures in order to be comfortable (the so-called 'comfort temperatures') during summer or winter. Therefore, the comfort 'zone' (the range of comfortable temperatures) is higher in summer than in winter.

A well-adapted building (curve A in Figure 2.1) has a good thermal insulation, appropriate passive solar gains (including moveable and efficient shading systems) and adaptive ventilation devices. In summer, it is protected against solar radiation and designed for passive cooling. In winter, it uses solar gain to increase the internal temperature. The result is a building that, in most

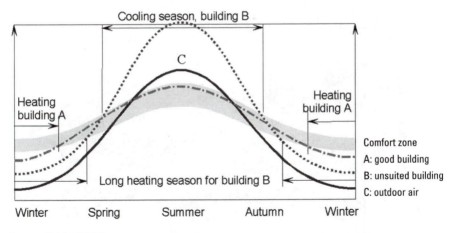

Source: Roulet (2004)

Figure 2.1 *Evolution of temperatures in a free-running building and its environment throughout the year (Northern hemisphere)*

European climates, provides comfort without energy sources other than the sun during most of the year. The energy use for heating is strongly reduced as a result of a shorter heating season. Cooling is not required as long as the internal heat load stays within reasonable limits.

On the other hand, a poorly adapted building (curve B in Figure 2.1) is not well insulated and protected against solar radiation. It is designed neither for an efficient use of solar energy, nor for passive cooling. Its free-floating internal temperature is then too low in winter and too high in summer. Expensive and energy-consuming systems have to be installed in order to compensate for this misfit between the building and its surrounding climate. Such poorly adapted buildings will require heating in winter and cooling in summer and are the cause of the belief that the use of large amounts of energy is necessary for comfort.

Exchanges of heat between the body and its environment

Perceived comfort temperature results from the energy balance of the body, which includes heat loss by convection and conduction to the surrounding air, by evaporation and by radiation to and from neighbouring surfaces. When too much heat is lost, the body perceives a sensation of cold through temperature sensors in the skin. When not enough heat is lost, the temperature of the skin rises, resulting in a sensation of warmth.

A healthy body always maintains equilibrium between heat gains (metabolic heat and heat gains from external environment by convection, conduction and radiation) and heat losses to the environment by convection, conduction, radiation and evaporation (or transpiration). This equilibrium is necessary to maintain the internal body temperature at a constant of nearly

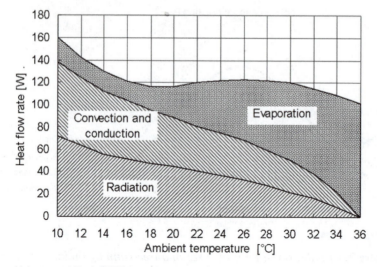

Source: Hebgen and Heck (1973)

Figure 2.2 *Heat lost by a sitting person placed in an isothermal environment*

37°C. It is reached by automatic changes of the blood circulation and skin temperature, on the one hand, and by conscious changes of clothing and activity on the other. Another way of ensuring thermal equilibrium is to change the environment by using available controls such as fans, heaters or window blinds.

Figure 2.2 demonstrates the heat lost by a sitting person placed in an isothermal environment. When the temperature is comfortable, heat loss is almost equally shared between radiation to surrounding surfaces, conduction/convection to the air and transpiration (evaporation). When temperature increases, evaporation becomes the predominant mode of heat loss, and at temperatures in excess of 37°C, becomes the only way to lose heat. At the same time, the production of metabolic heat may fall. When temperature decreases, evaporation is reduced but it is compensated for by an increase of radiation and convection losses. At low temperatures, the metabolism may increase (shivering) to compensate for heat losses by additional heat production.

This clearly shows that thermal comfort does not result from air temperature alone, but also from the temperature of the surrounding surfaces, humidity and air movement.

Thermal comfort at low air velocity and acceptable air humidity

Essentially, comfort is expressed by the satisfaction of a building's occupants. Therefore, the most appropriate way to measure comfort is to ask occupants if they feel comfortable. The EN-ISO 7730 (ISO, 1993) standard scale is most

Table 2.1 *EN-ISO thermal comfort scale*

-3	Cold	
-2	Cool	'Cold' dissatisfied
-1	Slightly cool	
0	Comfortable	Satisfied
1	Slightly warm	
2	Warm	'Hot' dissatisfied
3	Hot	

frequently used to determine this (see Table 2.1). When there are several people in a room, the mean vote is calculated.

Fanger (1982) proposed a method for calculating the mean vote of a group of people from air parameters (temperature, humidity and air velocity), clothing and activity. He called this the 'predicted mean vote' (PMV). Fanger also suggested that the percentage of dissatisfied people (hot or cold – see Table 2.1) is related to mean vote (see Figure 2.3). It should be noted that, according to this model, it is impossible to satisfy everybody: the minimum number of dissatisfied people is approximately 5 per cent.

Fanger (1982) also published a relationship between the physical parameters that influence thermal comfort and the mean vote, which can then be predicted. The Fanger equation of comfort is now accepted all over the world.

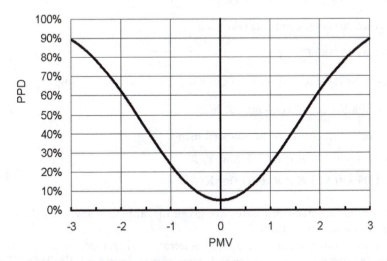

Source: Drawn using the relation given by Fanger (1982)

Figure 2.3 *Relationship between the percentage of people who do not feel comfortable (PPD) and the mean vote (PMV)*

Table 2.2 *Parameters influencing thermal comfort*

Air temperature	θ_a [°C] or T_a [K]
Mean radiant temperature	θ_{rt}[°C] or T_r[K]
Air velocity relative to the subject	v [m/s]
Water vapour partial pressure	p [Pa]
Metabolic activity of the subject	M [W]
Mechanical work of the subject	W [W]
Skin area	A [m²]
Specific metabolic activity	$m = M/A$ [W/m²]
Specific mechanical work	$w = W/A$ [W/m²]
Thermal resistance of clothing	R [m² K/W]
Clothing	H [Clo] $= R/0.155$
Clothed fraction	f

The Fanger equation is:

$$PMV = (0.303 \exp(-0.036\ m) + 0.028)$$
$$[m{-}w - 0.00305\ (5733 - 6.99\ (m{-}w) - p) - 0.42\ (m{-}w - 58.15)$$
$$-0.000017\ m\ (5787 - p) - 0.0014\ m\ (3307 - T_aD) - F]$$

$$(2.6)$$

where the clothing function F is:

$$F = (3.96\ 10^{-8}\ f(T_{cl}^{\ 4} - T_r^{\ 4}) + f\,h\ (T_{cl} - T_a) \tag{2.7}$$

the heat transfer coefficient h is taken as:

$$h = \max\ [2.38\ (T_{cl} - T_a)^{1/4}\ ;\ 12.06\ \sqrt{v}] \tag{2.8}$$

the absolute surface temperature of cloths, T_{cl}, is found by solving:

$$T_{cl} = 308.9 - 0.028\ (m - w) - R\ F \tag{2.9}$$

and the clothed fraction can be assessed using:

$$f = 1.00 + 1.290\ R \text{ if } R<0.078\text{m}^2 \text{ K/W}$$
$$f = 1.05 + 0.645\ R \text{ if } R<0.078\text{m}^2 \text{ K/W} \tag{2.10}$$

Some examples of metabolic rates are given in Table 2.3; several values for clothing are indicated in Table 2.4.

The solution of the Fanger equation is iterative; therefore, for all practical purposes, a computer is essential. International Standard EN/ISO 7730 provides a simple program in BASIC. Figure 2.4 shows the ideal operative temperature (plain lines) as a function of clothing and activity at which there will be only 5 per cent dissatisfied individuals. This figure is valid for low air velocities and acceptable relative humidity. Shaded and white areas are tolerance domains, in which the percentage of dissatisfied individuals will be less than 10 per cent.

Table 2.3 *Mean metabolic rate for various activities (EN-ISO 7730)*

Activity	Heat emission		
	(met)	*(W/m²)†*	*(W/person)**
Reclining	0.8	46	83
Seated, relaxed	1.0	58	104
Sedentary activity (office, dwelling, school, laboratory)	1.2	70	126
Standing light activity (shops, laboratory, light industry)	1.6	93	167
Standing, medium activity (domestic or machine work)	2.0	116	209
Walking at 4 km/h	2.8	162	292

Notes: * for a person with 1.8m² body area (e.g. 1.7m tall weighing 69kg)
† per body unit area
Metabolic rate expressed in physical units and in met (metabolism) units. 1 met = 58 W/m² body area

For example, a sitting person wearing a lounge suit would prefer, on average, an operative temperature of 22°C ± 2°C. If this person is more active – for example, when giving a lecture – a temperature of 18°C ± 3°C is preferred. This is why a temperature of about 20°C is preferred in schools and offices. A sitting person wearing shorts and a light shirt will prefer 26°C ± 1.5°C, while an average person naked and at rest is comfortable, on average, at 28°C ±1°C.

The operative temperature at a given location is, by definition, the temperature of an isothermal room in which a person has the same total heat loss as the actual location. An approximation is:

$$\theta_{op} = a\,\theta_e + (1 - a)\,\theta_r \tag{2.11}$$

where a is a factor depending upon the air velocity v relative to the subject:

Table 2.4 *Some standard clothing with their thermal resistance expressed in physical units and in clo (clothing) units*

Clothing	(clo)	(m²K/W)
Naked, standing	0.0	0.0
Shorts, bathing suit	0.1	0.015
Summer clothing: panties, shirt with short sleeves, light trousers or skirt, socks, shoes	0.5	0.08
Underpants, boiler suit, socks, shoes	0.7	0.11
Panties, shirt, trousers or skirt, vest, jacket, socks or stockings, shoes	1.0	0.15
Underwear with long sleeves and legs, shirt, trousers, vest, jacket, coat, socks or stockings, shoes	1.5	0.23

Note: Thermal resistance expressed in physical units and in clo (clothing) units. 1 clo = 0.15m²K/W.

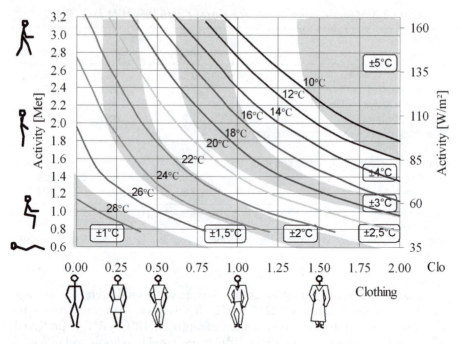

Source: Fanger et al (1980); Fanger et al (1985)

Figure 2.4 *Optimal operative temperatures for various clothing and activities*

$$a = 0.5 + 0.25v \tag{2.12}$$

This approximation can be used for air velocities up to 1 metre per second (m/s).

The Fanger equation is valid within the following domain:

- metabolism from 46 to 232 watts per square metre body area (W/m²) (0.8 to 4 units of metabolism (met));
- clothing from 0 to 2 units of thermal resistance of clothing (clo) (or clothing thermal resistance from 0 to 0.310 (m²K/W));
- air temperature between 10 and 30°C;
- mean radiant temperature from 10 to 40°C;
- relative air velocity less than 1 m/s;
- water vapour partial pressure between 0 and 2700Pa.

The practical consequence for administrative buildings and dwellings, where the activity is close to 1.1 met, is that the optimal operative temperature in winter (about 1 clo) is between 20 and 24°C, while in summer, with lighter clothing, the optimal operative temperature is between 23 and 26°C.

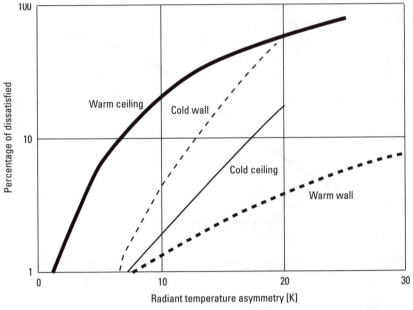

Source: adapted from Fanger et al (1985)

Figure 2.5 *Effect of radiant temperature asymmetry at optimal operative temperature*

Effects of thermal gradients

The operative temperature is an average. Even if it is optimal, temperature gradients may induce discomfort (Fanger et al, 1988).

Radiant temperature asymmetry is the difference in mean radiant temperature between the two sides of a small, plane surface, each face seeing one half of the surrounding space. Note that the warm ceiling is clearly less appealing than the cold one, and that warm walls are more comfortable than cold ones (see Figure 2.5).

Even at optimal operative temperature, a temperature difference of 4K between head and ankles is uncomfortable for 10 per cent of office workers (Figure 2.6). This is of particular importance when applying displacement ventilation, or when an open window allows cold air to enter a warm room. In both cases, the cold air falls down in a cold air layer close to the ground.

Draught risk

The percentage of people complaining of draughts depends upon the air temperature, air velocity and turbulence intensity. Because of turbulence, air velocity at a given place varies with time. If v_i are several successive measurements of the air velocity, the mean velocity and its standard deviation are:

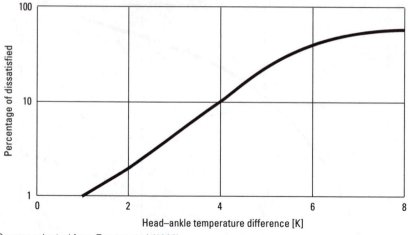

Source: adapted from Fanger et al (1988)

Figure 2.6 *Effect of a temperature difference between head and ankle*

$$v = \frac{\sum\limits_{i=1}^{N} v_i}{N} \quad and \quad \sigma = \sqrt{\frac{\sum\limits_{i=1}^{N} (v_i - v)^2}{N-1}} \tag{2.13}$$

The turbulence intensity is the ratio σ/v.

The percentage of dissatisfied persons, PD, can be calculated from the empirical relationship published by Fanger et al (1988):

$$PD = max \left(\frac{0}{v - 0.05} \right)^{0.6223} (3.143 + 36.96 \cdot \sigma) \cdot (34 - \theta_a) \tag{2.14}$$

where θ_a is the air temperature. From this, one can deduce the minimum temperature needed to limit the percentage of dissatisfied persons:

$$\theta_{a,min} = 34 - \frac{PD}{\left(\dfrac{0}{v - 0.05} \right)^{0.6223} (3.143 + 36.96 \cdot \sigma)} \tag{2.15}$$

This relationship is illustrated in Figure 2.7, calculated so that less than per cent of individuals are dissatisfied. Note that turbulence intensity in most rooms exceeds 0.3.

At comfortable temperatures, air velocity should therefore not exceed 0.15 metres per second. Most mechanical ventilation systems are designed to fulfil this condition. In naturally ventilated buildings, the occupants generally monitor the openings in order to avoid uncomfortable draughts. In warm environments, however, it is recommended that the air velocity is increased by using fans or large openings.

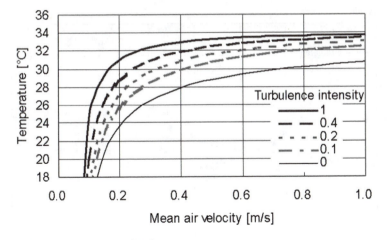

Source: Drawn using equation (2.15)

Figure 2.7 *Minimum air temperature so that less than 10 per cent of people complain of draughts for various air velocities and turbulence intensities*

Adaptive comfort

The comfort models presented above are based on measurements in a steady state, regarding occupants as passively reacting to thermal stimuli. Everyday experience, however, shows that the ideal temperature is not a constant. It depends upon the activity and clothing of the occupants and should therefore vary according to these parameters. Given the opportunity, people will change the indoor climate to suit their preferences and vice versa, and will adapt themselves to the ambient temperature by changing their clothing or adapting their activity. In addition, occupants accept larger temperature variation in some environments more than in others. Within the frame of the ASHRAE research project 884, comfort data from 160 buildings all over the world were compiled. De Dear and Brager (2002) have split these buildings into two types: naturally ventilated and air-conditioned buildings. In air-conditioned buildings, perceived comfort temperature fitted well with the PMV calculated according to EN-ISO 7730 (Fanger, 1982) (see Figure 2.8a). In naturally ventilated buildings however, EN-ISO 7730 does not predict the comfort temperature correctly. It seems that occupants have adapted themselves, using means not taken into account in the EN-ISO 7730 model (see Figure 2.8b). McCartney and Nicol (2002) arrive at similar conclusions from experiments in European buildings.

From these experiments, adaptive comfort models were developed, as shown in Figure 2.9. The McCartney model for Europe is within the 90 per cent acceptance interval of the de Dear and Brager (2002) model. There is, therefore, no significant difference, and we can adopt the de Dear model:

$$\theta_{op} = 17.8 + 0.31\theta_e \tag{2.16}$$

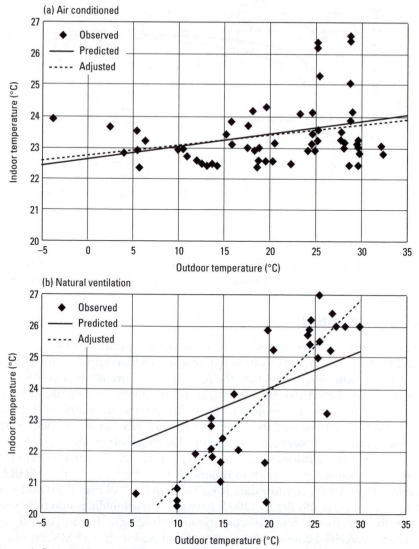

Source: de Dear and Brager (2002)

Figure 2.8 *(a) Observed and predicted indoor comfort temperatures
from ASHRAE RP-884 database for air-conditioned buildings;
(b) Observed and predicted indoor comfort temperatures from
RP-884 database for naturally ventilated buildings*

where θ_{op} is the internal operative temperature and θ_e is the outdoor mean
temperature. The acceptance interval is ±2.5K for 90 per cent acceptance and
±3.5K for 80 per cent.

As shown in Figure 2.10, the predictions of EN-ISO 7730 (ISO, 1993) do
not fit with the adaptive model, even when the seasonal use of clothing is taken
into account.

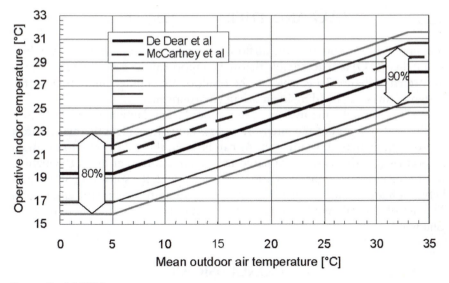

Source: Roulet (2004)

Figure 2.9 *Adaptive comfort models from 80 per cent and 90 per cent bands are acceptance intervals for the de Dear model*

The adaptive comfort model not only provides design rules for better comfort in naturally ventilated buildings, but also allows substantial energy savings, especially in summer.

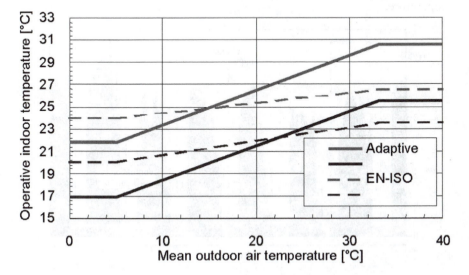

Figure 2.10 *Ninety per cent accepted comfort ranges according to the adaptive comfort model and EN-ISO 7730 standard, assuming 1.2 met and adapted clothing (1 clo in winter and 0.5 clo in summer)*

IAQ AND THERMAL COMFORT

It is important to note that the airflow rates required to provide good indoor air quality (IAQ) and acceptable thermal comfort can be very different. This is illustrated in Figure 2.11, which is the result of a computer simulation for the design of an office building in an urban environment.

In this example, the hygienic ventilation during daytime is provided by a mechanical system; but the intensive night cooling to control thermal comfort is provided by natural ventilation. As can be seen, the airflow rate to maintain a good IAQ in this case is evaluated to one air change per hour; the airflow rate of the intensive night ventilation, calculated with the software ESP-r, varies between 8 and 12 air changes per hour, according to the climatic conditions. The use of natural ventilation for night cooling is discussed in more detail in Chapter 7.

CONCLUSIONS

The role of ventilation is mainly to dilute and evacuate the contaminants produced indoors. The ventilation rate increases with the contaminant source intensity and decreases with the acceptable contaminant concentration.

The well-accepted Fanger model allows the prediction of thermal comfort in conditioned spaces, depending on the activity and clothing of occupants. In naturally ventilated spaces, however, occupants are more tolerant than in conditioned spaces, and the optimal comfort temperature depends on outdoor temperature.

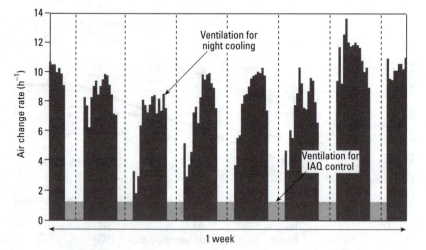

Figure 2.11 *Airflow rates to control IAQ and thermal comfort*

REFERENCES

Chatelet, A., Fernandez, P., et Lavigne, P. (1998) *Architecture Climatique*, Edisud, Aix-en-Provence, France

de Dear, R. J. and Brager, G. S. (2002) 'Thermal comfort in naturally ventilated buildings: Revisions to ASHRAE Standard 55', *Energy and Buildings*, vol 34, pp549–561

Fanger, P. O. (1982) *Thermal Comfort*, R. E. Krieger, Melbourne, Florida

Fanger, P. O., Banhidi, L., Olesen, B. W. and Langkilde, G. (1980) 'Comfort limits for heated ceilings', *ASHRAE Transactions*, vol 86, no 2, pp141–156

Fanger, P. O., Ipsen, B. M., Langkilde, G., Olesen, B. W., Christensen, N. K. and Tanabe, S. (1985) 'Comfort limits for asymmetric thermal radiation', *Energy and Buildings*, vol 8, pp225–236

Fanger, P. O., Melikov, A. K., Hansawa, H. and Ring, J. (1988) 'Air turbulence and the sensation of draught', *Energy and Buildings*, vol 12, pp21–30

Hebgen, H. and Heck, F. (1973) *Außenwandkonstruktion mit optimalem Wärmeschutz*, Bertelsmann-Fachverlag DüsseldorfISO (International Organization for Standardization) (1993) *ISO-7730: Moderate Thermal Environments – Determination of the PMV and PPD Indices and Specifications of the Conditions for Thermal Comfort*, ISO, Geneva

ISO (1993) *ISO-7730: Moderate thermal environments: Determination of the PMV and PPD indices and specification of the conditions for thermal comfort*, ISO, Geneva. Also adopted as CEN standard as EN-ISA 7730

McCartney, K. J. and Nicol, J. F. (2002) 'Developing an adaptive control algorithm for Europe', *Energy and Buildings*, vol 34, pp623–635

prEN 13779 (2004) *Ventilation for Buildings – Performance Requirements for Ventilation and Air-conditioning Systems*. CEN (Commission Européenne de Normalisation), Technical committee 156 (Secretariat: British Standards Institution)

Roulet, C.-A. (2004) *Santé et Qualité de l'environnement dans les Bâtiments*, PPUR, Lausanne

3

The Physics of Natural Ventilation

Cristian Ghiaus and Francis Allard

BASIC THEORY OF FLUID DYNAMICS

Lagrangian and Eulerian descriptions

In describing the motion of a rigid body, we use the three spatial coordinates of the centre of mass and the three angular coordinates of rotation about the mass centre of the position and of the angular orientation of the body at each instant of time. Knowing these six coordinates as functions of time, we can find their time derivatives in order to determine the components of the velocity of the mass centre and the angular velocity about the mass centre. An additional differentiation will determine the linear and angular accelerations of the body. This mode of describing the motion of an identified body of finite mass is called the *Lagrangian* description.

Since a fluid is not rigid, but easily deformable, we need to take into account the motion of the fluid relative to the mass centre, which is certainly not a simple rotation as it is in a rigid body. The solution to this dilemma is to abandon the requirement of following the fate of each fluid particle and focus on the velocity $\mathbf{v}$ of the fluid particle that occupies a point in space, $\mathbf{x} = (x_1, x_2, x_3)$, at the time t. A *Eulerian* description of the flow field consists of the specification of the velocity $\mathbf{v}$ as a function of position $\mathbf{x}$ and time t:

$$\mathbf{v} \equiv \mathbf{v}(t, \mathbf{x}) = \begin{bmatrix} v_1(t, x_1, x_2, x_3) \\ v_2(t, x_1, x_2, x_3) \\ v_3(t, x_1, x_2, x_3) \end{bmatrix} \equiv \mathbf{v}_1(t, x_1, x_2, x_3) \equiv \mathbf{v}(t, x_i) \equiv v_j(t, x_i) \Big|_{\substack{i=1,2,3; \\ j=1,2,3}} \quad (3.1)$$

By a suitable differentiation with respect to time, we can find the acceleration of the fluid particle at any position $\mathbf{x}$ and time t and, if necessary, the displacement of the particle from its position at an earlier time by integration.

In the Eulerian description of fluid motion, other physical variables of interest, such as pressure **p** and density ρ, are also considered to be functions of position **x** and time t. Mathematically speaking, **v**, p, ρ etc. are considered to be the dependent variables of the flow that are functions of the independent variables **x** and t. This general description is termed a field description, and the dependent variables are called field variables. Thus, we use the terms such as velocity field and pressure field to imply the dependence of velocity and pressure on the independent variables **x** and t. For a field vector **G**, we will have:

$$\mathbf{G} \equiv \mathbf{G}(t,\mathbf{x}) \equiv \mathbf{G}_1(t,x_i) = G_j(t,x_i)\Big|_{\substack{i=1,2,3;\\ j=1,2,3}} \tag{3.2}$$

and for a scalar G:

$$\mathbf{G} \equiv \mathbf{G}(t,\mathbf{x}) \equiv G_j(t,x_i)\Big|_{i=1,2,3} \tag{3.3}$$

Material derivative

The standard forms of Newton's law of motion and the laws of thermodynamics apply to a fixed mass of identified matter whose properties change as time progresses. The natural mode for expressing these laws is the Lagrangian description of motion because it directly describes the history of an identified particle. Since we use the Eulerian description for a moving fluid, we need to establish the Eulerian expression of the rate of change of any property of a fluid particle as it moves through the flow field. The time rate of change of a fluid property, as measured by an observer moving with the particle, is called the *material derivative* of that property.

As an example, consider the rate of change of density of a fluid particle that is located at position **x** at time t. We note that ρ represents a property describing a particle in motion and not a property characterizing a geometrical point. During the time interval dt, the particle moves the distance $d\mathbf{x} = \mathbf{v}dt$. The total increment in density, $d\rho$, is the sum of the part due to the time increment dt and that due to the spatial increment $d\mathbf{x}$. Using Cartesian coordinates to express the amount of $d\rho$:

$$\begin{aligned}
\frac{d\rho(t,\mathbf{x})}{dt} &= \frac{\delta\rho}{\delta t} + \frac{\delta\rho}{\delta x_1}\cdot\frac{dx_1}{dt} + \frac{\delta\rho}{\delta x_2}\cdot\frac{dx_2}{dt} + \frac{\delta\rho}{\delta x_3}\cdot\frac{dx_3}{dt} \\
&= \frac{\delta\rho}{\delta t} + v_1\frac{\delta\rho}{\delta x_1} + v_2\frac{\delta\rho}{\delta x_2} + v_3\frac{\delta\rho}{\delta x_3} \\
&= \frac{\delta\rho}{\delta t} + v_j\frac{\delta\rho}{\delta x_i}
\end{aligned} \tag{3.4}$$

Or, expressed as a function of the vector space basis $x_1 = [1\ 0\ 0]^T$, $x_2 = [0\ 1\ 0]^T$, $x_3 = [0\ 0\ 1]^T$:

$$d\rho(t,\mathbf{x}) \equiv d\rho(t,x_1,x_2,x_3) = \frac{d\rho}{\delta t}\,dt + \frac{\delta\rho}{\delta x_1}\,dx_1 + \frac{\delta\rho}{\delta x_2}\,dx_2 + \frac{\delta\rho}{\delta x_3}\,dx_3$$

$$= \frac{\delta\rho}{\delta t}\,dt + (x_1 dx_1 + x_2 dx_2 + x_3 dx_3)\left(\frac{\delta\rho}{\delta x_1}x_1 + \frac{\delta\rho}{\delta x_2}x_2 + \frac{\delta\rho}{\delta x_3}x_3\right)$$

$$= \frac{\delta\rho}{\delta t}\,dt + d\mathbf{x}\cdot\nabla\rho = \frac{\delta\rho}{\delta t}\,dt + \frac{d\mathbf{x}}{dt}\,dt\cdot\nabla\rho = \left(\frac{\delta\rho}{\delta t} + (\mathbf{v}\cdot\nabla)\rho\right)dt$$

$$\tag{3.5}$$

$$\frac{\delta\rho}{\delta t} = \left(\frac{\delta}{\delta t} + \mathbf{v}\cdot\nabla\right)\rho = \frac{\delta\rho}{\delta t} + v_1\frac{\delta\rho}{\delta x_1} + v_2\frac{\delta\rho}{\delta x_2} + v_3\frac{\delta\rho}{\delta x_3} \tag{3.6}$$

In order to emphasize that the material time derivative includes both spatial and time partial derivatives, and is not simply the partial time derivative, we will denote it by D/Dt:

$$\frac{D}{Dt} = \left(\frac{\delta}{\delta t} + \mathbf{v}\cdot\nabla\right) \tag{3.7}$$

Note that $\mathbf{v}\cdot\nabla$ is a scalar operator so that the material derivative of a scalar variable, such as density ρ, for example, is a scalar quantity:

$$\frac{D\bullet}{Dt} \equiv \frac{\delta\bullet}{\delta t} + (\mathbf{v}\cdot\nabla)\bullet = \frac{\delta\bullet}{\delta t} + v_1\frac{\delta\bullet}{\delta x_1} + v_2\frac{\delta\bullet}{\delta x_2} + v_3\frac{\delta\bullet}{\delta x_3} \tag{3.8}$$

The flow can be considered steady if the time derivative term of equation (3.8) is much smaller than the spatial derivative:

$$\frac{\delta\bullet}{\delta t} \ll (\mathbf{v}\cdot\nabla)\bullet \tag{3.9}$$

For a vector field variable, such as the acceleration of a particle, $\mathbf{a}$, the material derivative is:

$$\mathbf{a} = \frac{D\mathbf{v}}{Dt} = \frac{\delta\bullet}{\delta t} + (\mathbf{v}\cdot\nabla)\mathbf{v} \tag{3.10}$$

Conservation of mass

For a conservative flow, the mass conservation is:

$$\frac{\delta\rho}{\delta t} + \nabla\cdot(\rho\mathbf{v}) = 0; \quad \frac{\delta\rho}{\delta t} + \mathrm{div}(\rho\mathbf{v}) = 0 \tag{3.11}$$

Mass conservation equation (3.11) may be written in a different form by expanding the divergence term:

$$\frac{\delta\rho}{\delta t} + (\mathbf{v} \cdot \nabla)\rho + \rho\nabla \cdot \mathbf{v} = 0 \tag{3.12}$$

or:

$$\frac{D\rho}{Dt} + \rho\nabla \cdot \mathbf{v} = 0 \tag{3.13}$$

An *incompressible flow* is one for which the rate of density change of a fluid particle, D/Dt, is negligible compared with the component terms of $\rho\nabla \cdot \mathbf{v}$. Using Cartesian coordinates, we may write this condition as:

$$\left|\frac{D\rho}{Dt}\right| << \rho \left(\left|\frac{\delta v_1}{\delta x_1}\right| + \left|\frac{\delta v_2}{\delta x_2}\right| + \left|\frac{\delta v_3}{\delta x_3}\right| \right) \tag{3.14}$$

When this condition is satisfied, the material derivative term in equation (3.13) may be dropped and the equation of mass conservation becomes:

$$\nabla \cdot \mathbf{v} = 0 \tag{3.15}$$

This condition for incompressible flow may be expressed in a different manner. Since equation (3.13) is always true, substituting equation (3.14) into it leads to the conclusion that:

$$\frac{D\rho}{Dt} = 0 \tag{3.16}$$

This form expresses the incompressibility of the flow by stating that the density of a fluid particle does not change as it moves through the flow field.

It is important to emphasize that an incompressible flow does not require that the density has the same constant value throughout the flow field, but only that the density is unchanging along a particle path. Different fluid particles may have different densities, yet each can have an unchanging density in an incompressible flow. If the density is the same at all locations at a particular time, it will remain so at subsequent times if the flow is incompressible. Such a flow is called a *constant density* flow. However, not all incompressible flows are constant density flows.

Forces on a fluid particle

A fluid particle is subject to two quite different types of forces. The *surface* of the particle experiences a force per unit area called the *stress*. The intermolecular force that gives rise to the surface stress is short range (i.e. it is appreciable only when the molecules are closer than about 1.10^{-10}m apart).

On the other hand, there are long-range forces that can be exerted throughout the volume of the fluid particle. These are called *body forces* because they act on the *entire particle*, not just the surface.

In a fluid, the *surface stress* depends upon both the relative *position* of the molecules near the surface and the relative average *motion* of these molecules. It is convenient to subdivide the surface stress into these two categories, the first of which is called the *pressure* **p** and the second is called the *viscous stress* τ. When a fluid has no relative motion, the only stress is the first kind, the pressure, which is always normal to the surface of the particle. However, when the fluid moves, there will be a viscous stress component whose direction and magnitude depend upon the rate of distortion of the moving fluid element. For nearly all fluids, this viscous stress is proportional to the fluid viscosity μ.

Let us be more precise. Consider a finite volume of fluid, V, completely enclosed by a surface S, which is completely surrounded by the same kind of fluid (see Figure 3.1). At a point on this surface, the fluid molecules on or close to the surface experience a force per unit area of surface, called the stress σ, caused by the molecules outside the surface. In general, the stress vector σ has a component normal to the surface (called a normal stress) and one parallel to the surface (called a shear stress), which are, respectively, parallel and perpendicular to the unit outward normal **n**. By Newton's law of action and reaction, the stress acting on the fluid inside S is equal and opposite to the stress at this point acting on the fluid outside S.

The stress at a point within a fluid is more complex than is implied by Figure 3.1 because the stress vector σ depends upon the direction of the surface normal S. In order to describe the state of stress at a point **P** in a fluid (or a solid, for that matter), we must specify the three components of the stress vector for each of three mutually perpendicular orientations of a surface passing through the point. These nine quantities form what is called the *stress tensor*. In a fluid, some of the components of the stress tensor depend upon the rate at which a fluid element is being distorted, and these components are proportional to the fluid viscosity.

Pressure force

In a static fluid, where there is no motion, the stress vector σ of the surface is normal because there is no preferred direction in the fluid, which is isotropic in structure. At a point **P** in a static fluid, σ must therefore have the direction of **n** and have the same magnitude for all directions of **n** (Pascal's law). Because we know that fluids can sustain only a compressive stress, or pressure, we identify the magnitude of σ with the pressure **p** and its direction as opposite to **n**:

$$\sigma = -p\mathbf{n} \tag{3.17}$$

Using Pascal's law given by equation (3.17), we can determine the force exerted on a volume V of fluid by the stress acting on its surface S if we integrate the pressure force per unit area, $\sigma = -p\mathbf{n}$, over the surface to find the *pressure force* vector:

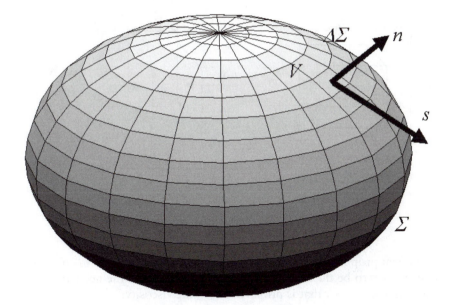

Figure 3.1 *Fluid inside a volume* V *enclosed by the surface* S; *at a point on the surface, where the unit outward normal is* n, *the stress is* σ

$$(-p\mathbf{n})\mathrm{d}S = p_1 \cdot \mathrm{d}x_2 \cdot \mathrm{d}x_3 \cdot \mathbf{x}_1 + [-(p_1 + \mathrm{d}p_1) \cdot \mathrm{d}x_2 \cdot \mathrm{d}x_3 \cdot \mathbf{x}_1]$$

$$+p_2 \cdot \mathrm{d}x_3 \cdot \mathrm{d}x_1 \cdot \mathbf{x}_2 + [-(p_2 + \mathrm{d}p_2) \cdot \mathrm{d}x_3 \cdot \mathrm{d}x_1 \cdot \mathbf{x}_2]$$

$$+p_3 \cdot \mathrm{d}x_1 \cdot \mathrm{d}x_2 \cdot \mathbf{x}_3 + [-(p_3 + \mathrm{d}p_3) \cdot \mathrm{d}x_1 \cdot \mathrm{d}x_2 \cdot \mathbf{x}_3]$$

$$= -\left(-\frac{\delta p_1}{\delta x_1}\mathbf{x}_1 - \frac{\delta p_2}{\delta x_2}\mathbf{x}_2 - \frac{\delta p_3}{\delta x_3}\mathbf{x}_3\right) \cdot \mathrm{d}x_1 \cdot \mathrm{d}x_2 \cdot \mathrm{d}x_3$$

$$= (-\nabla\cdot\rho) \cdot \mathrm{d}V$$

(3.18)

Gravitational force

The gravitational force is a body force whose magnitude is the product of the mass of a fluid element multiplied by the gravitational acceleration. For a volume of fluid $\mathrm{d}V$, the mass is $\rho\mathrm{d}V$ so that the gravitational force per unit volume becomes $(\rho\mathrm{d}V)\mathbf{g}$.

Viscous stress

In hydrostatics, the only stress on an element of fluid surface is a normal stress, called the pressure, which is the same regardless of the orientation of the surface element (Pascal's law). However, in a viscous flow the stress σ will, in general, not be normal to the surface – in fact, it will usually have a tangential

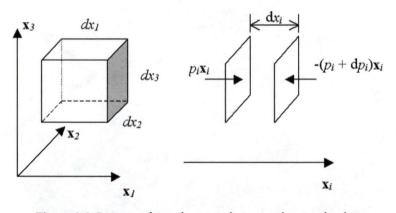

Figure 3.2 *Pressure force for an infinitesimal unit of volume*

component proportional to the viscosity. We find it convenient to consider the fluid stress σ to be the sum of a pressure stress $(-p)\mathbf{n}$ in the normal direction and a *viscous stress* τ that is proportional to the viscosity:

$$\sigma \equiv (-p)\mathbf{n} + \tau \tag{3.19}$$

A viscous stress arises when the shape of a fluid element is changed in a flow. For a Newtonian fluid, a shear stress on the lower and upper surfaces of a fluid element is generated in proportion to the velocity gradient and the fluid viscosity:

$$\tau_{ij} = \mu \frac{\delta v_i}{\delta x_j} \tag{3.20}$$

The symbol τ_{ij} denotes that the shear stress acts in the $\mathbf{x}_i$ direction on a surface element whose normal vector is in the $\mathbf{x}_j$ direction. The tensor of viscous stress is:

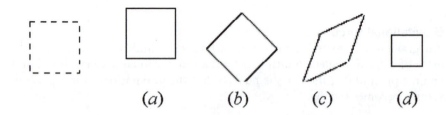

Figure 3.3 *The motion of a fluid element, initially defined by the dashed figure, can be described as a combination of (a) translation, (b) rigid body rotation, (c) shear compression and (d) pure compression. Only the deformations of (c) and (d) give rise to viscous stresses*

$$\tau_{ij} = \begin{bmatrix} \tau_{11} & \tau_{12} & \tau_{13} \\ \tau_{21} & \tau_{22} & \tau_{23} \\ \tau_{31} & \tau_{32} & \tau_{33} \end{bmatrix} \tag{3.21}$$

where:

$$\tau_{ij} = \tau_{21} = \mu \left(\frac{\delta v_1}{\delta x_2} + \frac{\delta v_2}{\delta x_1} \right)$$

$$\tau_{ij} = 2\mu_{21} \frac{\delta v_1}{\delta x_1} \ , \ \tau_{22} = 2\mu \frac{\delta v_2}{\delta x_2} \ , \ \tau_{33} = 2\mu \frac{\delta v_3}{\delta x_3} \ , \text{if } \nabla \cdot \mathbf{v} = 0 \tag{3.22}$$

In order to derive an expression for the viscous force per unit volume, f, consider the fluid element of volume dx_1, dx_2, dx_3 shown in Figure 3.4. Let us consider only the viscous stresses acting in the $\mathbf{x}_1$ direction, τ_{11}, τ_{12} and τ_{13}. The normal viscous stress τ_{11} increases with distance x_1 from a value of τ_{11} at one face of the element to a value of $\tau_{11} + (\delta\tau_{11}/\delta x_1)dx_1$ at $x_1 + dx_1$. The net difference between these stresses, $\delta\tau_{11}/\delta x_1$, acts over an area $dx_2\ dx_3$ and contributes an amount $(\delta\tau_{11}/\delta x_1)dx_1 dx_2 dx_3$ to the x_1 component of the force acting on the fluid element, or an amount $\delta\tau_{11}/\delta x_1$ to the x_1 component of the force per unit volume, $\mathbf{f} \cdot \mathbf{x}_1$. There will be similar contributions from the stresses τ_{12} and τ_{13} due to their increases in the $\mathbf{x}_2$ and $\mathbf{x}_3$ directions, respectively, giving a total $\mathbf{x}_1$ component of the viscous force per unit volume of:

$$\mathbf{f} \cdot \mathbf{x}_1 = \frac{\delta\tau_{11}}{\delta x_1} + \frac{\delta\tau_{12}}{\delta x_2} + \frac{\delta\tau_{13}}{\delta x_3} \tag{3.23}$$

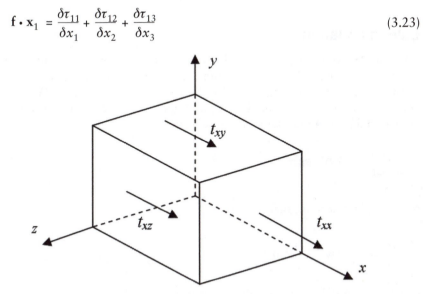

Figure 3.4 *The x_1 component of the viscous force acting on a fluid element of volume dx_1, dx_2, dx_3 consists of the viscous shear stresses τ_{12} and τ_{13} acting on the surfaces normal to the x_2 and x_3 axes and the viscous normal stress τ_{11} acting on the surfaces normal to the x_1-axis*

For an incompressible fluid, we may replace the viscous stresses τ_{11}, τ_{12} and τ_{13} by their values:

$$\mathbf{f} \cdot \mathbf{x}_1 = \frac{\delta}{\delta x_1}\left(2\mu\frac{\delta v_1}{\delta x_1}\right) + \frac{\delta}{\delta x_2}\left(\mu\left[\frac{\delta v_1}{\delta x_2} + \frac{\delta v_2}{\delta x_1}\right]\right) + \frac{\delta}{\delta x_3}\left(\mu\left[\frac{\delta v_1}{\delta x_3} + \frac{\delta v_3}{\delta x_1}\right]\right)$$

(3.24)

This expression can be simplified if we assume that μ is constant everywhere in the flow field and can be taken outside the partial derivatives to give:

$$\mathbf{f} \cdot \mathbf{x}_1 = \mu\left(\frac{\delta^2 v_1}{\delta x_1^2} + \frac{\delta^2 v_1}{\delta x_2^2} + \frac{\delta^2 v_1}{\delta x_3^2}\right) + \mu\frac{\delta}{\delta x_1}\left(\frac{\delta v_1}{\delta x_1} + \frac{\delta v_2}{\delta x_2} + \frac{\delta v_3}{\delta x_3}\right)$$

$$= \mu\nabla^2 v_1 + \mu\frac{\delta}{\delta x_1} = (\nabla \cdot \mathbf{v})$$

(3.25)

$$= \mu\nabla^2 v_1 \text{ if } \mu = \text{const. and } (\nabla \cdot \mathbf{v}) = 0$$

In vector form, the viscous force term is:

$$\mathbf{f} = (\mu\nabla^2 v_1)\,\mathbf{x}_1 + (\mu\nabla^2 v_2)\,\mathbf{x}_2 + (\mu\nabla^2 v_3)\,\mathbf{x}_3$$

$$= \mu\nabla^2 \mathbf{v} \text{ if } \mu = \text{const.}; \nabla \cdot \mathbf{v} = 0 \quad \text{incompressible flow}$$

(3.26)

Euler's equation

Newton's law of motion for a fluid particle stands: the product of mass, ρdV, multiplied by the acceleration of a fluid particle, $\mathbf{a} = D\mathbf{v}/Dt$, is equal to the sum of the forces acting on the particle, the pressure force $(-\nabla p)\cdot dV$ and the gravity force $(\rho dV)\mathbf{g}$; dividing by dV, we obtain Euler's equation for a perfect inviscid fluid (i.e. a fluid with no viscosity):

$$\rho\frac{D\mathbf{v}}{Dt} = -\nabla p + \rho\mathbf{g}$$

(3.27)

or, taking into account that $\mathbf{a} = \dfrac{D\mathbf{v}}{Dt} = \dfrac{\delta\mathbf{v}}{\delta t} + (\mathbf{v} \cdot \nabla)\mathbf{v}$

$$\frac{\delta\mathbf{v}}{\delta t} + (\mathbf{v} \cdot \nabla)\mathbf{v} = -\frac{1}{\rho}\nabla p + \mathbf{g}$$

(3.28)

which corresponds to three scalar equations:

$$\frac{\delta v_i}{\delta t} + v_i\frac{\delta v_i}{\delta x_i} = -\frac{1}{\rho}\frac{\delta p}{\delta x_j} + \mathbf{g}\bigg|_{\substack{i=1,2,3;\\ j=1,2,3}}$$

(3.29)

These three equations and the mass conservation equation allow us to solve the problem for four variables (v_1, v_2, v_3, t).

The left side of Euler's equation is the acceleration of a fluid particle, while the right side is the sum of the forces per unit mass of fluid. Note that the fluid density appears only in the denominator of the pressure force term. For a given amount of acceleration, a high density liquid fluid particle requires a much greater pressure gradient ∇p than does a low density gas particle. On the other hand, a droplet of water and one of mercury would fall freely in a vacuum ($\nabla p = 0$) with the same acceleration g, despite their different densities.

To solve an inviscid fluid flow problem utilizing Cartesian coordinates, we must integrate Euler's equation to find the four dependent scalar variables (v_1, v_2, v_3, p) as functions of the independent variables (x_1, x_2, x_3, t), assuming ρ is a constant. Since we need four scalar equations to find the four dependent variables, we must append to the three scalar components of Euler's equation the equation of mass conservation of an incompressible fluid:

$$\frac{\delta v}{\delta t} + (v \cdot \nabla)v = -\frac{1}{\rho} \nabla p + g$$

$$\nabla \cdot v = 0 \tag{3.30}$$

Pressure in a fluid in a gravitational field

In the absence of any motion ($v = 0$), Euler's equation reduces to the equation for static equilibrium:

$$-\nabla p + \rho g = 0 \tag{3.31}$$

This equation of hydrostatic equilibrium expresses the force balance at each point in a stationary fluid. It shows that the pressure p must increase in the direction of g (since $\nabla p = \rho g$) and that the magnitude of the pressure gradient is ρg. The denser the fluid, the greater is the increase of pressure with depth. Furthermore, any horizontal plane in the fluid is a surface of constant pressure because ∇p has no component in the horizontal direction.

The differential equation of hydrostatic equilibrium (3.31) may be integrated explicitly along any line lying entirely within the fluid and connecting two points, 1 and 2, *whenever the density is constant within the fluid*. Denoting the line element by dc, the line integral of equation (3.31) becomes:

$$-\int_1^2 \nabla p \cdot dc + \int_1^2 \rho g \cdot dc = 0 \tag{3.32}$$

The first of these terms is:

$$\int_1^2 \nabla p \cdot dc = p_2 - p_1 \tag{3.33}$$

If we are assuming that the acceleration of gravity does not change with position **x**, which is acceptable as long as the vertical dimension of the fluid is small compared to the radius of the Earth, the acceleration of gravity can be expressed as the gradient of the scalar product of **g** and the position vector **x**:

$$\nabla(\mathbf{g} \cdot \mathbf{x}) = \frac{\delta(g_1 x_1)}{\delta x_1}\mathbf{x}_1 + \frac{\delta(g_2 x_2)}{\delta x_2}\mathbf{x}_2 + \frac{\delta(g_3 x_3)}{\delta x_3}\mathbf{x}_3 = g_1\mathbf{x}_1 + g_2\mathbf{x}_2 + g_3\mathbf{x}_3 = \mathbf{g}$$

(3.34)

Noting that ρ is constant, we now can evaluate the second integral:

$$\int_1^2 \rho\mathbf{g} \cdot dc = \rho\int_1^2 \nabla(\mathbf{g} \cdot \mathbf{x}) \cdot dc = \rho(\mathbf{g} \cdot \mathbf{x}|_2 - \mathbf{g} \cdot \mathbf{x}|_1) = \rho\mathbf{g}(\mathbf{x}_2 - \mathbf{x}_1) = \rho g h \quad (3.35)$$

or:

$$p_1 + \rho g z_1 = p_2 + \rho g z_2$$

(3.36)

Incompressible flow

If the fluid density is constant throughout the flow field and unvarying with time (an instance of incompressible flow), it is possible to simplify the form of Euler's equation by defining a new independent variable:

$$p^* = p + \rho g z$$

(3.37)

which is the sum of potential energies of pressure and position. Euler's equation becomes:

$$\rho\frac{D\mathbf{v}}{Dt} = -\nabla p^*$$

(3.38)

The variable p^* is a measure of the amount by which the pressure p differs from a hydrostatic pressure distribution and ∇p is the net force per unit volume available to accelerate the flow.

By introducing the variable p^*, gravity was eliminated explicitly from Euler's equation. Once we have solved Euler's equation and obtained $p^*(\mathbf{x}, t)$, we can then determine $p^*(\mathbf{x}, t)$ from equation (3.37).

Bernoulli's equation

To solve an inviscid fluid flow problem utilizing Cartesian coordinates, we must integrate Euler's and mass conservation equations:

$$\frac{\delta\mathbf{v}}{\delta t} + (\mathbf{v} \cdot \nabla)\mathbf{v} = -\frac{1}{\rho}\nabla p + \mathbf{g}$$

(3.39)

$$\nabla \cdot \mathbf{v} = 0$$

No general integral of these equations has yet been found. However, if we limit our attention to flows of simple geometry and initial and boundary conditions, we can find some analytical solutions that are useful in a practical way.

Bernoulli has derived what subsequently proved to be a single scalar integral of Euler's equation, one that applies to any inviscid flow provided that the fluid density does not vary arbitrarily, but only in a prescribed manner. This integral, called *Bernoulli's equation*, provides useful, although not complete, information about the fluid flow. For a complete description of the fluid flow, we would need four scalar integrals of Euler's equation and the mass conservation equation.

By using the vector identity:

$$\mathbf{v} \times (\nabla \times \mathbf{v}) = (\mathbf{v} \cdot \nabla)\mathbf{v} + \nabla\left(\frac{v^2}{2}\right) \tag{3.40}$$

Euler's equation becomes:

$$\frac{\delta \mathbf{v}}{\delta t} + \nabla\left(\frac{v^2}{2}\right) + \frac{1}{\rho}\nabla p - \mathbf{g} = \mathbf{v} \times (\nabla \times \mathbf{v}) \tag{3.41}$$

Two of the terms in this equation can be integrated directly along any line between two points in space:

$$\int_1^2 \nabla\left(\frac{v^2}{2}\right) \cdot dc = \frac{v^2}{2}\bigg|_2 - \frac{v^2}{2}\bigg|_1 \tag{3.42}$$

$$\int_1^2 \mathbf{g} \cdot dc = \int_1^2 \nabla (\mathbf{g} \cdot \mathbf{x}) \cdot dc = gh_2 - gh_1 \tag{3.43}$$

The constancy of density along a streamline is ensured by the condition that the density gradient $\nabla \rho$ is perpendicular to $\mathbf{v}$, or $\mathbf{V} \cdot (\nabla \rho) = 0$:

$$\int_1^2 \left(\frac{1}{\rho}\nabla p\right) \cdot ds = \frac{1}{\rho}\int_1^2 \nabla p \cdot ds = \frac{1}{\rho}(p_2 - p_1) \text{ if } \mathbf{v} \cdot (\nabla \rho) = C \tag{3.44}$$

(constant density along a streamline)

In order to integrate the right-hand term, we choose the line C to be a streamline (i.e. dc is parallel to V at each point along the line). To emphasize this choice, we denote the streamline element by ds. By this choice, the integral on the right side of equation (3.41) is zero because its integrand is perpendicular to $\mathbf{v}$ and therefore the scalar product of the integrand with ds is identically zero:

$$\int_1^2 \mathbf{v} \times (\nabla \times \mathbf{v}) \cdot d\mathbf{s} = 0, \text{ if } d\mathbf{s} \times \mathbf{v} = 0 \text{ *(integral along a streamline)*}$$

$$(3.45)$$

We obtain Bernoulli's equation, which expresses the energy conservation of a perfect fluid ($\mu = 0$) in conservative flow ($\nabla \cdot \mathbf{v} = 0$) along a streamline:

$$\int_1^2 \frac{\delta \mathbf{v}}{\delta t} \cdot d\mathbf{s} + \left(\frac{\mathbf{v}^2}{2} + \frac{p}{\rho} gx_3 \right) + \left(\frac{\mathbf{v}^2}{2} + \frac{p}{\rho} gx_3 \right)_2 = 0$$

$$(3.46)$$

if $\mathbf{v} \cdot (\nabla \rho) = 0$, $d\mathbf{s} \times \mathbf{v} = 0$

where $\mathbf{g} \cdot \mathbf{x} = -gx_3$.

For permanent flow ($\delta \mathbf{v}/\delta t = 0$), Bernoulli's equation becomes:

$$\frac{\mathbf{v}^2}{2} + \frac{p}{\rho} gx_3 = \text{constant}$$

if $\delta \mathbf{v}/\delta t = 0$, stationary flow

$$(3.47)$$

$\mathbf{v} \cdot (\nabla \rho) = 0$, constant density along a streamline

$d\mathbf{s} \times \mathbf{v} = 0$, integration along a streamline

Navier–Stokes equation of motion

Partial differential equations

If we add an additional term, $\mathbf{f}/\rho$, to the right side of Euler's equation to account for the viscous force which was neglected in deriving Euler's equation, we obtain the Navier–Stokes equation. It expresses the Newton law for an infinitesimal particle as the force balance of pressure force $-\nabla p/\rho$, viscous force $\mathbf{f}/\rho$, and gravitational force $\mathbf{g}$ per unit mass:

$$\begin{cases} \dfrac{D\mathbf{v}}{Dt} = -\dfrac{1}{\rho}\nabla p + \dfrac{\mu}{\rho}\nabla^2\mathbf{v} + \mathbf{g}, \text{ if } \mu = \text{const.} \\ \nabla \cdot \mathbf{v} = 0 \text{ (incompressible flow)} \end{cases}$$

$$(3.48)$$

where $\mu/\rho = \nu$ is the cinematic viscosity. When the fluid density is constant throughout the flow field, it is convenient to introduce the variable $p^* = p - \rho\mathbf{g}\cdot\mathbf{x}$, so that the gravity term is combined implicitly with the pressure term:

$$\frac{D\mathbf{v}}{Dt} = -\frac{1}{\rho}\nabla p^* + \frac{\mu}{\rho}\nabla^2\mathbf{v} \text{ if } \rho, = \text{constant}; \; \nabla \cdot \mathbf{v} = 0$$

$$(3.49)$$

(incompressible flow)

The Navier–Stokes equation is a partial differential equation with four independent variables (x_1, x_2, x_3, t) and four dependent variables (v_1, v_2, v_3, p^*). Together with the mass conservation equation, there are four scalar equations (three components of the Navier–Stokes equation and the mass conservation equation) that may be solved for the four unknown dependent variables:

$$\begin{cases} \nabla \cdot \mathbf{v} = 0 \text{ (incompressible flow)} \\ \dfrac{D\mathbf{v}}{Dt} = -\dfrac{1}{\rho}\nabla p^* + \dfrac{\mu}{\rho}\nabla^2 \mathbf{v}, \text{ if } \rho,\mu = \text{const.} \end{cases} \tag{3.50}$$

Needless to say, there is no general solution to this set of equations.

Expressed in differential form, the momentum conservation principle is restricted to inviscid flow (Euler's equation) or incompressible viscous flow (incompressible Navier–Stokes equation).

Boundary conditions

Before we can solve viscous flow problems by integrating the equations of motion and mass conservation, we must specify the physical conditions that constrain the flow at its boundaries, called *boundary conditions*, and the state of the flow at an initial time (if the flow is time dependent), called the *initial condition*. These conditions are generally recognizable from the nature of the flow:

- *Inflow*: at an inflow boundary, the velocity of the fluid is specified: $\mathbf{v} = \mathbf{v}_{boundary}$.
- *Outflow*: at an outflow boundary, a Neumann condition is used for the velocity, and the value of the pressure is specified, $p = p_{boundary}$.
- *Slip*: a slip condition means that the normal component of the velocity is zero: $n \cdot \mathbf{u} = 0$.
- *No slip*: a no-slip condition means that the velocity of the fluid equals the velocity of the boundary, usually zero. This is normally used for walls: $\mathbf{v} = \mathbf{v}_{boundary}$.
- *Straight out*: at a straight-out outflow boundary, the pressure and the tangential components of the velocity are zero: $t \cdot \mathbf{u} = 0$; $p = 0$.
- *Neutral*: a neutral boundary is treated as if there were no boundary, $n \cdot (\mu(\nabla \cdot \mathbf{u} + (\nabla \cdot \mathbf{u}))^T) = 0$.

The Navier–Stokes equation of motion was derived by Claude-Louis-Marie Navier in 1827 and independently by Siméon-Denis Poisson in 1831. Their motivations of the stress tensor were based on what amounts to a molecular view of how stresses are exerted by one fluid particle against another. Later, Barré de Saint Venant (in 1843) and George Gabriel Stokes (in 1845) derived the equation, starting with the linear stress rate-of-strain argument.

Conservation of energy for incompressible viscous flow

The principles that govern the motion of an incompressible viscous flow are embodied in the conservation of mass:

$$\nabla \cdot \mathbf{v} = 0 \text{ or } + (\mathbf{v} \cdot \nabla)\rho = 0 \tag{3.51}$$

and the Navier–Stokes equation:

$$\frac{\delta \mathbf{v}}{\delta t} + (\mathbf{v} \cdot \nabla)\mathbf{v} = -\frac{1}{\rho}\nabla p + \frac{\mu}{\rho}\nabla^2 \mathbf{v} + \mathbf{g}, \text{ if } \mu = \text{const.} \tag{3.52}$$

For a low-velocity flow with negligible viscous dissipation, and considering that the effects of thermal dilatation are negligible, the energy conservation equation can be written as:

$$\rho C_p \left(\frac{\delta T}{\delta t} + (\mathbf{v} \cdot \nabla)T \right) = \nabla \cdot (k \nabla T) + S_h \tag{3.53}$$

where:

- T [K] is the temperature;
- ρ [kg/m³] is the density;
- C_p [J/kg.K] is the specific heat capacity;
- k [W/m.K] is the thermal conductivity;
- S_h [W/m³] is the volumetric rate of heat generation.

The term $\rho C_p(\mathbf{v} \cdot \nabla)T$ represents the diffusion and the term $\nabla \cdot (k \nabla T)$ represents the conduction heat transfer within fluid. If C_p is constant, $h = c_p T$ and:

$$\frac{\delta T}{\delta t} + (\mathbf{v} \cdot \nabla)T = \alpha \nabla \cdot (\nabla T) + \frac{S_h}{\rho C_p} \tag{3.54}$$

where $\alpha = k/\rho C_p$.

There are two types of boundary conditions:

1 imposed temperature: $T = T_{boundary}$; and
2 imposed heat flux: $q_{boundary} = \bar{n} \cdot \lambda \nabla T$.

Here, n is the unit vector normal to the exterior of the boundary $\delta\Omega$.

Mixed or natural convection

In forced convection, the fluid moves due to external conditions and buoyancy is negligible. The movement is described by the mass, momentum and energy conservation equations:

$$\begin{cases} \dfrac{\delta\rho}{\delta t} + (\mathbf{v} \cdot \nabla)\rho = 0 \\[2ex] \dfrac{\delta\mathbf{v}}{\delta t} + (\mathbf{v} \cdot \nabla)\mathbf{v} = -\dfrac{1}{\rho}\nabla p + \dfrac{\mu}{\rho}\nabla^2\mathbf{v} + \mathbf{g}, \text{ if } \mu = \text{const.} \\[2ex] \dfrac{\delta T}{\delta t} + (\mathbf{v} \cdot \nabla)T = \alpha\nabla \cdot (\nabla T) + \dfrac{S_h}{\rho C_p} \end{cases} \qquad (3.55)$$

In natural and mixed convection, the fluid moves to buoyancy forces resulting from the density gradient. By using the approximation of Boussinesq:

$$\rho_0 - \rho = \rho\beta(T - T_0) \qquad (3.56)$$

where the subscript 0 stands for the ambient values, the set of partial differential equations that describe this phenomena is:

$$\begin{cases} \mathbf{v} \cdot \nabla = 0 \\[2ex] \dfrac{\delta\mathbf{v}}{\delta t} + (\mathbf{v} \cdot \nabla)\mathbf{v} = -\dfrac{1}{\rho}\nabla p + \dfrac{\mu}{\rho}\nabla^2\mathbf{v} + \beta T\mathbf{g}, \text{ if } \mu = \text{const.} \\[2ex] \dfrac{\delta T}{\delta t} + (\mathbf{v} \cdot \nabla)T = \alpha\nabla \cdot (\nabla T) + \dfrac{S_h}{\rho C_p} \end{cases} \qquad (3.57)$$

Example (Figure 3.5): for the visualization of the flow with mixed convection in a room, see the file *heat_flow_in_room.mpg* on the CD that accompanies this book.

Turbulence

The nature and origin of turbulence

Most flows that occur in nature and in engineering applications are turbulent. For instance, the atmospheric boundary layer, jet streams in the upper troposphere and cumulus clouds are all in turbulent motion, as are the flow of water in rivers or the wakes of ships, cars or aircrafts. In fact, in fluid dynamics, laminar flow is an exception, not the rule; there must be very small dimensions and very high viscosity in order to encounter laminar flow.

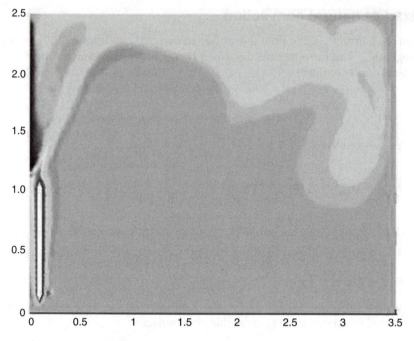

Source: Comsol Inc, www.comsol.com

Figure 3.5 *Heat flow in a room*

Everyone who has seen the development of a cigarette smoke plume in a quiet indoor environment has some idea about the nature of a turbulent flow. However, the precise description of a turbulent flow is quite impossible; all we can do is to draw the main characteristics of turbulent flows (Tennekes and Lumley, 1972):

- *Irregularity or randomness*: one main characteristic of turbulent flows is the randomness in time and space of all of its physical characteristics. This characteristic makes the deterministic approach impossible and leads to the statistical analysis of turbulent flows.
- *Diffusivity*: the diffusivity of turbulence creates rapid mixing of the flows and, as a consequence, increases the rate of momentum, heat and mass transfers.
- *Three-dimensional*: turbulence is rotational and three dimensional; it is characterized by high levels of fluctuating vorticity.
- *Dissipation*: turbulence is a dissipative phenomenon and requires a constant supply of energy to compensate the viscous losses. Usually this energy is provided by shear or buoyancy phenomena.
- A *characteristic of flows*: turbulence is not a feature of fluids but a feature of fluid flows. Since every flow is different, every turbulent flow is unique even though turbulent flows have many characteristics in common.

The origin of turbulence

In flows that are originally laminar, turbulence arises from instabilities occurring at large Reynolds numbers. In duct flows, turbulence may appear at a Reynolds number (based on the mean velocity and the diameter of the duct) around 2000. Boundary layers in zero pressure gradients become unstable at a Reynolds number close to 600 (based on the non-disturbed velocity of the flow and the displacement thickness). For mixing layers, turbulence may occur even at very low Reynolds numbers due to an inviscid instability mechanism that does not exist in duct flows or boundary layers.

Since turbulence is a dissipative phenomenon, it cannot maintain itself without some energy provided by the environment. The main source is usually shear in the flow itself; but buoyancy can also play this role in most of the flows existing in the building environment. If this source vanishes, the flow will tend to become laminar. Another way of preventing a laminar flow from becoming turbulent is to provide for a mechanism that will consume kinetic energy. This phenomenon may exist in atmospheric flows with stable density stratification. If the transition to turbulence is still poorly understood, direct numerical simulation and experiments have shown that turbulence is usually initiated by a primary instability mechanism. Instabilities that trigger off the creation of eddies in a flow induce turbulence. This primary instability will generate secondary motions, usually three dimensional, that will become unstable themselves. This kind of sequence generates turbulent spots which grow rapidly and randomly and create a developed turbulent flow.

As turbulence is a continuum phenomenon (even the smallest scales occurring in a turbulent flow are far larger than the molecular scale), it is governed by the equations of fluid dynamics that can be used to model a turbulent flow.

However, turbulent flows are characterized by a random evolution in time and space, a strong three-dimensional diffusion of all quantities (temperature, velocities, pollutant concentration, etc.) and energy transfer between eddies. The size of these eddies, which is proportional to the geometry taken into consideration, may be characterized at the macro-scale. Energy is transferred from the large-scale eddies to the smaller-scale eddies: this is called the energy cascade. This phenomenon occurs until the smallest scale is reached. At this scale, there is a balance between the inertial forces due to turbulence and the molecular viscous forces. This scale η_k, called 'Kolmogorov micro-scale', can be calculated as follows:

$$\eta_k = l\, Re^{-3/4} \tag{3.58}$$

where the Reynolds number Re is defined as:

$$Re = \frac{u\,l}{v} \tag{3.59}$$

where u is a turbulent velocity scale and v is the kinematic viscosity of the fluid. If direct numerical simulation is applied, at least $Re^{9/4}$ discretization nodes are necessary to account for Kolmogorov micro-scale. For most high Reynolds number turbulent flows, such as those encountered in natural ventilation applications, this surpasses the possibilities of high-performance computers. The energy transfer from the large-scale energy containing eddies to the smaller ones must therefore be modelled.

The following equations are given for two dimensions for the sake of simplicity. They are valid for three dimensions.

Time averaging of the instantaneous flow equations: Reynolds decomposition

In order to model the random feature of turbulent flows, one can introduce into the governing equations of the flow field a time decomposition (also called Reynolds decomposition) of the instantaneous flow variables $\phi(t)$:

$$\phi(t) = \bar{\phi} + \phi'(t) \tag{3.60}$$

where $\bar{\phi}$ is the mean value of $\phi(t)$ and $\phi'(t)$ is the instantaneous fluctuation of $\phi(t)$ (see Figure 3.6). The mean value of $\phi(t)$ is obtained by integrating $\phi(t)$ over a period T that is long in comparison with the oscillation periods of the fluctuations:

$$\bar{\phi} = \frac{1}{T} \int_{t}^{t+T} \phi(t_1) dt_1 \tag{3.61}$$

In addition, the mean value of $\phi'(t)$ is zero:

$$\overline{\phi(t)} = 0 \tag{3.62}$$

The following mathematical rules (called Reynolds' rules) are used to time average the instantaneous flow equations:

$$\overline{u + v} = \bar{u} + \bar{v} \tag{3.63}$$

$$\overline{\frac{\delta u}{\delta x_i}} = \frac{\delta \bar{u}}{\delta x_i} \tag{3.64}$$

$$\overline{\bar{u} u'} = 0 \tag{3.65}$$

$$\overline{\bar{u} \cdot \bar{v}} = \bar{u} \cdot \bar{v} \tag{3.66}$$

$$\overline{u \cdot v} = \bar{u} \cdot \bar{v} + \overline{u'} \tag{3.67}$$

Introducing Reynolds decomposition into the continuity equation and time averaging the resulting equation involves:

$$\frac{\delta \bar{u}}{\delta x} + \frac{\delta \bar{v}}{\delta y} = 0 \tag{3.68}$$

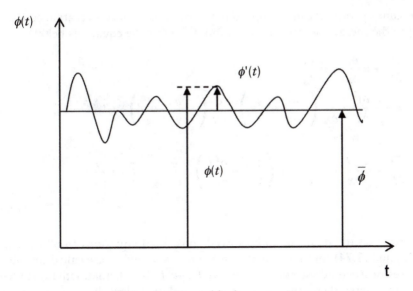

Figure 3.6 *Reynolds decomposition*

By subtracting this equation (the time-averaged continuity equation) from the instantaneous continuity equation, one obtains:

$$\frac{\delta u'}{\delta x} + \frac{\delta v'}{\delta y} = 0 \tag{3.69}$$

Applying the same procedure (introduction of Reynolds decomposition and time averaging) to the x-momentum conservation equation yields:

$$\frac{\delta \bar{u}}{\delta t} + \bar{u}\frac{\delta \bar{u}}{\delta x} + \overline{u'\frac{\delta u'}{\delta x}} + \bar{v}\frac{\delta \bar{u}}{\delta y} + \overline{v'\frac{\delta u'}{\delta y}} = -\frac{1}{\rho}\frac{\delta \bar{P}}{\delta x} + v\left(\frac{\delta^2 \bar{u}}{\delta x^2} + \frac{\delta^2 \bar{u}}{\delta y^2}\right) \tag{3.70}$$

In this equation, the fluctuating terms can be manipulated according to the following manner:

$$\overline{u'\frac{\delta u'}{\delta x}} + \overline{v'\frac{\delta u'}{\delta y}} = \overline{u'\frac{\delta u'}{\delta x}} + \overline{v'\frac{\delta u'}{\delta y}} + \overline{u'\left(\frac{\delta u'}{\delta x} + \frac{\delta v'}{\delta y}\right)} = \frac{\delta}{\delta x}(\overline{u'u'}) + \frac{\delta}{\delta y}(\overline{u'v'})$$

$$\tag{3.71}$$

Equations (3.70) and (3.71) lead to:

$$\frac{\delta u}{\delta t} + \bar{u}\frac{\delta \bar{u}}{\delta x} + \bar{v}\frac{\delta \bar{u}}{\delta y} = -\frac{1}{\rho}\frac{\delta \bar{P}}{\delta x} + \frac{\delta}{\delta x}\left(v\frac{\delta \bar{u}}{\delta x} - \overline{u'u'}\right) + \frac{\delta}{\delta y}\left(v\frac{\delta \bar{u}}{\delta y} - \overline{u'v'}\right)$$

$$\tag{3.72}$$

The same operations can be applied to the y-momentum conservation equation and to the energy conservation equation; this gives the equations below:

$$\frac{\delta\bar{v}}{\delta t} + \bar{u}\frac{\delta\bar{v}}{\delta x} + \bar{v}\frac{\delta\bar{v}}{\delta y}$$

$$= -\frac{1}{\rho}\frac{\delta\bar{P}}{\delta y} + \frac{\delta}{\delta x}\left(v\frac{\delta\bar{v}}{\delta x} - \overline{u'v'}\right) + \frac{\delta}{\delta x}\left(v\frac{\delta\bar{v}}{\delta y} - \overline{v'v'}\right) + g\beta_T(\bar{T} - T_0) \qquad (3.73)$$

$$\frac{\delta\bar{T}}{\delta t} + \bar{u}\frac{\delta\bar{T}}{\delta x} + \bar{v}\frac{\delta\bar{T}}{\delta y} = \alpha\left(\frac{\delta^2\bar{T}}{\delta x^2} + \frac{\delta^2\bar{T}}{\delta y^2}\right) + \frac{\delta}{\delta x}(-\overline{u'T'}) + \frac{\delta}{\delta y}(-\overline{v'T'})$$

$$(3.74)$$

The final set of equations to be solved consists of equations (3.68), (3.72), (3.73) and (3.74). In these equations, $-\overline{u'u'}, -\overline{u'v'}, -\overline{v'v'}$ are called turbulent stresses or Reynolds stresses, while $-\overline{u'T'}, -\overline{v'T'}$ are denominated turbulent heat transfers; these turbulent stresses and turbulent heat transfers are representative of the influence of the fluctuations on the mean flow. The unknowns are $\bar{u}, \bar{v}, \bar{P}, \bar{T}$ and $-\overline{u'u'}, -\overline{u'v'}, -\overline{v'v'}, -\overline{u'T'}, -\overline{v'T'}$. There are too many unknowns for the available equations. Closure hypotheses therefore need to be found in order to solve this set of equations.

These equations can be closed in roughly two ways:

1   $-\overline{u'u'}$, and $-\overline{u'_jT'}$ are determined from algebraic relationships, which leads to zero, one and two equation turbulence models.
2   Conservation equations for the turbulent stresses and the turbulent fluxes are solved; these are second-order models.

It is still difficult to implement second-order models because many equations must be solved (at least nine additional equations for a three-dimensional configuration), and convergence is not easy to obtain (Chen, 1996).

The turbulent viscosity concept
In 1877, Boussinesq made an analogy between the molecular stresses τ_{ij} in Newtonian fluids, expressed as:

$$\tau_{ij} = y\left(\frac{\delta u_i}{\delta x_j} + \frac{\delta u_j}{\delta x_i}\right) \qquad (3.75)$$

($\frac{\delta u_i}{\delta x_j}$ and $\frac{\delta u_j}{\delta x_i}$ are the gradients of instantaneous velocity), and the turbulent stresses $-\overline{u'_iu'_j}$:

$$\overline{u'_i u'_j} = v_t \left(\frac{\delta \overline{u}_i}{\delta x_j} + \frac{\delta \overline{u}_j}{\delta x_i} \right) \tag{3.76}$$

where $\frac{\delta \overline{u}_i}{\delta x_j}$ and $\frac{\delta \overline{u}_j}{\delta x_i}$ are the gradients of mean velocity and v_t is the turbulent viscosity. Unlike the kinematic viscosity of the fluid, the turbulent viscosity is not an intrinsic property of the fluid but a local property of the flow. Thus, t may be calculated at any point in the flow. It should be noticed here that this analogy works for isotropic turbulent flows.

Another analogy can be conducted between the molecular heat transfer φ_j:

$$\varphi_i = \left(\alpha \frac{\delta T}{\delta x_i} \right) \times (\rho C) \tag{3.77}$$

where C is the heat capacity of the fluid and the turbulent heat transfer:

$$(-\overline{u'_j T'}) \times (\rho C) = \left(\alpha_t \frac{\delta \overline{T}}{\delta x_j} \right) \times (\rho C) \tag{3.78}$$

where a_t, the turbulent thermal diffusivity, is also a local property of the flow.

The use of equations (3.76) and (3.78) notably decreases the number of unknowns; but v_t and a_t must, nevertheless, be calculated everywhere in the flow.

Constant turbulent viscosity
This is the simplest imaginable model, which consists of considering constant turbulent viscosity. However, it is known that the turbulent viscosity is far from constant, making this model inappropriate for the majority of industrial flows.

Mixing length (zero-equation) model
This model was introduced by Prandtl in 1925 in analogy with the kinetic theory of gases. The turbulent viscosity is considered proportional to a mean fluctuating velocity and to a mixing length, l_m, which corresponds to the mean free distance of the particles. As a supplementary hypothesis, Prandtl considered that the mean fluctuating velocity is equal to the gradient of the mean velocity multiplied by the mixing length. The gradient of the mean velocity is calculated from the tensor of deformation, d:

$$\nabla_M \overline{u} = [tr(\underline{\underline{d}}\,\underline{\underline{d}})]^{1/2} \tag{3.79}$$

where $tr(.)$ represents the trace operator. In Cartesian coordinates, the tensor $\underline{d}$ is defined by:

$$d_{ij} = \frac{1}{2}\left(\frac{\delta \bar{u}_i}{\delta x_j} + \frac{\delta \bar{u}_j}{\delta x_i}\right) \tag{3.80}$$

and $\underline{\underline{dd}}$ may be calculated by:

$$(\underline{\underline{dd}})_{ik} = d_{ij}d_{jk} \tag{3.81}$$

or, taking the trace and given the symmetry of $\underline{d}$:

$$tr(\underline{\underline{dd}})_{ik} = d_{ij}d_{ij} = \frac{1}{2}\left(\frac{\delta \bar{u}_i}{\delta x_j} + \frac{\delta \bar{u}_j}{\delta x_i}\right)\frac{\delta \bar{u}_i}{\delta x_j} \tag{3.82}$$

The invariance of $\nabla_M \bar{u}$ in any system of coordinates is due to the properties of tensor $\underline{d}$ and trace operator. The turbulent viscosity is then given by:

$$\mu_t = \rho K L_m^2 = [(\underline{\underline{dd}})]^{1/2} \tag{3.83}$$

where K is von Karman constant ($K = 0.41$).

The k-ε (two-equation model)

This is the most widely used model in air-flow simulation in rooms. Introduced by Harlow and Nakayama (1968), it became popular primarily because it was believed that the use of the kinetic energy dissipation rate, ε requires no extra terms near the wall. The time-averaged turbulent energy per unit mass is the combination of the kinetic energies of many eddies of different sizes. The allocation of this kinetic energy to motions of different length scales is called the *turbulent energy spectrum*. The amount of turbulent energy in a flow is limited by the loss of energy due to viscous dissipation. The distribution of turbulent kinetic energy among motions of different length scales is commonly given as a function of the wave number, κ which is inversely proportional to eddy size. Kolmogoroff showed that the smallest eddy has a wave number, κ_K, which is related to the rate of loss of turbulent energy, ε and the flow Reynolds number by:

$$\kappa_K = (\varepsilon/v^3) \cong Re^{3/4}/D \tag{3.84}$$

The smallest eddies are therefore several orders of magnitude smaller than the largest energy-containing eddies since the Reynolds number of a turbulent flow is necessarily large. This fundamental physical property of turbulent flow makes it extremely difficult to completely describe a turbulent flow, even using the largest and fastest computers available today. Instead, we must compromise by using much less information, such as k and ε, to characterize the effects of turbulence and must be content to obtain approximate solutions to the mean flow field.

The k-ε model consists of the turbulent kinetic energy equation:

$$\frac{Dk}{Dt} = \frac{1}{\rho} \nabla^2 \left[k \left(\mu_l + \frac{\mu_t}{\sigma_k} \right) \right] + \frac{\mu_t}{\rho} G - \varepsilon \tag{3.85}$$

and the dissipation rate equation:

$$\frac{D\varepsilon}{Dt} = \frac{1}{\rho} \nabla^2 \left[\varepsilon \left(\mu_l + \frac{\mu_t}{\sigma_\varepsilon} \right) \right] + C_{l\varepsilon} \frac{\mu_t}{\rho} G \frac{\varepsilon}{k} - C_{2\varepsilon} \frac{\varepsilon^2}{k} \tag{3.86}$$

where G represents the turbulent generation rate:

$$G = 2 \left[\left(\frac{\delta u}{\delta x} \right)^2 + \left(\frac{\delta v}{\delta y} \right)^2 + \left(\frac{\delta w}{\delta z} \right)^2 \right] + \left(\frac{\delta u}{\delta y} + \frac{\delta v}{\delta x} \right)^2 + \left(\frac{\delta v}{\delta z} + \frac{\delta w}{\delta y} \right)^2 + \left(\frac{\delta w}{\delta x} + \frac{\delta u}{\delta z} \right)^2$$

$$3.87$$

and the turbulent viscosity:

$$\mu_t = C_\mu \rho \frac{k^2}{\varepsilon} \tag{3.88}$$

The parameters are considered with constant values: $C_\mu = 0.09$, $\sigma_k = 1.0$, $\sigma_k = 1.3$, $C_{l\mu} = 1.44$, $C_{2\varepsilon} = 1.92$.

THE ATMOSPHERIC BOUNDARY LAYER

Theoretically, the basic laws of fluid dynamics can be used for any kind of flow. However, for practical reasons, simple models were developed and are largely used.

General description

Recordings of the time variation of the wind velocity (see Figure 3.7) show that the wind flow is characterized by strong turbulence. In the low atmospheric layers, turbulence is generated by any ground obstacle, as well as by thermal airflow instabilities. Turbulence decreases with increasing height.

The instantaneous wind velocity should therefore be calculated using a statistical approach. We will discuss its main hypotheses here.

As seen before, applying the Reynolds decomposition, the wind velocity can be written as the sum of an average and a fluctuating term. For the longitudinal component $u(t)$ we obtain:

$$u(t) = \bar{u} + u'(t) \tag{3.89}$$

where:

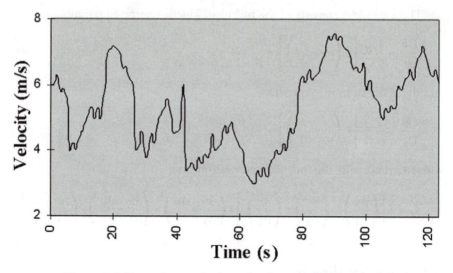

Figure 3.7 *Typical record of wind velocity near the ground*

- $u(t)$ is the instantaneous speed;
- $\bar{u}$ is the average speed; and
- $u'(t)$ is the fluctuating part.

The average wind velocity is given by:

$$\bar{u} = \frac{1}{T}\int_{t_0}^{t_0+T} u(t)dt \tag{3.90}$$

The averaging process is supposed to be independent of time, and the period T is such that the average operator should converge in a quadratic mean. In the low atmosphere, the experimental value of T ranges typically between ten minutes and one hour.

The vertical and lateral mean velocity components of a homogeneous flow on a flat ground are zero due to adherence and permeability conditions. The components of the instantaneous velocity vector $v(t)$ are:

$$\bar{u} + u'(t), \bar{v} + v'(t), \bar{w} + w'(t) \tag{3.91}$$

where:

- $u'(t)$ is the longitudinal fluctuation;
- $v'(t)$ is the lateral fluctuation; and
- $w'(t)$ is the vertical fluctuation.

If the effects of thermal stratification on the wind velocity can be neglected (general case for building applications), then, in a first approximation, the flow direction is assumed to be constant in the immediate vicinity of the ground (in a 100m height layer). By orienting the x-axis according to the mean flow direction, the mean velocity will only depend upon the height z above the ground.

For a horizontal homogeneous steady flow, by neglecting the molecular viscosity term, the Navier–Stokes equations lead to:

$$u\frac{\delta u}{\delta x} + v\frac{\delta v}{\delta y} + w\frac{\delta w}{\delta z} = 0 \qquad (3.92)$$

The continuity equation for a three-dimensional incompressible flow gives:

$$\frac{\delta u}{\delta x} + \frac{\delta v}{\delta y} + \frac{\delta w}{\delta z} = 0 \qquad (3.93)$$

By introducing the Reynolds decomposition of the velocity vector (3.89) into the Navier–Stokes equations, we obtain:

$$\frac{\delta(u'w')}{\delta z} = 0 \qquad (3.94)$$

It can be noticed from this equation that the turbulent momentum flux is constant with height.

Integrating equation (3.94) between the ground (z = 0) and height z yields:

$$-u'v' = \frac{\tau_0}{\rho} \qquad (3.95)$$

where τ_0 is the friction stress at the ground. τ_0 is usually equal to Δu^{*2}, u^* being a velocity scale called the 'friction velocity'. Reynolds decomposition enables us to introduce turbulence effects into the mean airflow equations. Reynolds stresses should, nevertheless, be expressed in terms of mean velocity in order to close the system of equations.

The first-order closure is based on the analogy between turbulent and molecular motions. Locally, the fluctuating velocity u' varies linearly with the distance of displacement l, while w' is in the same order of magnitude as u'. This is Prandtl mixing length theory expressed by:

$$u' \cong -\frac{\delta\overline{u}}{\delta z}l \qquad (3.96)$$

where:

$$cl^2\left(\frac{\delta\overline{u}}{\delta z}\right)^2 = u^{*2} \qquad (3.97)$$

and $\sqrt{cl} = kz$, where k = 0.41 (von Karman constant).

The mean velocity can therefore be calculated from the following equation:

$$\frac{\delta \overline{u}}{\delta z} = \frac{u^*}{kz}$$ (3.98)

The mean velocity equals zero ($\overline{u} = 0$) at the reference height $z = z_0$, where z_0 is the roughness length (a characteristic of the ground surface).

The mean wind velocity is thus a logarithmic function of the height above the ground:

$$\overline{u}(l) = \frac{u^*}{k} \ln \left(\frac{z}{z_0} \right)$$ (3.99)

The values of u^* and z_0 can be obtained experimentally.

The velocity profile in semi-logarithmic coordinates is a straight line of slope k/u^* and y-component at origin $\ln z_0$.

The roughness height is an aerodynamic characteristic of the ground surface. For an identical geostrophic velocity and an identical height above the ground, the average velocity will decrease for an increasing roughness of the ground. The roughness height is thus a function of the nature of the ground and the geometry of existing obstacles. Table 3.1 presents an experimental value range obtained on homogeneous sites of great horizontal extension (Wieringa, 1991).

A logarithmic variation law of the wind speed with the height is obviously applicable only above a height z^* where the flow can 'see' irregularities of the ground. z^* corresponds to the effective thickness of the turbulent substratum and is usually equal to 1.5 h_0, where h_0 is the average obstacle height (Sacré, 1988).

Furthermore, when the density of obstacles is high (i.e. they occupy more than 25 per cent of the total ground area), the apparent level of the ground beside the flow is raised. This problem is solved by introducing the concept of displacement height in the formulation of the vertical velocity profile:

Table 3.1 *Roughness height and class*

Type of surface	Roughness height (m)	Roughness class
Sea, snow and sand	0.0005	I
Sea with very strong wind	0.005	II
Short grass	0.01	III
Cultivated open fields	0.05	IV
High plants and open country	0.10	V
Countryside and spread habitat	0.25	VI
Peripheral urban zone	0.50	VII
Mean city centre and forest	1.00	VIII
Metropolis centre and tropical forest	4.00	IX

$$\bar{u}(z) = \frac{u^*}{k} \ln\left(\frac{z - d_0}{z_0}\right) \tag{3.100}$$

In a first approximation, $d_0 = 0.7\, h_0$.

Data transfer in a homogeneous site

In practice, available data on wind characteristics come from standard meteorological measurements that are taken at stations near airports. In an airport environment, the roughness class is IV. A reference velocity u_{ref} is defined as the mean velocity measured at a height of 10m on a site of homogeneous roughness for which z_{0ref} equals 0.05m:

$$\bar{u}_{ref} = \frac{u_{ref}^*}{k} \ln\left(\frac{10}{z_{0ref}}\right) \tag{3.101}$$

The main difficulty is expressing the speed of the observable wind on the studied site according to what is measured at the meteorological station ($\bar{u}_{ref}$). In a first approximation, the velocity of the geostrophic wind can be assumed to be identical above the two sites.

This relationship between the two speeds can then be written as:

$$\bar{u}(z) = \lambda(z_0)\bar{u}_{ref} \ln\left(\frac{z}{z_0}\right) \tag{3.102}$$

with:

$$\lambda(z_0) = \frac{u^*}{u_{ref}} \frac{1}{\ln\left(\dfrac{10}{z_{0ref}}\right)} \tag{3.103}$$

where $\dfrac{u^*}{u_{ref}}$ remains to be determined. An approximate formula for u^*/u^*_{ref} is (ESDU 82026, 1982):

$$\frac{u^*}{u^*_{ref}} = \frac{\ln\left(\dfrac{10^5}{z_{0ref}}\right)}{\ln\left(\dfrac{10^5}{z_0}\right)} \tag{3.104}$$

that gives the values in Table 3.1.

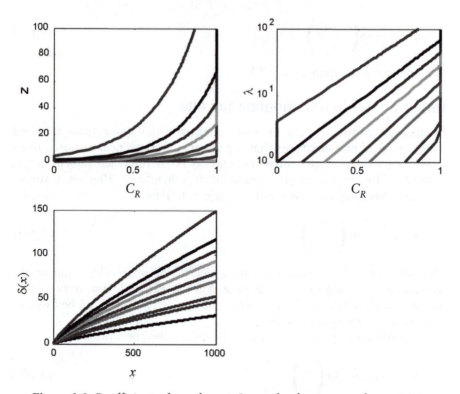

Figure 3.8 *Coefficient of roughness, C_R, and reference roughness, $\lambda(x)$*

Similarity considerations at the scale of the atmospheric boundary layer allow one to express the geostrophic wind velocity:

$$u_g = \sqrt{u_g^2 + u_{gv}^2} \tag{3.105}$$

Taking into account the characteristic parameters of the boundary layer (the roughness length z_0, the Coriolis parameter f and the friction velocity u^*) Simiu (1973) proposes the following formula for the geostrophic wind velocity:

$$u_g^2 = \frac{u^{*2}}{k}\left(\left(\ln\left(\frac{u^*}{fz_0}\right) - B\right)^2 + A^2\right) \tag{3.106}$$

This relationship results from a balance between the force of the geostrophic pressure gradient and the friction force on the surface of the ground. A and B have been estimated experimentally: $A = 4.5$ and $B = 1.7$. This expression gives a rough estimate of the atmospheric boundary layer height ($\delta = 0.3\ u^*/f$) and of the angular deviation between the geostrophic flow and the flow at ground level:

$$\sin \alpha = -\frac{A u^{*}}{k u_{g}} \tag{3.107}$$

By setting the geostrophic velocity to correspond to the studied site equal to the one at the meteorological station, the following non-linear relationship between the corresponding friction velocities was deduced:

$$\frac{u^{*}}{u^{*}_{ref}} = \frac{\sqrt{\left(\ln\left(\dfrac{u^{*}_{ref}}{fz_{0ref}}\right) - B\right)^{2} + A^{2}}}{\sqrt{\left(\ln\left(\dfrac{u^{*}}{fz_{0}}\right) - B\right)^{2} + A^{2}}} \tag{3.108}$$

Table 3.2 gives the values of the coefficient $\lambda(z_0)$ for the different types of roughness described in Table 3.1 (λ is the reference roughness $z_{0ref} = 0.05$ calculated with the help of the approximate formula proposed by ESDU (1988)):

$$\frac{u^{*}}{u^{*}_{ref}} = \frac{\ln\left(\dfrac{10^{5}}{z_{0ref}}\right)}{\ln\left(\dfrac{10^{5}}{z_{0}}\right)} \tag{3.109}$$

The site environment is rarely homogeneous; each site is thus characterized in a few kilometres extension by its topographical position (hill, valley, etc.) and the nature of the terrain (geographical distribution of urban zones, the close-cropped countryside, etc.), and in a few hundred metres by the presence of nearby obstacles (hedges, trees, houses, etc.).

In order to take these particular site characteristics into consideration, three specific coefficients are usually introduced for the definition of the average local wind velocity as a function of the reference mean velocity. These

Table 3.2 $\lambda(z_0)$ *values*

Type of surface	Coefficient $\lambda(z_0)$	Roughness class
Sea, snow and sand	0.14	I
Sea with very strong wind	0.15	II
Short grass	0.17	III
Cultivated open fields	0.19	IV
High plants and open country	0.20	V
Countryside and spread habitat	0.21	VI
Peripheral urban zone	0.22	VII
Mean city centre and forest	0.24	VIII
Metropolis centre and tropical forest	0.25	IX

coefficients take into account local change of roughness, local modification of topographical relief and the presence of a singular obstacle:

$$\bar{u}(x,z) = u_{ref}C_R(x,z)C_T(x,z)C_S(x,z) \qquad (3.110)$$

where:

- C_R (x, z) is the roughness coefficient;
- C_T (x, z) is the topographical coefficient; and
- C_S (x, z) is the wake coefficient.

These three coefficients result from empirical studies and can be found in various references.

General aspects of wind in the urban environment

In the urban environment, the presence of numerous obstacles significantly increases the roughness of the ground compared to the rural environment, and thus increases the friction effect on the airflow. The vertical variation of wind velocity as a function of the nature of the ground presented in the previous section applies above the city from a height approximately equal to double that of the average roof level. Below this height it is the viscous sub-layer or the transition layer where viscous phenomena and local characteristics prevail. This is the reason why the prediction of local urban flows is quite impossible in a general way. Chapter 4 proposes a classification of urban winds at street level for some specific configurations.

However, the city itself will induce some modifications of the atmospheric boundary layer. For moderate to strong winds, and for the same height above ground (20m), a reduction of 20 to 30 per cent in the average wind speed is observed when moving from the countryside into the urban environment. Conversely, the turbulence intensity increases by 50 to 100 per cent. As a result of strong winds, the friction due to the city also creates a cyclonic rotation of the flow.

Another effect of the urban boundary layer, in the case of moderate winds, is to provoke an upward movement of the air. This vertical velocity can reach 1m/s.

Weak winds are 5 to 20 per cent more frequent in a city than in the countryside. However, for wind velocities less than a threshold of 4m/s, the wind velocity is higher in the centre than in the periphery of the city. This can be attributed, on the one hand, to turbulence generated by the numerous obstacles and, on the other hand, to the relatively unstable state which characterizes the urban boundary layer compared to the rural atmosphere.

Furthermore, as the temperature increases while moving from the countryside into the city centre, the air converges to the centre of the city under the effect of the pressure gradient induced by the horizontal temperature gap. Thus, the continuity of the flow creates an upward movement which stops at a given height. The countryside breeze that blows mainly at the end of the night and in the morning can reach 2 to 3m/s.

NATURAL AIRFLOWS IN BUILDINGS

Wind effect

Airflow around buildings affects worker safety, process and building equipment operation, weather and pollution protection at inlets, and the ability to control environmental factors of temperature, humidity, air motion and contaminants. As seen before for an isolated obstacle, wind causes surface pressures that vary around buildings, changing intake and exhaust system flow rates, natural ventilation, infiltration and exfiltration, and interior pressure. The mean flow patterns and wind turbulence passing over a building can even cause a recirculation of exhaust gases to air intakes.

The flow in the internal viscous boundary layer is dominated by the effect of viscosity. Depending upon the Reynolds number, the flow in this region is either laminar or turbulent. When this turbulent flow hits a sharp edge, such as a corner of a rectangular building, the separation occurs immediately. Nevertheless, the effect of the Reynolds number is extremely small for rectangular buildings because it is no longer the dominating factor in controlling the separation and wake width (Aynsley et al, 1977).

Bernoulli's equation

The relationship for free stream flow between velocity and related pressure at different locations of the flow field can be obtained from Bernoulli's equation. This equation results from the integration along a streamline of the momentum equation (3.47):

$$p_{stat} + \rho g \, y + 0.5 \, \rho \, v^2 + \rho g \, j = constant \tag{3.111}$$

where:

$$u = -\frac{v}{g} \int \left(\frac{\delta^2 u}{\delta x^2} + \frac{\delta^2 u}{\delta y^2} \right) dx + \left(\frac{\delta^2 v}{\delta x^2} + \frac{\delta^2 v}{\delta y^2} \right) dy \tag{3.112}$$

Here, j represents the friction losses along the trajectory.

Assuming a non-viscous fluid and a constant density along a streamline at a given height, Bernoulli's equation can be simplified to:

$$p_{stat} + 0.5 \, \rho \, v^2 = constant \tag{3.113}$$

If the streamline is stopped by an obstacle that will not modify the flow pattern, we define its dynamic pressure P_{dyn} as the pressure resulting on this theoretical obstacle:

$$p_{dyn} + 0.5 \, \rho \, v^2 \tag{3.114}$$

Pressure coefficient concept

On a real obstacle, the pressure due to a streamline will be proportional to this dynamic pressure:

$$P = C_p \, P_{dyn} \tag{3.115}$$

where C_p represents an empirical coefficient which depends upon the flow characteristics close to the obstacle and on the obstacle itself.

Thus, the pressure coefficient C_p at point $M(x,y,z)$ on a building surface with the reference dynamic pressure P_{dyn} corresponding to height z_{ref} for a given wind direction θ can be described by:

$$C_{ps}(z_{ref}, \theta) = [P - Po(z)] . [P_{dyn}(z_{ref})]^{-1} \tag{3.116}$$

with:

$$P_{dyn}(z_{ref}) = 0.5 \, \rho_{out} \, v^2(z_{ref}) \tag{3.117}$$

where:

- P is the measured resulting pressure;
- P_0 is the reference atmospheric pressure.

Figure 3.9 shows an example of C_p distribution on a building.

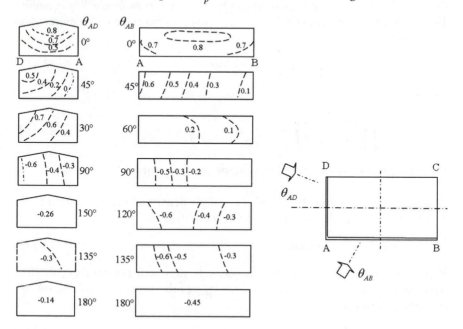

Source: Linddament (1986)

Figure 3.9 *Example of C$_p$ distribution on a building*

Numerous papers on wind pressure distribution as input data for infiltration models have been published (Kula and Feustel, 1988); but only a few deal with wind pressure distribution modelling as a method to calculate C_p. Allen (1984) has described a calculation method showing how the variation of pressure coefficients with wind angle can be represented by a Fourier series. Results are shown only for wall average C_p except for a location at a relative building height of 0.85m where horizontal distribution is plotted in relation to a specific environmental situation. In addition, the dependence of Fourier series with side ratio and wind shelter is demonstrated. A general remark is given about the necessity of further investigation, mainly concerning the fluctuating pressures arising from turbulence, different building shapes and the sheltering effect of neighbouring buildings.

Bala'zs (1987) developed a software package called CPBANK, including a set of C_p data files related to different predefined building geometries and exposures. A program handles a search of C_p values for a selected set of wind directions related to any building similar to CPBANK types. The reference data are taken from a series of results of tests performed in the wind tunnel laboratory of the Hungarian Institute of Building Science (ETI).

Swami (1987) developed two algorithms: one for low-rise buildings, another one for high-rise buildings. For low-rise buildings, data from eight different investigators were analysed and surface average pressure coefficients were found by a non-linear regression with wind incidence angle and side ratio as variables (correlation coefficients: 0.8). For high-rise buildings, local pressure coefficients were used by fitting more than 5000 data points. The regression is represented by only one equation with the location coordinates of a surface element as variables.

The conclusion of the test was that the Swami and Chandra algorithm, though valuable for estimates of either the surface average pressure coefficients on low-rise buildings or the C_p along the vertical centreline on a façade of an isolated high-rise building (in the case of normal approaching wind and suburban terrain roughness), would not be able to fulfil the wider needs of multi-zone airflow models.

Modelling wind pressure distribution according to a parametric approach means finding an algorithm that calculates the variation of C_p on the envelope surfaces of a building when varying wind direction, and architectural and environmental conditions. Because of the stochastic behaviour of the distribution of pressure coefficients around a building, such an algorithm should be drawn by empirical correlations of time-averaged C_p values from wind tunnel tests chosen as reference data sets. If tables and graphs, unlike wall-averaged values of C_p, are given for wide intervals of wind angle (Wiren, 1985; Liddament, 1986), a parametric wind pressure distribution model can yield C_p values at any point on the surface for any specific wind angle. Three types of parameters were taken into account, as shown in Table 3.3.

Table 3.3 *Parameters affecting C_p distribution*

Wind	Environment	Building geometry
Wind velocity profile exponent	Plan area density (PAD)	Frontal aspect ratio (FAR)
Wind incident angle	Relative building height (RbH)	Side aspect ratio (SAR)
		Element positioning coordinates
		Roof slope tilt angle

Buoyancy-driven flows

A source term due to buoyancy appears in the y-momentum conservation equation; this means that a density field coupled with a gravity field will generate a flow. This phenomenon is well known and is called natural convection. The variation of density in our problems will generally be due to thermal or concentration gradients in the fluid.

Hydrostatic pressure field and stack effect

In any fluid without motion and submitted to a gravity field, a pressure field due to the density field exists. At position y, the pressure gradient (hydrostatic gradient) given by the vertical momentum conservation equation is:

$$\frac{dP}{dy} = -\rho g \tag{3.118}$$

The pressure at position y is then given by:

$$p(y) = p_0 - p_{gy} \tag{3.119}$$

This pressure field is called the hydrostatic pressure field.

Between two different media with different characteristics in terms of density, we will obtain, at the same height, a pressure difference:

$$p_2(y) - p_1(y) = p_2(0) - p_1(0) + (\rho_1 - \rho_2) g\, y \tag{3.120}$$

If the two media are linked by an orifice, then a flow due to this pressure drop through the orifice will be generated.

In urban microclimates, where wind velocities are usually weak, this phenomenon cannot be neglected and will very often provide an interesting potential source for the natural ventilation of buildings. In ventilation applications, the air density is mainly a function of temperature and the moisture content of air. Figure 3.10 depicts a leakage between two zones, M and N.

In Figure 3.10, the reference heights are z_M and z_N. The reference pressure, temperature and humidity are, respectively, P_M, T_M, H_M and P_N, T_N and H_N. The relative heights of the leakage in each zone are, respectively, z_i and z_j.

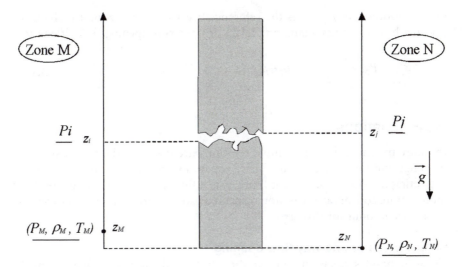

Source: Linddament (1986)

Figure 3.10 *Stack effect*

The local pressure difference between the two sides of the opening is $P_i - P_j$ with respect to the reference pressure of each zone:

$$P_i - P_j = P_M - P_N + P_{st} \qquad (3.121)$$

where P_{st} is the pressure difference created by the stack effect:

$$P_{st} = \rho_M g(z_M - z_i) - \rho_N g(z_N - z_j) \qquad (3.122)$$

In this equation, ρ_M and ρ_N are the air density in zones M and N, respectively.

Combined action of wind and temperature difference

For the calculation of the total pressure difference across the opening, the terms of the dynamic pressure must be added to those representing the stack effect. Thus, combining equations (3.121) and (3.122):

$$\Delta P = P_M - P_N + \frac{\rho_M C_p U_M^2}{2} - \frac{\rho_N C_p U_N^2}{2} + (\rho_M - \rho_N) gz \qquad (3.123)$$

where:

- U_M, U_N is the wind speed at the two sides of the opening (m/s); and
- ρ_M, ρ_N are air densities of the interconnected zones (kg/m³).

For exterior openings, $U_N = 0$ and U_M is taken equal to the wind speed U at the building height, while ρ_N is the indoor air density, ρ_i and ρ_M is the density of the outdoor air, ρ_o. P_N is the reference pressure of the zone to which the opening belongs. Thus, equation (3.123) for exterior openings is written as:

$$\Delta P_{ext} = P_N - \frac{\rho_i C_p U^2}{2} + (\rho_i - \rho_o) gz \tag{3.124}$$

Flow equations

In many practical designs, simple relations are used for the initial sizing of openings and flow calculations. These equations are based on pressure forces, neglecting the viscous stress (see 'Forces on a fluid particle'). Consequently, the momentum conservation is not respected; some formulas have correction factors to account for this error.

Simple crack or one-way flow opening

Using Bernoulli's equation, one can directly get a theoretical expression of the velocity of a flow due to a pressure difference. The theoretical mass flow rate induced by this pressure difference is:

$$m'_t = \rho A \sqrt{\frac{2\Delta P}{\rho}} \tag{3.125}$$

where A is the area of the cross-section of the flow tube.

In fact, the flow is obviously affected by the geometrical characteristics of the opening. For a simple geometrical configuration, it is possible to introduce a discharge coefficient C_d relating the real mass flow rate, m', to the theoretical one.

Thus:

$$m' = C_d \rho A \sqrt{\frac{2\Delta P}{\rho}} \tag{3.126}$$

The discharge coefficient is a function of the temperature difference, wind speed and the shape of the opening. A number of expressions have been proposed for its calculation, especially for internal openings. Inter-zonal heat and mass flow measurements in a real building (Riffat, 1989) have given the following expression for the discharge coefficient, in the case of internal openings:

$$C_d = 0.0835(\Delta T/T)^{-0.3} \tag{3.127}$$

For steady-state and buoyancy-driven flow, the discharge coefficient for internal openings can be calculated from the following expression (Kiel and Wilson, 1989):

$$C_d = (0.4 + 0.0075\Delta T) \tag{3.128}$$

Experimental results have been analysed in order to express the discharge coefficient of the internal openings as a function of the temperature difference, air speed and opening height (Santamouris and Argiriou, 1997). It was proven that the value of C_d is a strong function of the opening dimensions. For small internal openings, a representative value for the discharge coefficient is 0.65. For large internal openings, C_d has a value close to unity. A proposed mean value for a standard opening is $C_d = 0.78$.

An evaluation of the discharge coefficient as a function of the opening height is attempted by Pelletret et al (1991). For opening heights of 1.5<H<2m, the proposed relation is: $C_d = 0.21H$. According to Limam et al (1991), the values of C_d can be selected within the range of 0.6–0.75, with reasonable accuracy.

Darliel and Lane-Serff (1991) have carried out experiments in a 18.6cm x 60cm x 40cm box and in a 199cm x 9.4cm channel using water. They have measured a C_d coefficient close to 0.311, which corresponds to a C value close to 0.103, while their theoretical estimations using a hydraulic theory proposed that $C = 0.121$.

Measurements of airflow through large openings separating two zones in a test cell (Limam et al, 1991) have shown that the coefficient of discharge (C_d) varies between 0.67 and 0.73, which corresponds to a C value between 0.223 and 0.243. This experiment was carried out using a cold and hot vertical plate situated at the end of each zone. Therefore, an important boundary layer flow should have been developed.

Khodr Mneimne (1990), in a full-scale experiment using an electrical heater as a heating source, has found that, for openings between 0.9m and 2m, a mean C_d value equal to 0.87 should be used.

Based on the experimental work, carried out in the DESYS Test Cell at Centre Scientifique et Technique de Bâtiment (CSTB), France (Allard et al, 1990), it has been concluded that a value of C_d equal to 0.42 for 5 x 10^8<Gr<3.6 x 10^9 can be used with satisfactory accuracy.

Furthermore, it appears that for leakages or openings of complex geometry, the dependency of the pressure difference is even more complicated. Therefore, an empirical power law function is usually considered:

$$m' = K\Delta P^* \tag{3.129}$$

The flow exponent, n, ranges between 0.5 (fully developed turbulent flow) and 1 (laminar flow). The flow coefficient, K, includes in its definition the geometrical characteristics of the leakage (the discharge effect) and it can be interpreted physically as the flow rate induced by a unitary pressure difference. These flow equations and their coefficients K and n are usually determined by a measurement using blower door techniques.

Large openings

We call large opening an internal or external opening which can be characterized by a two-way flow. In order to represent the behaviour of a large

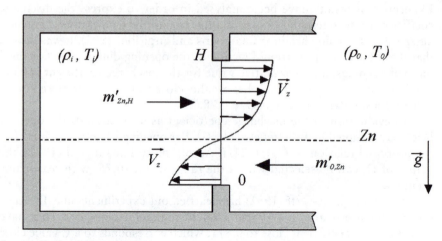

Figure 3.11 *Gravitational flow through a vertical opening*

opening, we can use the concept that we already did for a one-flow opening, an explicit definition of the flow by a Bernoulli flow regime assumption, or any other correlation of natural or mixed convection corresponding to the studied configuration. In order to integrate the behaviour of such an opening, the easiest way, however, is to represent its behaviour by non-linear flow equations based on the evaluation of the pressure field on both sides of the opening. Thus, the first possibility is then to describe the large opening with a series of parallel, small one-way flow openings and to use the preceding method relative to such small openings. This method has been used by Walton (1982) and Roldan (1985).

Another approach is to directly interpret the whole behaviour of this large opening in terms of a set of non-linear equations describing this typical scheme. Since the pioneering work of Brown and Solvason (1963), many authors have dealt with this solution (Pelletret et al, 1991). Figure 3.11 describes this basic problem.

For an incompressible, inviscid and steady flow, using Bernoulli's equation, the horizontal velocity V_z along a streamline is given by:

$$V_z = \left[2 \left(\frac{\rho_0 - \rho_i}{\rho_0} \right) g\, z \right]^{0.5} \tag{3.130}$$

If z_N is the height of the neutral plane, the mass flow rate below this neutral plane is given directly by integrating the velocity profile between the origin and z_N:

$$m'_{0,Zn} = Cd \int_0^{Z_n} \rho_0 V_z W \, dz \tag{3.131}$$

where Cd, the discharge coefficient, takes into account the local contraction of the flow through the opening and the friction effects along its solid limits. The position of the neutral plane is then given by writing the mass conservation in each zone. If zone i is closed, then the conservation of mass in zone i leads to:

$$\frac{Zn}{H - Zn} = \left(\frac{\rho_i}{\rho_0}\right)^{1/3} \tag{3.132}$$

At the end, a direct integration delivers the value of the outgoing airflow:

$$m'_{0,Zn} = Cd \, \frac{W}{3} (8gH^3 \rho'_i \, \Delta\rho)^{0.5} \tag{3.133}$$

where:

$$\rho'_i = \frac{\rho_i}{\left[1 + \left(\frac{\rho_i}{\rho_0}\right)^{1/3}\right]^3} \tag{3.134}$$

In this model, the air density is mainly a function of the air temperature and humidity. This basic model, which has been used by numerous authors, can be coupled with an air supply on one side of the opening or with a thermal gradient on both sides of the opening (Allard and Utsumi, 1992). In this case, two possible positions of the neutral level may be derived (see Figure 3.12) since the pressure profile on each side of the opening becomes a second-order polynomial.

Mass conservation equation

Under assumed steady-state conditions, the conservation of mass inside each zone must be ensured by considering all elementary flows passing through the various leaks:

$$m'_{vent} + \sum_{k=1}^{Nk} m'_k = 0 \tag{3.135}$$

where Nk is the total number of distinct leakage openings in the zone, m'_{vent} is the extracted or supplied mass flow rate due to a mechanical system and m'_k is the individual mass flow rate through leakage openings number k.

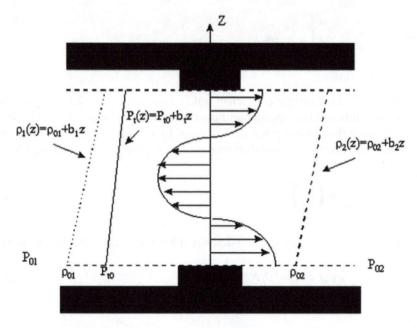

Source: Santamouris (1998)

Figure 3.12 *Airflow through large openings (density gradient)*

Network models

Empirical models are based on simplified formulae and they must be carefully applied within the limits of their validity. In addition, due to the simple assumptions upon which they are based, they must be expected to provide estimates of the bulk airflow rates in a building that can be regarded as a single zone. However, in real conditions, the approximation of a building by a single zone volume is of little value since the interaction of various zones through internal openings is of great importance. In this case, a multi-zone airflow network analysis is required.

According to the concept of airflow network modelling, a building is represented by a grid that is formed by a number of nodes standing for the simulated zones and the exterior environment. Interaction between various zones is denoted by flow paths that link their respective nodes. Thus, the rooms of a building are represented by nodes and the openings are represented by linking flow paths. Interaction with the outdoor environment is represented by flow paths linking interior with exterior nodes. All nodes, interior and exterior, are attributed a pressure value.

As discussed in the previous sections, the airflow rate through a building opening is directly related to the pressure difference across it. Pressures at exterior nodes are known. Following the concept of network modelling, the pressure values of interior nodes have to be determined in order to finally deduce the airflow rates.

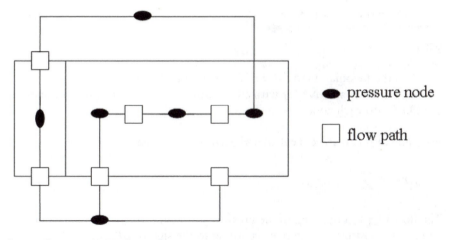

Source: Santamouris (1998)

Figure 3.13 *Network representation of a multi-zone building*

Mathematical solution

Network modelling is based on the concept that each zone of a building can be represented by a pressure node. Boundary nodes are also used to represent the environment outside the building. Nodes are interconnected by flow paths, such as cracks, windows, doors and shafts, to form a network. Figure 3.13 shows a network representation of a multi-zone building.

According to the network approach, a building with N zones is represented by a network of N pressure nodes. Some of them communicate with exterior nodes of known pressure, while others are only connected to interior nodes. Interior node pressures are unknown. Airflow paths can be either cracks, or windows and doors. Calculation of unknown pressures is derived by application of mass balance equations (3.135) in each zone representing a pressure node.

Application of mass balance on each internal node of the network leads to a set of simultaneous non-linear equations, the solution of which gives the internal node pressures. Thus, a non-linear system of N equations is formed (Allard and Herlin, 1989). Solution of this system is based on Newton–Raphson's iterative method. According to this method, a set of initial pressures is attributed to the unknown pressures. Until convergence is reached, the right-hand terms of the equations in the system expressed by equation (3.135) are different from zero. in order to minimize these values (residuals), a new estimate of the pressure at each node is computed at each iteration. For iteration k, the new set of pressures is derived from:

$$p_n^{k+1} = p_n^k - X_n^k \tag{3.136}$$

where the matrix of the pressure corrections $[X]$ is defined for each iteration by the equation:

$$[J][X] = [F] \tag{3.137}$$

where:

- [J] is the Jacobian matrix $(N \times N)$ for the simulated building; and
- [F] is the matrix $(N \times 1)$ with the residuals from application of equation (3.135) to each zone.

Each line of this matrix is calculated according to equation (3.135):

$$f(Pn) = \sum_{m=1}^{N} \rho_{mm} Q_{mm} \tag{3.138}$$

The flow Q_{nm} is a function of the pressure difference, ΔP_{nm}, across the opening and can be positive or negative according to the sign of ΔP_{nm}:

$$\Delta P_{nm} = P_n - P_m \tag{3.139}$$

If $\Delta P_{nm} > 0$, then $Q_{nm} > 0$, $\rho_{nm} = \rho_n$ and the air flows from node n to node m (outflow).

If $\Delta P_{nm} < 0$, then $Q_{nm} < 0$, $\rho_{nm} = \rho_m$ and the air flows from node m to node n (inflow).

The Jacobian matrix is symmetrical (Feustel et al, 1989). The elements of the matrix are calculated by the following derivatives applied to each node n communicating with a node m:

$$\text{Diagonal elements: } J(n,n) = \delta(P_n) / \delta P_n \tag{3.140}$$

$$\text{Off-diagonal elements: } J(n,m) = J(m,n) = \delta(P_n) / \delta P_m \tag{3.141}$$

According to the complexity of the application, a predefined value for the maximum acceptable residual is defined (usually, this value is set to 0.001). Calculation of the Jacobian elements is performed at each iteration and the worst (highest) residual is chosen among the elements of matrix [F]. If its absolute value is greater than the chosen acceptable one, then a new set of corrections is calculated and the derived new set of pressures is attributed to the unknown pressure nodes. Iterations continue until convergence is reached.

Most of the developed nodal codes use this methodology (e.g. Roldan, 1985; Feustel et al, 1989; Walton, 1989; Dascalaki and Santamouris, 1995).

CONCLUSIONS

In this chapter, we have described the basics of fluid dynamics and turbulence necessary to model turbulent flows in naturally ventilated buildings. However, if the atmospheric boundary layer is a good model to predict and evaluate the effects of the wind on a stand-alone building in a dense urban environment, the building façades are submitted to very local effects. The definition of a reference wind appears much more complicated and the definition of local pressure coefficients is quite impossible. Nevertheless, the so-called multi-zone models could be very helpful in predicting the airflows due to buoyancy that are characteristic of low wind situations. In the following chapters we will go deeper into the definition of local wind in canyon streets and will propose a methodology to overcome the difficulty of predicting natural ventilation flows in an urban environment.

REFERENCES

Allard, F. and Alvarez, S. (1998). 'Fundamentals of natural ventilation', in Allard, F. (ed), Natural Ventilation in Buildings, James and James, London

Allard, F. and Herrlin, M. (1989) 'Wind induced ventilation', ASHRAE Transactions, vol 95, pp722–728

Allard, F. and Utsumi, Y. (1992) 'Air flow through large openings', Energy and Buildings, vol. 18, pp113–145

Allard,. F., Bonnotte, D. and Liman, K. (1990) 'Air flow through large openings: Experimental study of the discharge coefficient'. IEA Annex 20 Expert Meeting, Oslo, 10–13 June, 19pp

Allen, C. (1984) 'Wind pressure data requirements for air infiltration calculations', Technical Note AIVC 13, Air Infiltrations and Ventilation Centre, Bracknell, UK, January

Aynsley, R. M., Melbourne, W. and Vickery, B. J. (1977) 'Wind tunnel testing techniques', Architectural Aerodynamics, Applied Science Publishers Ltd, London

Bala'sz, K. (1987) 'Effect of some architectural and environmental factors on air filtration of multi-storey buildings', 3rd ICBEM Proceedings, Presses Polytechnique Romande, Lausanne, Switzerland, vol 3, pp21–28

Brown, W. G. and Solvason, K. R. (1963) 'Natural convection in openings through partitions-1, vertical partitions'. International Journal of Heat and Mass Transfer, vol 5, pp859–868

Chen, Q. (1996) 'Prediction of room air motion by Reynolds stress models', Building and Environment, vol 31, pp233–244

Darliel, S. B. and Lane-Serff, G. F. (1991)'The hydraulics of doorway exchange flows', Building and Environment, vol 26, pp121–135

Dascalaki, E. and Santamouris, M. (1995) Manual of PASSPORT-AIR, Final Report, PASCOOL Research Programme, European Commission, DG XII, Brussels

Engineering Sciences Data Unit (ESDU) 82026 (1982) Strong Winds in the Atmospheric Boundary Layer: Part 1, Mean Hourly Wind Speeds, Engineering Sciences Data, London

Feustel, H. and Raynor-Hoosen, A. (eds) (1989) 'COMIS fundamentals', AIVC Technical Note 29, Code TN 29, Air Infiltration and Ventilation Centre, Bracknell, 115pp

Grosso, M. (1996) Final Report on CPCALC, PASCOOL Project, European Commission, DG XII, Brussels

Harlow, F. H. and Nakayama, P. I. (1968) 'Transport of turbulence energy decay rate', LA-3854, Los Alamos Science Laboratory, University of California, California

Khodr Mneimne, H. (1990) *Transferts Thermo-Aerouliques Entre Pieces à Travers les Grandes Ouvertures,* PhD thesis, Nice University, France

Kiel, D. E. and Wilson, D. J. (1989) 'Combining door swing pumping with density driven flow', *ASHRAE Transactions,* vol 95, no 2, pp590–599

Kula, H. G. and Feustel, H. E. (1988) *Review of Wind Pressure Distribution as Input Data for Infiltration Models,* Lawrence Berkeley Laboratory Report LBL-23886, Berkeley, US

Liddament, M. W. (1986) *Air Infiltration Calculation Techniques: An Application Guide,* Air Infiltration and Ventilation Centre, Bracknell, UK

Limam, K., Innard, C. and Allard, F. (1991) *Étude Experimentale des Transferts de Masse et de Chaleur à Travers les Grandes Ouvertures Verticales,* Conference Groupe d' Étude de la Ventilation et du Renouvellement d'Air, INSA, Lyon, France, pp98–111

Oke, T. (1987) City Size and Urban Heat Island. Perspectives on Wilderness: Testing the theory of Restorative Environments, Proceedings of the Fourth World Wilderness Congress, vol 7, pp767–779.

Pelletret, R., Allard, F., Haghighat, F. and van der Maas, J. (1991) *Modeling of Large Openings,* Proceedings 12th AIVC Conference, Ottawa, Canada

Riffat, S. B. (1989) 'A study of heat and mass transfer through a doorway in a traditionally built house', ASHRAE Transactions, vol 95, pp584–589

Roldan, A. (1985) *Étude Thermique et Aéraulique des Enveloppes de Bâtiments,* PhD thesis, INSA de Lyon, France

Sacré, C. (1988) *Ecoulements de l'Air au-dessus d'un Site Complexe, Première Partie: Etat des Connaissances Actuelles,* Rapport CSTB EN-CLI 88, 12L., Centre Scientifique et Technique du Bâtiment, Marne la Vallée, France

Santamouris, M. (1998) 'Prediction methods', in Allard, F. (ed), *Natural Ventilation in Buildings,* James and James, London

Santamouris, M. and Argiriou, A. (1997) 'Passive cooling of buildings – Results of the PASCOOL program'. *International Journal of Solar Energy,* vol 18, pp231–258

Simiu, E. (1973) 'Logarithmic profiles and design wind speeds', *Journal of the Engineering Mechanics,* vol 99, pp1073–1083

Swami, M. V. (1987) 'Procedures for calculating the natural ventilation airflow rates in buildings'. ASHRAE Research Project 448-RP, Final Report FSEC-CR-163-86, Florida Solar Energy Centre, Cape Canaveral, USA

Tennekes, H. and Lumley, J. L. (1972) *A First Course in Turbulence,* MIT Press, Cambridge, Massachusetts

Walton, G. N. (1982) *A Computer Algorithm for Estimating Infiltration and Inter-room Air Flows,* US Department of Commerce, National Bureau of Standards, Gaithersburg, Maryland

Walton, G. N. (1989) *AIRNET: A Computer Program for Building Air Flow Network Modeling,* NISTR, 89-4072, National Institute of Standards and Technology, Gaithersburg, Maryland

Wieringa, J. (1991) 'Updating the Davenport roughness classification', *Journal of Wind Engineering and Industrial Aerodynamics,* Eighth International Conference on Wind Engineering, London, Ontario, Canada

Wiren, B. G. (1985) 'Effects of surrounding building on wind pressure distributions and ventilation losses for single-family houses', *National Swedish Research Bulletin,* December, vol M85, p19, National Swedish Institute for Building Research, Gavle, Sweden

4

Wind and Temperature in the Urban Environment

Chrissa Georgakis and Mat Santamouris

INTRODUCTION

The urban environment has drawbacks for the application of natural ventilation – for example, lower wind speed, higher temperatures due to the effect of the urban heat island, noise and pollution. The Natural Ventilation in the Urban Environment (URBVENT) project quantified some of these barriers.

The wind in street canyons has much lower values when compared with undisturbed wind. When undisturbed wind features values larger than 4 metres per second (m/s), a correlation exists between it and the wind in street canyons. When a 4m/s or stronger wind blows perpendicular to a street canyon, a vortex develops in the canyon. If the wind occurs parallel to the canyon axis, the main flow inside the canyon is in the same direction. Based on existing information completed with experimental data, an empirical model was developed for all types of wind flow for undisturbed wind speed values lower and higher than 4m/s. The temperature measured inside the canyon streets was approximately 5°C lower than that of the canopy layer, partially compensating for the effect of the urban heat island.

Airflow measurements conducted in the URBVENT project for perpendicular, parallel and oblique direction to the canyon axis for five different urban canyons in the centre of Athens complete the available information and resulted in a concise model.

WIND DISTRIBUTION IN THE URBAN ENVIRONMENT

The urban wind field is complex. Small differences in topography may cause irregular airflows. As the air flows from the rural to the urban environment, it must adjust to the new boundary conditions defined by cities. The wind variation with height was divided into two specific sub-layers (Oke, 1987): the 'obstructed sub-layer', or urban canopy sub-layer, which extends from the ground surface up to the building's height, and the 'free surface layer', or urban boundary layer, which extends above the rooftops.

The flow in the obstructed (or canopy) sub-layer is driven by the interaction of the flow field above and is influenced by the local effects of topography, building geometry and dimensions, streets, traffic and other local features, such as the presence of trees. In a general way, wind speed in the canopy layer is much lower when compared to the undisturbed wind speed.

Airflow in street canyons

Airflow around isolated buildings is well known. It is characterized by a bolster eddy vortex due to flow down the windward façade, while behind is a lee eddy drawn into the cavity of low pressure due to flow separation from the sharp edges of the building top and sides. Further downstream is the building wake characterized by increased turbulence, but lower horizontal speeds than the undisturbed flow.

Urban canyons are characterized by three main parameters: H, the mean height of the buildings in the canyon, W, the canyon width, and L, the canyon length. Given these parameters, the geometrical descriptors are limited to three simple values. These are the aspect ratio of the canyon H/W, the aspect ratio of the building, L/H, and the building density $J = A_r/A_l$, where A_r is the plan of the roof area of the average building and A_1 is the 'lot' area or unit ground area occupied by each building.

Airflow in urban canyons was studied by numerical simulations, in field experiments in real urban canyons and on scale models in wind tunnels. Most of the existing studies deal with determining the pollution characteristics within the canyon and place emphasis on situations where the ambient flow is perpendicular to the canyon long axis, when the highest pollutant concentration occurs in the canyon.

Theoretical analysis of airflow inside street canyons

Undisturbed wind perpendicular to the canyon

When the predominant direction of the airflow is approximately normal (e.g. ±15°) to the long axis of the street canyon, three types of airflow regimes are observed as a function of the building (L/H) and canyon (H/W) geometry (Oke, 1987). When the buildings are well apart, ($H/W > 0.05$), their flow fields do not interact. At closer spacing, the wakes are disturbed. When the height and spacing of the array combine to disturb the bolster and cavity eddies, the flow is characterized by secondary flows in the canyon space where the downward flow of the cavity eddy is reinforced by a deflection down the windward face of the next building downstream. At even greater H/W and density, a stable circulatory vortex is established in the canyon because of the transfer of momentum across a shear layer of roof height, and a flow regime occurs where the bulk of the flow does not enter the canyon. Because high H/W ratios are very common in cities, skimming airflow regime has attracted considerable attention.

The vortex velocity depends upon wind speed out of the canyon. For wind speed higher than 1.5 to 2m/s, DePaul and Sheih (1986) reported that the speed of the vortex increases with the speed of the cross-canyon wind. In a $H/W = 1$ symmetric canyon, it was found that the transverse vortex speed inside the canyon is proportional to the above-roof transverse component and independent of the above-roof longitudinal component (Yamartino and Wiegand, 1986). In an asymmetric canyon of a mean H/W value close to 1.52, Arnfield and Mills (1994) found that vortex circulation speeds were unrelated to the u-component of the roof-level wind.

The vortex inside the canyon is driven by a downward transfer of momentum across the roof-level shear zone. A flow normal to the canyon axis has to create a vortex where the direction of the airflow near the ground should be directly opposite the wind direction outside the canyon. Depending upon the undisturbed wind speed and the canyon aspect ratio ($H/W > 2$), a secondary vortex may be observed and for even higher ratios ($H/W > 3$) a third weak vortex. This is verified for the case of a symmetric and a step-up canyon configuration (Hoydysh and Dabberdt, 1988; Nakamura and Oke, 1988). In a step-up asymmetric canyon, the vortex direction was consistent with the mechanism described above, although a reversed vortex was detected in some cases with low wind speeds below the threshold value of 2m/s (Arnfield and Mills, 1994). In deep canyons, wind tunnel research has found that two vortices are developed, an upper one driven by ambient airflow and a lower one driven in the opposite direction by the circulation above it (Chang et al, 1971).

The air velocity inside the canyon also depends upon the undisturbed wind velocity. Nakamura and Oke (1988) report that for wind speeds up to 5m/s, the general relation between the two wind speeds appears to be linear, $u_{in} = p \times u_{out}$. For wind speeds normal to the canyon axis, and for a symmetric canyon with $H/W = 1$, they found that p varies between 0.66 and 0.75 provided that winds in and out are measured at about 0.06 H and 1.2 H, respectively, where H is the height of the buildings. For perpendicular wind speeds, DePaul and Sheih (1986) report that downdraft vertical velocities in a canyon are a function of height and reach a maximum close to 95 per cent of the ambient horizontal velocity, at heights near three-quarters of the height of the upwind building. The updraft velocity appeared to be relatively independent of height and had a maximum close to 55 per cent of the ambient velocity, at a height one half of the height of the upwind building. Vertical velocities measured in the centre of the canyon were close to zero. Horizontal velocities varied from zero up to 55 per cent of the free-stream wind speed. The highest horizontal velocities were obtained at the bottom and the higher parts of the canyon. Zero horizontal velocity was measured at about 75 per cent of the height of the lowest building; these results were in good agreement with the numerical predictions (Hotchkiss and Harlow, 1973). Hoydysh and Dabberdt (1988) reported that for a symmetric canyon, the average circumferential velocity was about one fourth of the free-stream wind speed (2m/s), while the corresponding mean ascending vertical velocity was 0.26m/s and the mean vertical ascending vertical velocity was 0.24m/s. For a step-up canyon configuration, the mean circumferential velocity was between 1.02 and 1.07m/s, while the corresponding mean ascending vertical velocity was 0.34m/s and the mean descending vertical velocity was 0.32m/s. Measurements indicated that as horizontal roof-level wind varies from 1 to 3m/s, the ascending and descending currents vary proportionally from 0.1 to 1m/s (Albrecht and Grunow, 1935). Numerical simulations in a symmetric canyon with an undisturbed wind speed of 5m/s flowing perpendicular to the canyon show that the strength of the vortex developed inside the canyon was less than the wind speed above the roof level by about an order of magnitude (Lee et al, 1994).

Undisturbed wind parallel to the canyon

When the incidence angle of the ambient wind is parallel to the main axis of the canyon (±15°), a secondary circulation feature develops inside the canyon. If the wind speed outside the canyon is below some threshold value (close to 2m/s), the coupling between the upper and secondary flow is lost (Nakamura and Oke, 1988) and the relation between wind speed above the roof and the air speed inside the canyon is characterized by a considerable scatter. For higher wind speeds, the main conclusions resulting from the existing studies is that parallel ambient flow generates a mean wind along the canyon axis (Wedding et al, 1977; Nakamura and Oke, 1988), with possible uplift along the canyon walls as airflow is retarded by friction to the building walls and street surface (Nunez and Oke, 1977). This is verified by Arnfield and Mills (1994), who found that for winds that blow along the canyon, the mean vertical canyon velocity is close to zero. Measurements performed in a deep canyon (Santamouris et al, 1999) have also shown an along-canyon flow of the same direction. The flow is characterized by an along speed almost always parallel to the axis of the canyon and a downward incidence angle relative to the canyon floor between 0° to 30°.

Yamartino and Wiegand (1986) reported that the along-canyon wind component, v, in the canyon is directly proportional to the above-roof along-canyon component through a constant of proportionality that is a function of the azimuth of the approaching flow. The same authors found that, at least in a first approximation, $v = U \cdot \cos\theta$, where θ is the incidence angle and U the horizontal wind speed out of the canyon. For wind speeds up to 5m/s, it was reported that the general relation between the two wind speeds appear to be linear, $v = p \cdot U$ (Nakamura and Oke, 1988). For wind speeds parallel to the canyon axis, and for a symmetric canyon with $H/W = 1$, it was found that p

varies between 0.37 and 0.68 under the condition that winds in and out of the canyon are measured at about 0.06 H and 1.2 H, respectively, where H is the height of the buildings. Low p values are obtained because of the deflection of the flow by a side canyon. Measurements performed in a deep canyon of H/W = 2.5 (Santamouris et al, 1999) have not shown any clear threshold value where coupling is lost. For wind speed lower than 4m/s, the correlation between the wind parallel to the canyon and the air velocity along the canyon was unclear. However, statistical analysis showed that there is a correlation between them.

The mean vertical velocity at the canyon top resulting from mass convergence or divergence in the along-canyon component of flow, w, can be expressed as $w = -H \cdot \delta v / \delta x$, where H is the height of the lower canyon wall, x is the along-canyon coordinate and v is the x-component of motion within the canyon, averaged over time and the canyon cross-section (Arnfield and Mills, 1994). A linear relationship between the in-canyon wind gradient $\delta v / \delta x$ and the along-canyon wind speed was found. According to Arnfield and Mills (1994), the value of $\delta v / \delta x$ varies between $-6.8 \times 10^{-2} \mathrm{s}^{-1}$ and $1.7 \times 10^{-2} \mathrm{s}^{-1}$, while according to Nunez and Oke (1977) $\delta v / \delta x$ varies between $-7.1 \times 10^{-2} \mathrm{s}^{-1}$ and $0 \mathrm{s}^{-1}$.

Concerning the relation between the perpendicular wind speeds at the top of the canyon and the along-canyon ambient wind speed, it was found that the vertical wind increases with the along-canyon free-stream velocity (Arnfield and Mills, 1994). When the free-stream wind travels down only a short section of the canyon and is still actively decelerating in response to the sudden imposition with the canyon facets, the relation between the two wind speeds is almost linear. A direct correlation exists between the vertical wind speed and the along-canyon free stream wind; but data were much more scattered for winds that penetrated a much longer canyon section and attained a partial equilibrium with the frictional effect on the walls and floor. In this case, deceleration is reduced as well as the vertical outflow, which results through the canyon top, an important down-lift flow being reported (Santamouris et al, 1999). The movement of the air downward close to the canyon walls could be the result of the effects of the finite length of the canyon associated with intermittent vortices shed on the building corners. The intermittent vortices are responsible for the mechanism of a downward advection flow from the building corners to the middle of the canyon (Yamartino and Wiegand, 1986; Hoydysh and Dabberdt, 1988).

Oblique wind outside canyons

If wind's incidence angle is not parallel or normal to the main axis of the canyon, the ambient flow is considered to be oblique. Existing results are available through limited field experiments and primarily through wind tunnel and numerical calculations.

The main results drawn from the existing research is that when the flow above the roof is at some angle of attack to the canyon axis, a spiral vortex is induced along the length of the canyon: a corkscrew type of action (Nakamura and Oke, 1988; Santamouris et al, 1999).

Wind tunnel research has also shown that a helical flow pattern develops in the canyon (Dabberdt et al, 1973; Wedding et al, 1977). For intermediate angles of incidence to the canyon long axis, the canyon airflow is the product of both the transverse and parallel components of the ambient wind, where the former drives the canyon vortex and the later determines the along-canyon stretching of the vortex (Yamartino and Wiegand, 1986).

Regarding the direction of the helical flow, Nakamura and Oke (1988) reported that in a first approximation the angle of incidence on the windward wall is the same as the angle of reflection of the wall which forms the return flow of the spiral vortex across the canyon floor. However, they found some evidence that the angle of incidence is greater than that of reflection. As reported, this could be caused by along-wind entrainment in the canyon.

Regarding the wind speed inside the canyon, Lee et al (1994) reported the results of numerical studies in a canyon with $H/W = 1$ and a free-stream wind speed equal to 5m/s, flowing at 45° relative to the long axis of the canyon. They reported that a vortex is developed inside the canyon whose strength was less than the wind speed above the roof level by about an order of magnitude. Inside the canyon, the maximum across-canyon air speed was 0.6m/s, and occurred at the highest part of the canyon. The vortex was centred at the upper middle part of the cavity and, in particular, to about 0.65 of the building height. The maximum wind speeds along canyon was close to 0.8m/s. Much higher along-canyon wind speeds are reported for the downward façade (0.6 to 0.8m/s) than for the upward façade (0.2m/s). The maximum vertical wind speed inside the canyon was close to 1m/s. Studies have shown that an increase of the ambient wind speed corresponds almost always to an increase of the along-canyon wind speed for the median and the lower and upper quartiles of the speed (Santamouris et al, 1999).

Regarding the distribution of pollutants concentration in symmetric, even, step-down and step-up canyons, when the wind flows at a certain angle to the canyon axis, Hoydysh and Dabberdt (1988) report results of wind tunnel studies. The authors have calculated the wind angle for which the minimum of the concentration occurs. They report that for the step-down configuration, the minimum of the concentration occurs for along-canyon winds (incidence angle equal to 90°). For the symmetric configuration, the minimum on the leeward façade occurs for an incidence angle of 30° while, on the windward, the minimum is achieved for angles between 20° to 70°. Finally, for step-up canyon configurations, the minimum on the leeward façade occurs at incidence angles between 0° to 40°, while for the windward façade the minimum is found for incidence angles between 0° to 60°.

A NEW CONCISE ALGORITHM FOR AIR SPEED IN STREET CANYONS

The existing knowledge on wind distribution in canyons completed by recent experimental investigation is integrated within a new model that predicts wind speed inside canyons at any height above ground level. This model uses as inputs the geometrical characteristics of the canyon, the wind speed and the direction outside canyon, and predicts wind speed inside canyon. The flow chart of the model is presented in Figure 4.1.

First, it is necessary to define if the space between the buildings is a street canyon or not. If the aspect ratio of the height and the width between buildings of the canyon, *H/W*, is greater than 0.7, this means that there is a canyon situation; otherwise, the space between buildings is not a canyon. Furthermore, if the ratio of the length and the width between buildings, *L/W*, is greater than

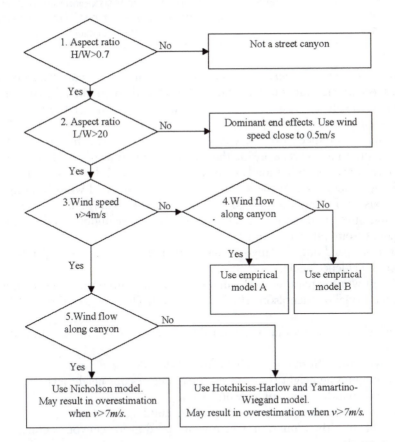

Source: Final Report of the URBVENT project, F. Allard (Coordinator), European Commission, Directorate General for Research, Brussels, June 2004

Figure 4.1 *Flow chart of the algorithm for estimating wind speed inside street canyons*

Table 4.1 *Values for air speed inside the canyon when wind blows along the canyon*

Wind speed outside canyon (U)	Typical values in the centre of the canyon	
	Lowest part	Highest part
U = 0	0m/s	0 m/s
0 < U < 1	0m/s	75 per cent of the corresponding maximum wind speed value recorded at the top of the canyon, for this cluster
1 ≤ U < 2	0m/s	75 per cent of the corresponding maximum wind speed value recorded at the top of the canyon, for this cluster
2 ≤ U < 3	0m/s	75 per cent of the corresponding maximum wind speed value recorded at the top of the canyon, for this cluster
3 ≤ U < 4	0m/s	75 per cent of the corresponding maximum wind speed value recorded at the top of the canyon, for this cluster

20, this signifies that there is a wind circulation in the canyon, based on the wind speed outside canyon. If the ratio *L/W* is less than 20, then the end effects dominate inside canyon and a mean wind speed value of 0.5m/s can be considered.

When wind speed outside canyon is less than 4m/s, but greater than 0.5m/s, although the flow inside the street canyon appeared to have chaotic characteristics, extended analysis of the experimental data resulted in two empirical models. When the direction of the undisturbed wind is along the main axis of the canyon, the values from Table 4.1 can be used. When the direction of the undisturbed wind is perpendicular or oblique to the canyon, the values from Table 4.2 can be used.

If wind speed outside canyon is higher than 4m/s, the model depends upon the wind incidence angle.

When wind is parallel to the main axis of the canyon (incidence angle ± 15°), the model of Nicholson (1975) can be used. The inputs of this model are:

- air velocity (caps wind speed) outside the canyon and the wind incidence angle (*gw*);
- canyon angle from north valued from 0° to 180° (*gc*);
- mean building height (*hb*) and the anemometer caps height (*zr*);
- canyon width from wall to wall;
- a parameter related to the density of the buildings; and
- height from the ground, in which wind speed inside canyon is going to be estimated.

The outputs of the model are:

Table 4.2 *Values for air speed inside the canyon when wind blows perpendicular or oblique to the canyon*

Wind speed outside the canyon (U)	Wind speed inside the canyon		Near the leeward façade
	Near the windward façade of the canyon		
	At the lowest part	At the highest part	
U = 0	0m/s	0m/s	0m/s
0 < U < 1	0m/s	75 per cent of the corresponding maximum wind speed value recorded at the top of the canyon, for this cluster	50 per cent of the calculated wind speed value close the windward façade
1 ≤ U < 2	0m/s	75 per cent of the corresponding maximum wind speed value recorded at the top of the canyon, for this cluster	50 per cent of the calculated wind speed value close the windward façade
2 ≤ U < 3	0m/s	75 per cent of the corresponding maximum wind speed value recorded at the top of the canyon, for this cluster	50 per cent of the calculated wind speed value close the windward façade
3 ≤ U < 4	0m/s	75 per cent of the corresponding maximum wind speed value recorded at the top of the canyon, for this cluster	50 per cent of the calculated wind speed value close the windward façade

- value of the air velocity inside the canyon parallel to canyon axis (up) at any height (from the ground to the mean building height).

The equations used for calculation of the up wind component along the main axis of the canyon are:

$$u = \frac{u^*}{k} \ln \left(\frac{z + p_d + z_0}{z_0} \right) \tag{4.1}$$

and:

$$u_p = U_0 \exp \left(\frac{y}{z_2} \right) \tag{4.2}$$

where:

- $\bar{u}$ is the mean wind in the free surface layer above roof tops;
- u^* is the frictional velocity;
- k is the von Karman constant (0.38);
- p_d is the zero-plane displacement;
- z_0 is the aerodynamic roughness length;
- U_0 is the constant reference speed;
- z_2 is the roughness length for the obstructed sub-layer; and
- y is the height from the ground in which we want to calculate the *up* air velocity parallel into the canyon's axis.

When wind incidence angle is perpendicular or oblique to the main axis of the canyon (± 15°), the air models of Hotchkiss and Harlow (1973) and Yamartino and Wiegand (1986) can be used. The inputs of these models are:

- air velocity (caps wind speed) outside the canyon and the wind incidence angle (g_w);
- canyon angle from north valued from 0° to 180° (g_c);
- mean building height (h_b) and the anemometer cap height (z_2);
- canyon width from wall to wall; and
- coordinates (cross and along canyon) of the location inside canyon in which wind speed is going to be estimated (x, y).

The outputs of the model are the:

- value of the air velocity inside the canyon parallel to the canyon main axis (u) at any height (from the ground to the mean building height);
- value of the air velocity inside the canyon cross to the canyon main axis (v) at any height (from the ground to the mean building height);
- value of the air velocity inside the canyon vertical to the canyon main axis (w) at any height (from the ground to the mean building height);
- air velocity inside the canyon at horizontal level $w_h = (u_2 + v_2)^{0.5}$; and
- total air velocity inside the canyon $w_t = (w_{h2} + w_2)^{0.5}$.

The equations used for calculation of cross and vertical wind components (V, w) are:

$$u_p = \frac{A}{k} \left[e^{ky} (1 + k \cdot y) - \beta \cdot e^{-ky} \cdot (1 - k \cdot y) \right] \sin (k \cdot x) \tag{4.3}$$

and:

$$w = -A \cdot y \cdot (e^{ky} - \beta \cdot e^{-ky}) \cos (k \cdot x) \tag{4.4}$$

with:

$$A = (k \cdot u_0) / (1 - \beta) \tag{4.5}$$

where k is von Karman's constant (0.38), $\beta = e^{-2kD}$ where D is the depth of the canyon, which is the same with the building's mean height, and u_0 is the wind speed value outside canyon. The along-canyon wind speed component is calculated by the following equation:

$$u = u_0 \cdot \log[(z + z_0) / z_0] / \log[z_r + z_0) / z_0] \tag{4.6}$$

where u_0 is the wind speed value outside canyon at reference height; z_r and z_0 represent surface roughness.

The horizontal wind speed inside the canyon is:

$$v_h = (u^2 + v^2)^{0.5} \tag{4.7}$$

The total wind speed inside the canyon in the location of coordinates (x,y) is:

$$v_t = (v_h^2 + w^2)^{0.5} \tag{4.8}$$

EXPERIMENTAL VALIDATION OF THE MODEL OF AIR SPEED IN STREET CANYONS

The model proposed above was derived from experiments conducted in the framework of the URBVENT project. Experiments were performed during the summer of 2001 in five different pedestrian streets in downtown Athens, located in different neighbourhoods.

Field experiments in urban canyons

The geometrical characteristics of each canyon street and the thermal measurements are given in Table 4.3.

The meteorological station of the University of Athens was placed in the centre of each urban canyon for three days, for 12 hours per day. The mobile meteorological station was installed on a vehicle equipped with a telescopic mast of 15.5m. On the telescopic mast, anemometers and thermometers were placed at four different heights (3.5m, 7.5m, 11.5m and 15.5m) in order to record and store every 30 seconds the following values in the middle of the canyon:

- air temperature, measured with miniature thermometers miniature screened against direct radiation, but allowing the free passage of air; and
- wind speed and direction.

Simultaneously, wind speed on three orthogonal axes was measured near the façades of the canyon, as well as the air temperature and wind speed and direction outside the canyon. Every hour, infrared measurements of the temperature of canyon façades were recorded. The above types of measurements have been performed with the following instruments:

Table 4.3 *Description of the experimental sites and definition of the measurement points during the experimental period of every canyon*

Canyon		Ermou	Miltiadou	Voukourestiou	Kaniggos	Dervenion
Orientation from the north	(degrees)	92°	45°	45°	12°	327°
Canyon width	(metres)	10m	5m	10m	9m	7m
Canyon length	(metres)	200m	100m	100m	70m	200m
Canyon height	(metres)	20m	15m	15m	22m	23m
Canyon aspect ratio	(H/W)	2	3	1.5	2.5	3.3
Air temperature measured inside the canyon	(metres from ground)	3.5m, 7.5m, 11.5m, 15.5m	3.5m, 7.5m, 11.5m, 15.5m	3.5m, 7.5m, 11.5m, 15.5m	3.5m, 7.5m, 11.5m, 15.5m	3.5m, 7.5m, 11.5m, 15.5m
Wind speed and direction inside the canyon	(metres from ground)	3.5m, 7.5m, 11.5m, 15.5m	3.5m, 7.5m, 11.5m, 15.5m	3.5m, 7.5m, 11.5m, 15.5m	3.5m, 7.5m, 11.5m, 15.5m	3.5m, 7.5m, 11.5m, 15.5m
Height of the two three-axes anemometer	(metres from ground)	7.5–10.5m	8–8m	5–12m	5–10m	20–9m
Height of the wind speed and direction anemometer outside the canyon	(metres)	26m	21m	21m	28m	29m
Height of the thermometer outside the canyon	(metres)	20m	15m	15m	22m	23m

Table 4.3 *continued*

Canyon		Ermou	Miltiadou	Voukourestiou	Kaniggos	Dervenion
Mean air temperature inside canyon, near the façades	(°C)	North wall 32°C; South wall 34°C; Ground 45°C	North-west wall 33°C; South-east wall 55°C; Ground 45°C	North-west wall 39°C; South-east wall 33°C; Ground 37°C	West wall 37°C; East wall 39°C; Ground 39°C	West wall 40°C; East wall 40°C; Ground 45°C
Mean air temperature distribution inside canyon during morning, noon and afternoon	(°C)	25°C 32°C 28°C	29°C 35°C 32°C	32°C 38°C 32°C	25°C 35°C 30°C	25°C 30°C 26°C
Mean air temperature distribution outside canyon during morning, noon and afternoon	(°C)	25°C 50°C 32°C	29°C 39°C 32°C	32°C 46°C 34°C	25°C 50°C 30°C	31°C 32°C 31°C
Duration of the experiment	(days)	28, 29 June, 3 August	31 July, 2, 3 August	7, 9, 10 August	27, 28, 29 August	4, 5, 6 September

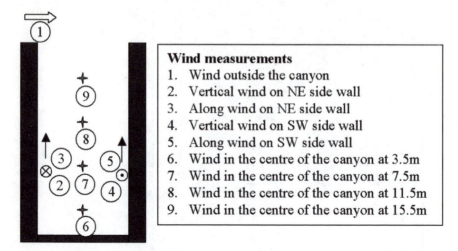

Source: Final Report of the URBVENT project, F. Allard (Coordinator), European Commission, Directorate General for Research, Brussels, June 2004

Figure 4.2 *Location of measurement points for wind speed*

- *Air temperature measurements outside the canyon*: a miniature ambient air temperature sensor was placed in the top of each canyon, on the roof of one building. The sensors were shielded inside a white-painted wooden cylinder, opened on two sides in order to allow air circulation.
- *Surface temperature measurements*: an infrared thermometer equipped with a laser beam measured the surface temperature. The surface temperatures of the exterior façades of the buildings were measured on a

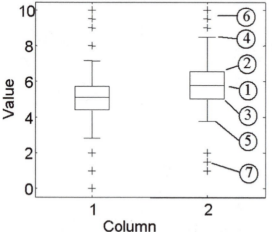

Legend
1. Median
2. Upper quartile
3. Lower quartile
4. Upper extend of data
5. Lower extend of data
6. Upper outliers
7. Lower outliers

Source: Final Report of the URBVENT project, F. Allard (Coordinator), European Commission, Directorate General for Research, Brussels, June 2004

Figure 4.3 *Data distribution in a box plot*

grid of 1m. All measurements were performed from the street level. The pavement and road temperatures were measured, as well, at different points along the width of the canyon in both sections defined above. All measurements were performed hourly for 12 hours.

- *Wind speed measurements near canyon façades*: a three-axis anemometer was used to measure the three components of the wind speed inside the canyon near the façades of the canyon. The anemometer was mounted on the exterior façade of a building in the canyon and at a distance of 1 to 2m from the wall.
- *Wind speed and direction measurements outside the canyon*: a cup anemometer was placed on the top of the canyon at a distance of 6m from its top level in order to measure the wind speed and direction out of the canyon.

Experimental analysis of airflow inside canyons

Wind speed was measured in nine points (see Figure 4.2) in five street canyons given in Table 4.3. The experimental results are given in the form of box plots. A box plot is a graphic representation of data distribution that shows the locations of percentiles (see Figure 4.3). The percentile of an element shows the percentage of elements in the sample with a lower value. The line in the middle of the box is the median, or the 50th percentile of the sample. The lower and upper lines of the box are the 25th and the 75th percentiles, representing the lower and upper quartile, respectively. The length of the box represents the inter-quartile range. The lower and upper 'whiskers' show the

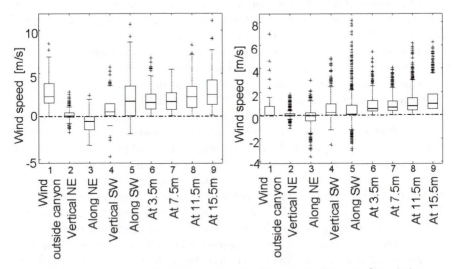

Source: Final Report of the URBVENT project, F. Allard (Coordinator), European Commission, Directorate General for Research, Brussels, June 2004

Figure 4.4 *Box plot of wind speed inside a deep and long street canyon when wind is perpendicular to the canyon axis: (a) 90° ± 15°; (b) 270° ± 15°*

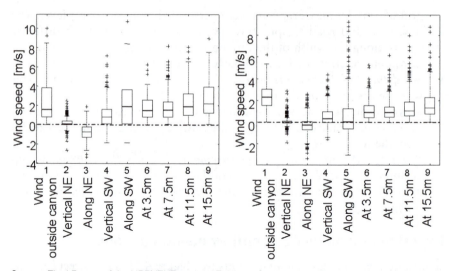

Source: Final Report of the URBVENT project, F. Allard (Coordinator), European Commission, Directorate General for Research, Brussels, June 2004

Figure 4.5 *Box plot of wind speed inside a deep and long street canyon when wind blows parallel to the canyon axis: (a) ± 15°; (b) 180° ± 15°*

range of data, if there are no outliers. Data are considered outliers if they are located 1.5 times the inter-quartile range away from the top or bottom of the box.

The measurements were performed in five street canyons in Athens under the conditions of hot weather and low wind velocity. The maximum wind velocity was 5m/s, but in 90 per cent of cases it was lower than 4m/s. The experimental data was grouped in three categories as a function of the wind direction: perpendicular, parallel or oblique to the canyon axis.

When the ambient flow was perpendicular to the main axis of the canyon (incidence angle from the direction of 90° ± 15° or 270° ± 15°), the flow inside canyon was along the main axis of the canyon (columns 3 and 5 in Figure 4.4). Mainly clockwise motions near the façades were observed, with a down lift near the windward façade and an up lift near the leeward façade of the canyon. The vertical velocity of the vortex was low, about 0.1m/s (columns 2 and 4 in Figure 4.4). No vertical distribution of wind in the centre of the canyon was observed in this situation, since at the four measured different heights of 3.5, 7.5, 11.5 and 15.5 metres values for horizontal wind speed were close to 1m/s (columns 6 to 9 in Figure 4.4). In some cases counter clockwise vortices were also observed, especially for aspects ratios (*H/W*) greater than three. When wind speed outside the canyon was lower than 4m/s, no specific flow inside the canyon was observed. For this case flow is due to intermittent vortices which established in the corners of the canyon (see Figure 4.4, columns 6 to 9).

In the case when ambient wind was parallel to the main axis of the canyon, the measured data inside the canyon showed flows from the same direction. The

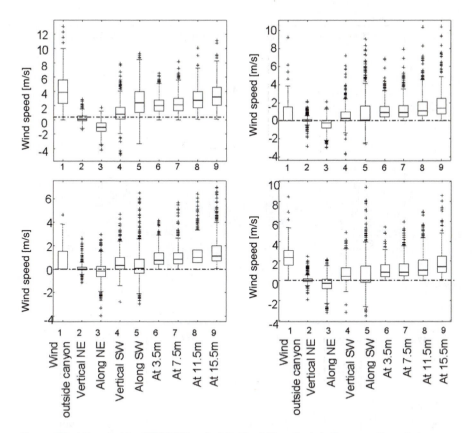

Source: Final Report of the URBVENT project, F. Allard (Coordinator), European Commission, Directorate General for Research, Brussels, June 2004

Figure 4.6 *Box plot of wind speed inside a deep and long street canyon when wind blows oblique to the canyon axis: (a) from east; (b) from south; (c) from west; (d) from north*

horizontal wind in the centre of the canyon was about 1m/s at all four heights (see Figure 4.5, columns 6 to 9). Up lift and down lift flows close to the canyon facades are mainly associated with thermal phenomena and are observed when the facades are heated by solar radiation (see Figure 4.5, columns 2 and 4). In general, a correlation was found between the undisturbed wind flow and the wind speed inside the canyon when wind speed was greater than 4m/s. However, when the undisturbed wind was very low (less than 4m/s), the coupling between the upper and the secondary flows inside the canyon is lost.

The most common case of flow is when the wind blew on oblique directions outside the canyon. When air is coming at a certain angle to the long axis of the canyon in most of the measured canyons the measured data indicate that a spiral vortex is induced along the length of the canyon, a corkscrew type of action.

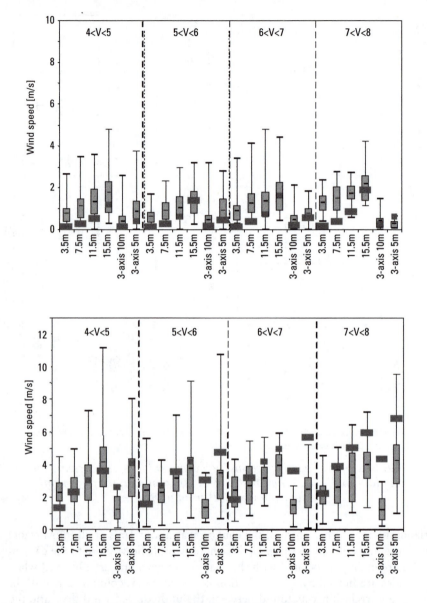

Source: Final Report of the URBVENT project, F. Allard (Coordinator), European Commission, Directorate General for Research, Brussels, June 2004

Figure 4.7 *Examples of validation of wind speed in street canyons: (a) Nicholson model; (b) Hotchkiss model. The experimental data are shown by box plots, the prediction of the model is figured in bold segments*

Validation of airflow model

The concise model for wind speed in street canyons, which was proposed in 'A new concise algorithm for air speed in street canyons', was compared with the experimental data. In Figure 4.7, the validation of the previously discussed model is presented. This analysis indicated a very good agreement between experimental and model values.

Occasionally, the described models lead to an overestimation of wind speed values outside a canyon of greater than 7m/s.

EXPERIMENTAL ANALYSIS OF AIR AND SURFACE TEMPERATURE IN URBAN CANYONS

The temperature distribution in the urban canopy layer is greatly affected by the radiation balance. Solar radiation incident on urban surfaces is absorbed and then transformed to sensible heat. Most of the solar radiation impinges upon roofs and on the vertical walls of buildings; only a relatively small part reaches ground level.

The temperature of the canyon surfaces results from the thermal balance of radiative, convective and conductive heat exchange. The surfaces absorb short-wave radiation depending upon their absorptivity and their exposure to solar radiation. They also absorb and emit long-wave radiation as a function of their temperature, emissivity and view factor. Heat is transferred to or from the surrounding air by convection and exchanged with the lower layers via conduction.

The optical and thermal characteristics of materials used in urban environments, especially the albedo for solar radiation and emissivity for long-wave radiation, have a very important impact on the urban energy balance. The use of high albedo materials reduces the amount of solar radiation absorbed in building envelopes and urban structures and keeps their surfaces cooler. Materials with high emissivity are good emitters of long-wave radiation and readily release the energy that has been absorbed as short-wave radiation. Lower surface temperatures decrease the temperature of the ambient air because heat convection intensity from a cooler surface is lower (Santamouris, 2001).

Analysis of the surface temperature between the two facing surfaces has shown the maximum simultaneous difference up to 10°C and 20°C at the middle and at the highest measured levels of the canyon, respectively. Comparison of the maximum difference of daily temperatures of the building façades and the surface temperature of the street shows that at street level, the temperature was 20°C and 50°C higher than the lower and the highest parts of the canyon, respectively. This is due to the higher amount of solar radiation received by a horizontal surface during the summer period, as well the higher absorptivity of the slabs used in the pedestrian streets and the materials used in for the building walls.

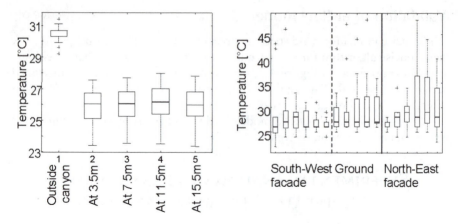

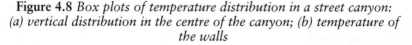

Source: Final Report of the URBVENT project, F. Allard (Coordinator), European Commission, Directorate General for Research, Brussels, June 2004

Figure 4.8 *Box plots of temperature distribution in a street canyon: (a) vertical distribution in the centre of the canyon; (b) temperature of the walls*

The air temperature outside the canyon was, during all the experimental period about 5°C higher than the corresponding temperature inside the canyon. The fact that air temperature inside the canyon was lower than outside can be explained as most of the canyons were deep and the penetration of solar radiation was limited.

In order to study the intensity of heat island in the five street canyons placed in the centre of Athens, comparisons have been made with temperatures recorded in the Station of Meteorological Service of the University of Athens. This is located in a suburban area at the University Campus in a tree planted area close to 7km distance from the centre of Athens. Both the Meteorological Station of the University of Athens and the street canyons are the same altitude. The air temperature differences between the spots inside the canyon and a reference station was close to 2°C. That was the order of magnitude of heat island intensity measured in Athens during the experimental campaign.

CONCLUSIONS

Air temperature, wind speed and direction measurements took place at four different height levels inside five different urban canyons during summer 2001 in the centre of Athens, in the frame of the URBVENT European Research project. The same figures were measured at the top of the canyon. The experiments lasted for three days, 12 hours each day. Data were collected and stored every 30 seconds. Surface temperature measurements were taken in the façades of the buildings and at street level during the same period on an hourly basis. The aim of these experiments was to better understand airflow phenomena and air temperature distribution in deep urban canyons.

The study of the thermal characteristics in the canyons revealed that there was a great difference between the surface temperatures of the facing walls of the canyon.

The air temperature stratification inside the canyons was found to be not significant. Air temperature outside the canyon was found always to be higher than the air temperature inside the canyon, with a maximum difference of 5°C. The ambient temperature inside the canyon was almost 2°C higher than the ones measured in a reference suburban station. The study of the air flow characteristics showed that for wind speed perpendicular to the axis of the canyon, the air flow inside the canyon was characterized by a vortex. When the flow outside the canyon was parallel to the canyon axis and above the threshold value of 4m/s, the flow inside the canyon was in the same direction.

REFERENCES

Albrecht, F. and Grunow, J. (1935) 'Ein Beitrag zur Frage der vertikalen Luftzirkulation in der Grossstandt', *Metorol*, vol Z52, pp103–108

Arnfield, A. J. and Mills, G. (1994) 'An analysis of the circulation characteristics and energy budget of a dry, asymmetric, east, west urban canyon. I. Circulation characteristics', *International Journal of Climatology*, vol. 14, pp119–134

Chang, P. C., Wang, P. N. and Lin, A. (1971) *Turbulent Diffusion in a City Street*, Proceedings of the Symposium on Air Pollution and Turbulent Diffusion, 7–10 December, Las Cruces, New Mexico, pp137–144

Dabberdt, W. F., Ludwig, F. L. and Johnson, W. B. (1973) 'Validation and applications of an urban diffusion model for vehicular emissions', *Atmospheric Environment*, vol 7, pp603–618

DePaul, F. T. and Sheih, C. M. (1986) 'Measurements of wind velocities in a street canyon', *Atmospheric Environment*, vol 20, pp445–459

Hotchkiss, R. S. and Harlow, F. H. (1973) *Air Pollution and Transport in Street Canyons*, US Office of Research and Monitoring, Washington, D.C.

Hoydysh, W. and Dabberdt, W. F. (1988) 'Kinematics and dispersion characteristics of flows in asymmetric street canyons', *Atmospheric Environment*, vol 22, no 12, pp2677–2689

Lee, I. Y., Shannon, J. D. and Park, H. M. (1994) *Evaluation of Parameterizations for Pollutant Transport and Dispersion in an Urban Street Canyon Using a Three-dimensional Dynamic Flow Model*, Proceedings of the 87th Annual Meeting and Exhibition, 19–24 June, Cincinnati, Ohio

Nakamura, Y. and Oke, T. R. (1988) 'Wind, temperature and stability conditions in an east-west oriented urban canyon', *Atmospheric Environment*, vol 22, pp2691–2700

Nicholson, S. E. (1975) 'A pollution model for street-level air', *Atmospheric Environment*, vol 9, pp19–31

Nunez, M. and Oke, T. R. (1977) 'The energy balance of an urban canyon', *Journal of Applied Meteorology*, vol 16, pp11–19

Oke, T. R. (1987) 'Street design and urban canopy layer climate', *Energy and Buildings*, vol 11, pp103–113

Santamouris, M. (2001) *Energy and Climate in the Urban Built Environment*, James and James Science Publishers, London

Santamouris, M., Papanikolaou, N., Koronakis, I., Livada, I. and Asimakopoulos, D. N. (1999) 'Thermal and airflow characteristics in a deep pedestrian canyon under hot weather conditions', *Atmospheric Environment*, vol 33, pp4503–4521

Wedding J. B., Lombardi, D. J. and Cermak, J. E. (1977) 'A wind tunnel study of gaseous pollutants in city street canyons', *Journal of the Air Pollution Control Association*, vol 27, pp557–566

Yamartino, R. J. and Wiegand, G. (1986) 'Development and evaluation of simple models for the flow, turbulence and pollution concentration fields within an urban street canyon', *Atmospheric Environment*, vol 20, pp2137–2156

5

Noise Level and Natural Ventilation Potential in Street Canyons

Michael Wilson, Fergus Nicol, John Solomon and John Shelton

INTRODUCTION

Noise, another barrier for the application of natural ventilation, was studied in the same urban environment as wind and temperature. Experimental data permitted the development of a simple model for estimating the noise attenuation with height above street level, as well as the aspect ratio. A monogram, which is useful for decisions in the initial stages of the design, was obtained by making the assumption that traffic intensity (and, consequently, noise level) depends upon street width. It was shown that the balconies reduce the noise level by approximately 2 decibels (dB) on the first floor and more than 3dB on the fourth floor.

High external noise levels are often used to justify the use of air conditioning in commercial and residential buildings. Methods of estimating noise levels in urban canyons are necessary if the potential for naturally ventilating buildings is to be assessed. These estimated noise levels can then be compared to the level of noise at which building occupants might be motivated to close windows in order to keep out the noise, but also to compromise the natural ventilation strategy.

A series of daytime noise measurements were made in 'canyon' streets in Athens with aspect ratios (height/width) varying from 1.0 to 5.0. The main purpose of the measurements was to examine the vertical variation in noise in the canyons in order to give advice on natural ventilation potential. A simple model of the noise level has been developed using a linear regression analysis of the measured data. The model can be used to predict the fall off (attenuation) of the noise level with height above the street level.

The attenuation is found to be a function of street width and height above the street; but the maximum level of attenuation (at the top of the canyon) is almost entirely a function of the aspect ratio, except in narrow streets. Background noise (L_{90}) suffers less attenuation than foreground noise (L_{10}) with height.

The attenuation results are compared to results from acoustic simulation. The simulation gives comparable values for attenuation in the canyons. The simulation is used to estimate the effectiveness of balconies for reducing external noise levels in canyon streets. Measurements in a survey throughout Europe are used to estimate the potential for natural ventilation in canyon streets in southern Europe.

The survey and simulations are used to assess the effect of noise on the natural ventilation potential of canyon-type streets, and to suggest limitations to the use of natural ventilation as a function of canyon geometry.

NOISE IN STREET CANYONS

This section describes noise measurements taken in streets in Athens. The rationale for these noise measurements is that the external noise climate is an important constraint to the opening of windows. This, in turn, means that the external noise level is a factor in the ventilation potential of an urban site. The ventilation potential is a measure of the viability of using natural ventilation in buildings at the site in question. This chapter provides guidance about the effect on the external noise as a function of the street width, aspect ratio and the distance of the site above street level. This requires some evaluation of the relative importance of the direct sound path from the source and the reverberant noise level within the street. Also important are the traffic density and its correlation with noise at street level.

Athens streets

Canyon-like streets in cities such as Athens vary considerably in their width and in height of the buildings that border them. The ratio of the height of the buildings (H) to the width of the street (W) is known as the 'aspect ratio' (AR) of the street. While the assumption is that the two sides of the street are of the same height, this is frequently not the case. In this study we have taken the average height of the street façades to give $AR = (H_1 + H_2)/2W$ (where H_1 and H_2 are the respective heights of the sides of the canyon – assumed to be comparable). The façades themselves also vary considerably, some being plain and some with balconies. Most residential streets have balconies; but even some office buildings are constructed with balconies. At ground level the situation can be more complex. The ground floor is often set back with colonnades. Paper stalls and other objects often litter the pavement.

The measurements of noise in Athens

Noise was measured outside the windows of buildings in nine street canyons in different areas of central Athens from 13–18 September 2001. The aim of these measurements was to assess the effect of the height of the measurement point above the canyon floor on the noise level. The measurements were taken in canyons with an aspect ratio ranging between 1 and 5 and with a variety of traffic loads. Table 5.1 indicates the date and time of the start of measurements, the numbers of different types of vehicles passing during the 15-minute recording session (heavy, light and motorcycle), the street width in metres, the aspect ratio, the presence of balconies (0 = none; 1 = one side of the street; 2 = both sides), the gradient of the street (+ for uphill), the typical traffic speed in kilometres per hour (km/h) and whether the traffic was travelling in one or both directions.

Because of traffic management policies in Athens, heavy goods vehicles are restricted to early deliveries. At the time of the measurements, the number of heavy vehicles was very low, consisting primarily of buses; but there was a high incidence of low-power motorcycles, around 50 per cent of which appeared to be the major source of noise (see Table 5.1). Vehicle speed varied, traffic lights regularly interrupted the flow and the roads were often congested. No sensible estimation of vehicle speed could be made (this made little sense, anyway, with regard to motorcycles).

Noise measurements

Noise was sampled every 0.125 seconds (s) with high-resolution logging sound meters (SIP95, manufactured by 01dB, Lyon). Four people were involved in each measurement:

- First, a building was selected for use in the measurement and access to the building was secured.
- One person was deployed on each of two floors of the building. Fieldworkers were positioned by an open window on the street side of the building and measured noise level at approximately 1m from the front of the building. In such circumstances, it is difficult to find consistent measuring positions, such as 1m in front of the façade. It was decided that fieldworkers would take measurements by stretching an arm through a window.
- A third person was deployed to measure noise at street level with the sound-level meter mounted on a tripod 1m in front of the façade. Measurements were made in front of a reflecting surface, if possible.
- The fourth person was deployed across the street to coordinate the noise-level measurements at the three sites and to time the simultaneous collection of data for 15 minutes at each site.
- The two fieldworkers at ground level separately counted the number of motorcycles, heavy vehicles, and cars and light goods vehicles using hand-held counters. The counts were continued for the full 15 minutes of the noise measurements and a note was made of any unusual events during that time (e.g. police sirens and church bells).
- Data were downloaded onto a laptop computer.

Table 5.1 *Basic data for the streets measured in central Athens*

Street	Date (2001)	Time	Vehicles passing in 15 minutes				Width (metres)	Aspect ratio (AR)	Balconies	Street gradient	Estimated speed (km/hour)	Traffic 1- or 2-way
			Heavy	Light	Motorcycle	Total						
AKE	17 September	11.55 am	32	386	356	774	19	1.6	0	0	0–40	2
AME	17 September	11.17 am	4	185	199	388	10	2.3	0	+5%	0–40	1
HAR	18 September	11.11 am	8	117	62	187	10	1.6	2	0	0–15	1
MI1	13 September	12.19 pm	3	83	107	193	9.5	2.5	0	−5%	8	1
MIM	13 September	13.19 pm	5	102	106	213	9.5	2.9	0	0	25–30	1
OCT	18 September	13.05 pm	50	236	278	564	20	1.9	1	0	0–30	2
OTE	14 September	11.53 am	16	153	359	528	22	1.0	0	0	10–15	2
PED	13 September	13.55 pm			2	2	3.5	5.0	1	0		0
SOL	17 September	12.32 pm	7	187	147	341	10	2.0	1	0	10–20	1

Table 5.2 *Height (in metres) of recording point above street level, and 15-minute L_{A90}, L_{Aeq} and L_{A10} for street level and each recording point for each street in the survey*

	Metres above street		L_{A90} dB			L_{Aeq} dB			L_{A10} dB		
	Low	High	Street	Low	High	Street	Low	High	Street	Low	High
AKE	11.5	25.5	72.1	71.5	69.8	78.6	76.8	74.3	81.7	79.5	76.6
AME	11.5	22	70.1	69.1	64.9	77.8	74.8	69.9	80.7	77.4	72.2
HAR	8	11.5	62.8	63.2	63.1	74.9	71.6	70.3	77.8	74.3	73.2
MI1		12	63.8	63.5	62.1	73.2	69.0	67.3	75.3	71.1	69.4
MIM	18.5	22.5	64	63.2	61.5	72.9	69.7	65.6	75.1	71.9	67.6
OCT*	33	–	70.6	68.7		81.0	77.0		81.0	76.9	
OTE	8	18.5	66.1	67.2	67.7	74.4	75.1	73.4	75.1	75.1	73.9
PED	15	22	62	59.8	55.4	66.1	63.2	57.8	68.5	65.5	59.9
SOL	11.5	15	66.9	66.3	64.8	76.0	73.2	71.9	79.1	76.1	74.7

Note: *In street OCT only one measuring point is shown because of a failure in one noise-level meter.

The noise spectrum in one of the streets was found to be similar to that used in BS EN-1793 (1998), but with a smaller contribution at higher frequencies. Both the average noise level and the range of loudness are reduced in places higher up the buildings.

Initial statistical analysis of measured data

The data collected in the field experiment were collated into a database. The 15-minute periods were subdivided into three 5-minute sub-periods so that the results obtained for one sub-period could be tested on another in order to examine the robustness of relationships.

The data in the database include, for each period, sub-period and measurement site, the following:

- the floor on which measurements were taken, f;
- the height of measuring point above ground, h (m);
- the street canyon aspect ratio, AR;
- the street width, W (m);
- the total number of vehicles per hour, n;
- the number of motorcycles per hour, mc;
- A-weighted values of L_{eq}, L_{10}, L_{90} (dB).

For each site, the reduction in noise level compared to ground level was calculated for each measure (ΔL_{eq}, ΔL_{10}, ΔL_{90}) (dB).

Regression analysis of the dependence of L_{eq} on n, W and h shows that only n and h are significant. In addition, the street width, W, and the traffic, n, are highly correlated ($R^2 = 0.78$). The terms in the regression equation and the coefficient of concordance R^2 are shown in Table 5.3.

Note that in Table 5.3 the regression coefficients for the three five-minute sub-periods are not significantly different from one another or from those for the whole 15-minute period. The noise level increases with the level of traffic and decreases with the height above the street.

The regression coefficients for the variation of the noise attenuation, ΔL_{eq}, with the height of the observer and the width of the street, are shown in Table 5.4. Other possible factors, such as the traffic, n, and the aspect ratio, AR, added little to the strength of the relationship.

Again, the linear regression coefficients for the three five-minute sub-periods are not significantly different from each other or from those for the whole 15-minute period. The noise attenuation increases with the height above the street and decreases with the street width.

These basic statistical analyses confirm the relation between noise level and traffic density, street dimensions and the position of the measurement point. In the following section, a simple model of the noise in urban canyons is developed and then calibrated using the data obtained in this study.

Table 5.3 *Regression coefficients (± standard error) in the equation* $L_{Aeq} = \alpha +$ $\beta n + \gamma h$*. All terms are significant at $\leqslant 1$ per cent*

Coefficient for		Five-minute sessions			All 15 minutes
		1	2	3	
γ	Height above street, h (metres)	0.00374 ± 0.00060	0.00366 ± 0.00056	0.00289 ± 0.00061	0.00377 ± 0.00055
β	Traffic level, n	−0.238 ± 0.055	−0.202 ± 0.052	−0.199 ± 0.050	−0.221 ± 0.051
α	Constant	69.0 ± 1.1	68.8 ± 1.1	70.5 ± 1.2	68.9 ± 1.051181
	R²	0.70	0.70	0.63	0.73

Table 5.4 *Regression coefficients (± standard error) in the equation* $L_{Aeq} = \alpha + \lambda w + \gamma h$*. All terms are significant at $\leqslant 1$ per cent*

Coefficient for		Five-minute sessions			All 15 minutes
		1	2	3	
λ	Street width, W (metres)	−0.286 ± 0.077	−0.257 ± 0.067	−0.288 ± 0.055	−0.249 ± 0.060
γ	Height above street, h (metres)	0.169 ± 0.057	0.157 ± 0.049	0.165 ± 0.034	0.161 ± 0.044
α	Constant	4.60 ± 1.33	4.46 ± 1.16	4.92 ± 0.88	4.26 ± 1.03
	R²	0.59	0.61	0.78	0.66

A SIMPLE MODEL OF NOISE IN CANYONS

The traffic noise, as measured at various locations in the canyons, is a combination of the direct sound and quasi-reverberation in the canyon. The term quasi-reverberation is used to denote a type of reverberation that is not diffuse but consists primarily of flutter echoes between the façades lining the street. Thus, the sound pressure, p, is:

$$p^2 \propto P(dc + rc) \tag{5.1}$$

where P is the sound power, dc is the direct component of the sound and rc is the reverberant component.

The direct component may be treated in two ways depending upon whether the traffic is considered as a line source (where the traffic stream is considered as the source) or point source (where each vehicle is separately responsible for the noise). Both of these possible scenarios were considered. For a line source, the direct component, dc, is inversely proportional to the distance from the source; for the point source, the direct component, dc, is inversely proportional to the square of the distance. If the street width is W and the height of the measuring position above the ground is h, assuming the source is in the middle of the road, the distance between source and receiver is:

$$d = ((W/2)^2 + h^2)^{1/2} \tag{5.2}$$

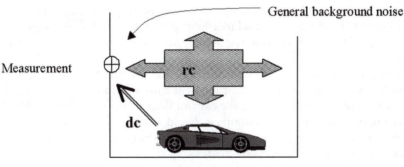

Figure 5.1 *Three noise sources: the direct component, dc, the reverberant component, rc, and the background noise*

For the reverberant sound, the noise is related approximately to the absorption area. This strictly applies to diffuse sound sources and is only approximate in this context. The main area for absorption is the open top of the canyon, which is assumed to be a perfect absorber and whose area per metre of street equals W, the width of the street. A further sophistication may be to include absorption of the road surface and façades. With an absorption coefficient of 0.05, this would lead to the absorption area:

$$W' = W' + 0.05W' + 2 \times 0.05H = 1.05W' + 0.1H \tag{5.3}$$

where W corresponds to the top of the canyon, $0.05W$ to the floor of the canyon, and $2 \times 0.05H$ to the walls. Alternatively, if we use the aspect ratio (AR) of the street, equation (5.3) becomes:

$$W' = W(1.05 + 0.1 \cdot AR) \tag{5.4}$$

The sound power is assumed proportional to the number of vehicles per hour, n. For line source, its expression is:

$$p^2 = a \frac{n}{d} + b \frac{n}{W'} + c \tag{5.5}$$

For point source, its expression is:

$$p^2 = a \frac{n}{d^2} + b \frac{n}{W'} + c \tag{5.6}$$

where a, b, and c are constants related to the direct component, the reverberant component and to any background environmental noise entering the canyon, respectively (see Figure 5.1). In general, the contribution of c will be small. Measurements on the rooftop of a building in a pedestrian area behind vehicular streets in the centre of Athens gave $L_{Aeq} = 55$dB. In the vehicular streets, few noise levels below $L_{Aeq} = 70$dB were recorded. L_{90} averaged 66dB. The expressions were developed into the form:

$$L_p = 10\log_{10}\left(n \left(\frac{n}{d_1} + \frac{b}{W'} \right) + c \right) \tag{5.7}$$

where, by the normal definition of sound level in dB, L_p is the noise level for a sound pressure level p and is equal to $10\log_{10}p$ and d_1 is d or d^2 (see equations (5.5) and (5.6)) depending upon the assumption about the shape of the noise source.

The purpose of this investigation is to provide a method for estimating the fall off in noise level with the height in street canyons. In equation (5.7), the value of L_p relates to height above the canyon floor, h, through the variable d_1. Estimating the values of the constants a, b and c will enable the change of L_p with h to be determined. The values of the constants a, b and c have been estimated using multiple regression analysis.

Correlation analysis suggested that the line source of sound was a better model for these data. The correlation between measured p^2 and calculated direct noise levels (ignoring the reverberant component) was 0.86 for the linear source assumption, against 0.68 for the point source. Further tests showed that there was little change in correlation whether W or W' were used. The advantage of using W is its simplicity, while W' would allow the computation of any increase in the absorption coefficient of the façade. However, there is no measured data to evaluate any change of absorption.

Calibrating the theoretical model

In order to determine how these results accord with the theoretical model presented above, values were calculated for n/d (referred to as D) and n/W' (RV) so that a linear regression could be conducted for p^2 from equations (5.5) and (5.6) with W' as defined in equation (5.4). Regression analyses were performed for p^2 against combinations of these variables, initially to determine which combination has the best explanatory power. The high coefficients of determination, R^2, compared to the straight linear regressions for L_{eq} on h and n shown in Table 5.3, suggest that the theoretical relationship developed above provides a good model of the spatial variation of p^2, related to the noise level, L, by:

$$L = 10 \log_{10} p^2 \tag{5.8}$$

The analysis suggests that there is an advantage in including the term in RV, although in these data the combined effect of the direct and the reverberant components may be as if the linear sound source was located further from the façade. Different values were calculated from the measured data by regression analysis depending upon whether the noise was considered to emanate from the middle of the road (as assumed above) or from other points in the street. Figure 5.2 suggests that in the case of L_{Aeq} and L_{A10}, the middle of the road is a good approximation; but in the case of L_{A90}, the direct sound acts as if it is coming from the other side of the street.

Regression analysis gives optimal values for the constants a, b and c (equation (5.5)) as follows: $a = 174314$, $b = 63391$ and $c = -4105672$. The regression equation (5.5), for p^2 on D_2 (the value of D when the traffic is assumed to be a line source in the middle of the street) and RV using the data from the whole 15 minutes (see Table 5.5) becomes:

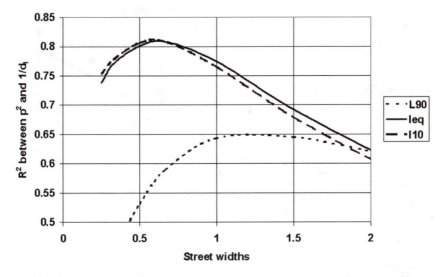

Source: Nicol and Wilson (2004)

Figure 5.2 *Variation of the value of R^2 with changing assumptions about the location of the stream of traffic. For L_{A10} and L_{Aeq}, the stream can be assumed to be roughly in the middle of the road (0.5); however, when calculating the L_{A90}, the traffic would have an apparent distance from the façade (d_1) between 1 and 1.5 times the width of the street*

$$p^2 = 17.4 \times 10^4 . D_2 + 5.34 \times 10^4 . RV - 411 \times 10^4 \quad (5.9)$$

Then:

$$L_{eq} = 10 \log_{10} p^2 \quad (5.10)$$

where L_{eq} is the noise level at height h above the street, and D_2 is a function of three variables, h, W and n, the number of vehicles (n is assumed to be proportional to the noise generated). Two of these variables (n and W) are also included in RV, together with the aspect ratio, AR, of the canyon. There is a

Table 5.5 *Comparison of regression coefficients of equation (5.5) for the first, second and third five-minute periods of the noise monitoring, with overall results*

Coefficient for	Five-minute sessions			All 15 minutes
	1	2	3	
D_2 (a)	16.44 ± 2.43**	17.92 ± 2.50**	18.92 ± 2.70**	17.43 ± 2.57**
RV (b)	6.1 ± 5.6	5.5 ± 8.0	17.5 ± 8.1*	5.34 ± 5.9
Constant (c)	−353 ± 379	−395 ± 546	−1553 ± 678*	411 ± 400
R^2	0.81	0.70	0.81	0.81

Notes: * and ** refer to significance of the coefficient at the 5 per cent and 0.1 per cent confidence level, respectively (all coefficients x 10⁴)

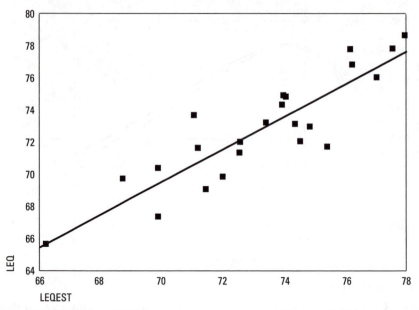

Source: Nicol and Wilson (2004)

Figure 5.3 *Measured noise level* L*eq* *(labelled LEQ) (dB) against the predicted* L*eq* *(LEQEST) (dB) (R² = 0.75)*

logical problem with a negative value for c since the value of p^2 cannot be negative. This value may be due to a curvature in the relationship which the linear regression cannot take into account. The effect of c on the value of p^2 is, in any case, generally small. Figure 5.3 shows that the measured value is well predicted by the calculated value ($R^2 = 0.75$).

In order to facilitate the visualization, a simplifying assumption has been made that the traffic level is a function of street width. In these data, the correlation between traffic intensity, expressed in number of vehicles per hour, n, and street width W (m) was $R = 0.88$ and the regression relationship (shown in Figure 5.4) was:

$$n = 137W - 306 \tag{5.11}$$

Using this simplifying assumption, values of expected noise level at different heights for a particular value of street width W can be calculated (see Figure 5.5).

CALCULATING THE NOISE ATTENUATION AT DIFFERENT HEIGHTS IN THE CANYON

Using the calculation for noise level at different heights in the canyon, it is possible to calculate the noise attenuation from street level at different heights

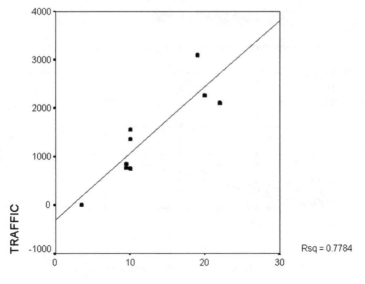

Source: Nicol and Wilson (2004)

Figure 5.4 *Correlation between traffic intensity,* n *(vehicles per hour), and street width,* W *(m); R^2 = 0.78*

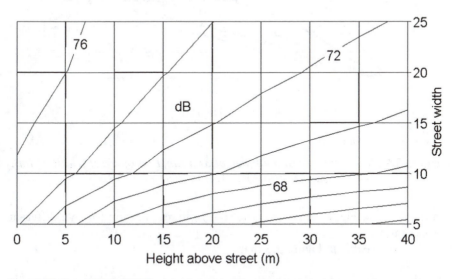

Source: Nicol and Wilson (2004)

Figure 5.5 *Predicted noise levels in decibels (dB) with different street widths and heights above the street*

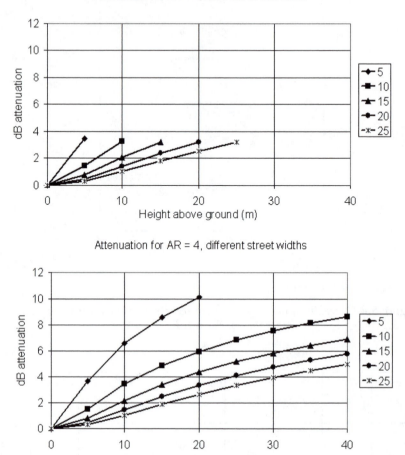

Source: Nicol and Wilson (2004)

Figure 5.6 *Noise attenuation with height as a function of street width* W *(m).*
(a) for aspect ratio AR – 1, *(b) aspect ratio* AR = 4

in the canyon. Figure 5.6 shows the change in attenuation for two different
aspect ratios.

It is noticeable in Figure 5.6 that:

- the attenuation for a given street width and measuring height is practically
  independent of *AR*;
- for a given *AR*, there is a maximum level of attenuation at the top of the
  canyon which is little affected by street width.

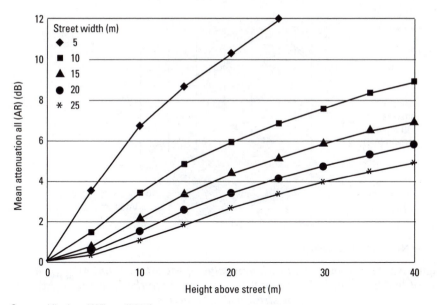

Source: Nicol and Wilson (2004)

Figure 5.7 *Mean value of the noise attenuation for different values of the street width and the height above the street*

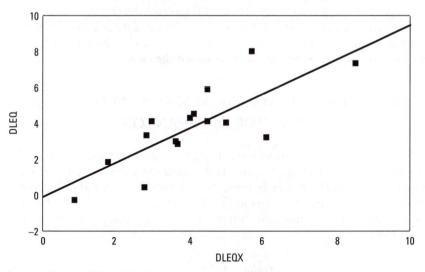

Source: Nicol and Wilson (2004)

Figure 5.8 *Measured values of attenuation (DLEQ) (dB) plotted against calculated values using equations (5.9) and (5.10) (DLEQX) (dB) ($R^2 = 0.58$)*

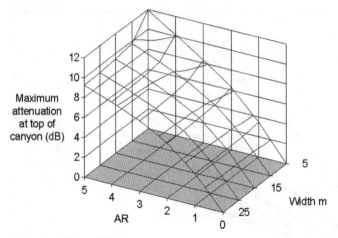

Source: Nicol and Wilson (2004)

Figure 5.9 *Variation of the maximum value of the attenuation,* ΔL_{AeqH}, *at the top of buildings bordering on an urban canyon, with the aspect ratio AR and the street width in metres*

Figure 5.7 shows the mean value of the attenuation in L_{eq} for different values of street width and height above the street. The error in using these mean values is generally less than 0.2dB. Figure 5.8 presents the relationship between the measured and calculated noise attenuation for the data collected in Athens (15-minute values) by subtracting the value at the given height from that at the street level. It suggests good agreement between the two.

CALCULATING THE MAXIMUM SOUND ATTENUATION AT THE TOP OF A CANYON

For a given value of the aspect ratio, there is a maximum value of the attenuation at the top of the canyon. This maximum value can be calculated using the theoretical approach presented above. Consider the difference between L_{eq} at the top of the canyon ($h = H$) and the bottom ($h = 0$). Because L_{eq} is a logarithmic function, the difference is, in fact, $10\log_{10}$ of the ratio of the two values of p^2:

$$\Delta L_{AeqH} = L_{Aeq0} - L_{AeqH} = 10\log_{10}\left(\frac{p_0^{\ 2}}{p_{\ H}^2}\right)$$ (5.12)

where:

$$p_0^{\ 2} = a\,\frac{n}{W/2} + b\,\frac{n}{W(1.05+0.1\cdot AR)} + c = \frac{n}{W}\left(2a + \frac{n}{1.05+0.1\cdot AR} + c\,\frac{W}{n}\right)$$

(5.13)

Table 5.6 *Values obtained from regression analysis of the coefficients* a, b *and* c *in equation (5.5) (with significance (p)) and the R^2 for the regression on p^2*

	a	(p)	b	(p)	c	(p)	R^2
p^2 (L_{90})	$2.16 \cdot 10^4$	0.013	$4.89 \cdot 10^4$	0.014	$-1.63 \cdot 10^6$	0.206	0.641
p^2 (L_{eq})	$1.74 \cdot 10^5$	0.000	$6.34 \cdot 10^4$	0.293	$-4.11 \cdot 10^6$	0.316	0.811
p^2 (L_{10})	$3.51 \cdot 10^5$	0.000	$1.04 \cdot 10^5$	0.376	$-9.78 \cdot 10^6$	0.225	0.813

and:

$$p^2{}_H = \frac{n}{W} \left(\frac{a}{\sqrt{AR^2+(1/2)^2}} + \frac{a}{1.05+0.1.AR} + c\frac{W}{n} \right) \qquad (5.14)$$

From $H = W \cdot AR$, and considering the relation between the street width and traffic intensity given in equation (5.11), it results in:

$$\Delta L_{Aeq} = 10Log_{10} \left(\frac{(2a + b/(1.05+0.1*AR) + cW/(137W{-}306))}{\dfrac{a}{\sqrt{AR^2+(1/2)^2}} + \dfrac{a}{1.05+0.1.AR} + cW/(137W{-}306)} \right)$$

$$(5.15)$$

Note that although ΔL_{AeqH} is a function of the aspect ratio, AR, and street width, W, its variation depends principally upon the aspect ratio except where the width of the street is small (see Figure 5.9).

A similar analysis to that presented above can be applied to the data for L_{10} and L_{90}. Table 5.6 gives the values of the constants *a*, *b* and *c* for the three different measures of noise. In the cases of L_{eq} and L_{10}, the terms for *b* are not statistically significant, suggesting that the direct component of noise predominates. In L_{90} both terms are significant.

The attenuation of L_{90} is relatively small, suggesting that the 'background' noise level falls more slowly and the loud noises more quickly with increasing height above the street. The maximum attenuation of L_{10} is affected more significantly by the aspect ratio than either L_{90} or L_{eq}.

SIMULATIONS OF NOISE ATTENUATION IN URBAN CANYONS

In order to back up the empirical results from the surveys of urban canyons in Athens (Nicol and Wilson, 2004), a number of simulations have been undertaken using a noise-level simulation package. In particular, three simulations were made assuming 5m, 10m and 15m street widths. The configuration of the buildings was five storeys (four above ground), with

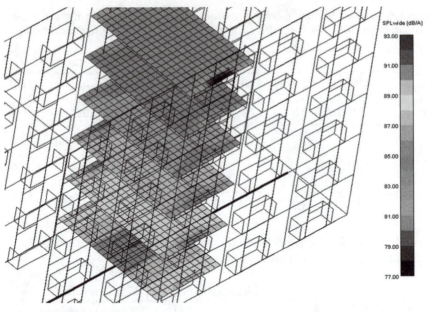

Figure 5.10 *Predicted noise levels at different heights within the canyon*
(10m wide street, aspect ratio of 2.1)

storey height 7m for the ground floor and 3.5m for upper floors; there were balconies on each floor. Each apartment façade had an open doorway of 2m x 2m located centrally, and a balcony 1.2m high, 3m wide and 1m deep. A line source of noise is assumed at the centre of the street.

Figure 5.10 shows the noise-level profiles at different levels: ground floor, mezzanine, first, second, third and fourth floors. Notice that the balconies produce an area of quiet outside the rooms, especially at the top of the building.

As the intensity of the line source assumed along the centre of the road has been set at an arbitrary (although realistic) value, a direct comparison between the noise levels could not be made. The methodology proposed by Nicol and Wilson (2004) suggests that the levels of traffic noise used in the simulation imply a very high traffic density. The value for the traffic density is almost the same for each street width, giving some confidence that the relationship between noise and street geometry presented in Nicol et al (2002) has some validity. The linear and constant relationship between the street width and the traffic intensity (and, consequently, the noise) is a key assumption of this methodology. It is evident that this relation cannot be constant. For example, the traffic is lower during the night time or on a pedestrian street. However, the traffic measured represents the highest intensity for a street with a given width, making the assumption valid and, consequently, useful for dimensioning in the worst situation.

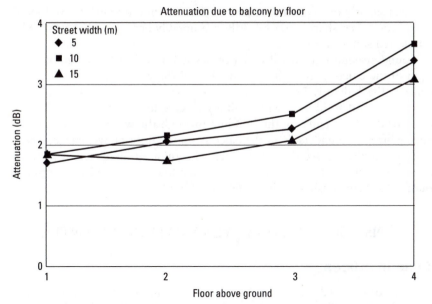

Figure 5.11 *Simulated contribution of balconies to reducing noise level at the surface of the building in five-storey buildings in street canyons*

Notes: The heights of the floors above street level are assumed to be 7m, 10.5m, 14m and 17.5m. Balconies are 1.2m deep and 3m wide and the values are averaged across the width of the façade

Attenuation with height above the street

The reduction of noise level is proportional to height above the street; therefore, the attenuation above the canyon floor should be constant for a particular position in the street, irrespective of the intensity of the noise source. This means that we would expect the relationship of attenuation to height within the street in these simulations to be comparable to that measured in an equivalent position in the empirical study.

The predicted attenuation is consistently lower than that measured in Athens. The attenuation within the balconies is always higher than outside them, and, in the case of 10m and 15m roads, the measured attenuation is between the noise level on the outside of the balconies and that within them.

Attenuation caused by balconies

The drop in noise level close to the building façade caused by the balcony can be estimated from the difference in noise level at 1.5m from the façade, compared to the noise at the level of the façade. This attenuation due to the balcony varies slightly with the street width but is almost entirely due to the height of the balcony above the street. Figure 5.11 shows the balcony contribution to noise attenuation. The height above the street is signified by the floor. The balcony contribution is just under 2dB at the first floor, and increases slightly on each of the next two floors. On the fourth (top) floor, the contribution rises sharply to over 3dB (presumably because of the relative lack of reflected sound from the canyon walls).

Sound attenuation caused by balconies will mostly be attributable to the depth of the balcony from the building line of the wall and the solidity of the front of the balcony. Balconies that are narrower or that do not have a continuous and solid wall will be likely to give less protection from noise. Much of the noise entering the building through the window will have been reflected from the underside of the balcony on the floor above, particularly on the floors higher above the street where the angle of incidence of the direct noise is higher. In these cases, an advantage may be gained from applying sound-absorbent finishes to the underside of balconies.

NOISE AND NATURAL VENTILATION POTENTIAL

Noise in offices

Noise is often used as an argument against natural ventilation and for supporting air conditioning. Noise is, thus, one of the factors when the potential for natural ventilation is under consideration. The European project Smart Controls and Thermal Comfort (SCATS) (Joule Programme) sought to develop control algorithms for both natural ventilation and air-conditioning systems based on the theory of adaptive thermal comfort (McCartney and Nicol, 2002). Instrumentation was built to undertake office surveys in 25 offices in five European countries, amounting to surveying 850 people, on a monthly basis over the year (Solomon et al, 1998). In research related to the noise limitations of natural ventilation in buildings in urban areas (Wilson, 1992; Wilson et al, 1993; Dubiel et al, 1996; Nicol et al, 1997), the noise was measured at each workstation and a question was answered concerning the noise environment. The response to the acoustic environment was measured on a seven-point scale. The implication of the results is that current noise standards are unnecessarily stringent and that an L_{Aeq} noise level of some 55dB to 60dB will be accepted. Although there is no direct evidence from Athens, research suggests that in countries such as Greece, where natural ventilation and open windows are common, tolerance of noise is generally greater (Dubiel et al, 1996).

Natural ventilation potential

Assuming that traffic in the canyons follows the relationship shown in equation (5.11), the expected daytime noise level becomes purely a function of the geometry of the street. Figure 5.5 shows the expected noise levels in Athens at different street widths and heights above the streets. Figure 5.12 shows the implication of this for natural ventilation potential of office units at a height h above street level.

The results introduced above from the SCATS project (McCartney and Nicol, 2002) suggest that the tolerable noise level in European offices is around

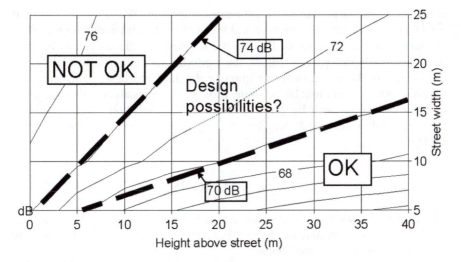

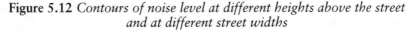

Notes: Configurations in which natural ventilation is possible are indicated (ok), as are those in which it is ruled out (not ok). Between these two extremes is a region in which there are possibilities for design solutions (based on Figure 5.5)
Source: Nicol and Wilson (2004)

Figure 5.12 *Contours of noise level at different heights above the street and at different street widths*

60dB. At the same time, the noise attenuation at an open window is accepted as 10dB to 15dB. Thus, an outdoor noise level of 70dB or less is likely to be acceptable. Using special methods and window designs, a further 3dB to 5dB attenuation is possible. For the traffic conditions of Athens, street widths that will give acceptable conditions at different heights above the street are indicated by 'ok'. Street widths that will give unacceptable conditions for buildings with open windows near street level are indicated by 'not ok'. Between these two, there are possibilities for acceptable conditions with careful design.

Because the noise measurements reported here were exclusively taken during the day, the implications on natural ventilation potential for evening or night time can only be estimated, although it should be remembered that in *unoccupied* offices, the outdoor noise level will be irrelevant to the use of night ventilation. The limitation to natural ventilation potential by noise will be important at night in residences. While overall noise levels will almost certainly be lower at night, the reduction will be offset by the greater sensitivity to noise. In addition, the occasional passing vehicle will be almost as loud, though as a point source its attenuation with distance above the street will be according to equation (5.6) and will be greater than for daytime noise. Notice that the attenuation of the loudest daytime noises (as suggested by the attenuation of the L_{10}) is greater than the attenuation of L_{eq} for similar reasons.

The effect on the urban noise climate of different street formations (e.g. point-block buildings, wider pavements and tree planting) will generally be to reduce noise, in particular the reverberant component. Wider streets and dual carriageways will increase the flow and speed of traffic and may have the effect of increasing the noise level. Part of the purpose of this study has been to develop a methodology that can be used in other contexts. In different cities (or, indeed, in Athens at different times of the day), the basic components of the noise environment will be the same, though the regression coefficients given in Table 5.6 could well be very different. The correlation between vehicle numbers and street width (see Figure 5.4) may not be so strong in other contexts.

CONCLUSIONS

This is an initial study of the daytime traffic noise in urban canyons in Athens. Further work is necessary; but from these measurements it is possible to draw a number of tentative conclusions:

- High levels of noise can be found in these canyon-type streets and show predominance in the low-frequency end of the noise spectrum despite a high proportion of motorcycles in the traffic mix.
- The noise level in canyon streets increases with traffic density and decreases with height above the canyon floor.
- The attenuation in noise level compared to that at street level increases with the distance from the canyon floor, but decreases with increasing street width.
- These relationships are well represented by a simple model of noise level comprising a direct component and a reverberant component.
- The direct component is assumed to be from a line source at or near the centre of the road whose power falls off with the inverse of the distance from this source.
- The reverberant component is assumed to act as if the street were a two-dimensional room, with the canyon roof acting as a perfect absorber.
- In addition, there may be a small additional noise component from the general environmental noise.
- The simple model, calibrated from the measured data, shows that the noise attenuation (L_{Aeq}) is almost entirely a function of street width and height above the canyon floor (see Figure 5.3)
- The maximum value of the attenuation (and, hence, the best possible noise attenuation) is almost entirely a function of aspect ratio (see Figure 5.6), with a small effect of street width in narrow streets.
- Similar considerations apply when predicting the attenuation of L_{10} and L_{90}. Relative to L_{eq}, the rate of attenuation with height is greater for L_{10} and less for L_{90}.
- Figure 5.12 indicates the potential for natural ventilation of offices as a function of street width and height above the street.

- This report compares the results of a simulation with measured values of noise in an Athenian urban canyon. The street dimensions used for the simulation are typical for canyons in central Athens.
- The comparison is between the values simulated and the results of a simple statistical model of canyon noise built from the measurements. The noise attenuation above street level can be compared and shows a similar reduction with height above street level for a given street width.
- The simulations have been used to predict the reduction in noise level at the building surface afforded by balconies. The simulation suggests that the noise reduction due to balconies is about 2dB lower in buildings, rising to 3–4dB near the top of the canyon.

REFERENCES

BS EN 1793-3 (1998) 'Road Traffic Noise Reducing Devices: Test Method for Determining the Acoustic Performance, Normalised Traffic Noise Spectrum', British Standards Institution, London

Dubiel, J., Wilson, M. and Nicol, F. (1996) 'Decibels and discomfort – an investigation of noise tolerance in offices', Proceedings of the Joint CIBSE/ASHRAE Conference in Harrogate, vol 2, Chartered Institution of Building Services Engineers, London, pp184–191

McCartney, K. and Nicol, F. (2002) 'Developing an adaptive control algorithm for Europe: Results of the SCATS project', *Energy and Buildings*, vol 34, no 6, pp623–635

Nicol, F., Wilson, M. and Dubiel, J. (1997) 'Decibels and degrees – interaction between thermal and acoustic interaction in offices', Proceedings of the CIBSE National Conference, Chartered Institution of Building Services Engineers, London

Nicol, J. F. and Wilson, M. P. (2004) 'The effect of street dimensions and traffic density on the noise level and natural ventilation potential in urban canyons'. *Energy and Buildings*, vol 36, no 5, pp 423–434

Solomon, J., Wilson, M., Wilkins, P. and Jacobs, A. (1998) 'An environmental monitoring system for comfort analysis', Proceedings of Conference EPIC 1998, ENTPE, Lyon, France, pp457–462

Wilson, M. (1992) 'A review of acoustic problems in passive solar design', Proceedings of Conference EuroNoise 1992, pp901–908

Wilson, M., Nicol, F. and Singh, R. (1993) 'Measurements of background noise levels in naturally ventilated buildings, associated with thermal comfort studies: Initial results', Proceedings of Institute of Acoustics, London, vol 15, no 8, pp283–295

www.unl.ac.uk/LEARN/port/1997/scats/scats_index.html

6

Outdoor–Indoor Pollutant Transfer

*Cristian Ghiaus, Vlad Iordache, Francis Allard and
Patrice Blondeau*

INTRODUCTION

Pollution is also considered to restrict the application of natural ventilation.
Two aspects are important when pollution is analysed: first, the economical
growth, after an initial increase of the pollution level, induces a reduction of
the pollution when the financial and technological resources become available;
second, the type and level of outdoor pollution are different compared to
indoor pollution. These two aspects make outdoor pollution less restrictive in
the application of natural ventilation.

Economic growth has a tendency to ameliorate outdoor air quality, after
its initial negative effect (see Figure 6.1a). While material progress is sought,
pollution increases with economic growth. But when financial and
technological resources are enough, the cost of pollution counts in the
evaluation of quality of life, and actions to reduce it are enforced. It is also
noticeable that the decrease of overall outdoor pollution occurs regardless of
income. The World Health Organization (WHO) issued health-based
guidelines for air quality in which recommended values are given for the 'key'
pollutants: sulphur dioxide (SO_2), nitrogen dioxide (NO_2), carbon monoxide
(CO), ozone (O_3), suspended particle matter and lead. Guideline values are
given for these pollutants (WHO, 2000).

These outdoor pollutants are different from indoor pollutants. Indoor
pollutants include environmental tobacco smoke, biological and non-
biological particles, volatile organic compounds, nitrogen oxides, lead, radon,
carbon monoxide, asbestos, various synthetic chemicals and others. Indoor air
pollution has been associated with a range of health effects, from discomfort
and irritation to chronic pathologies and cancers. In an effort to conserve
energy, modern building design has favoured tighter structures with lower rates

of ventilation (WHO, 2000). The impact of indoor pollution on health is much more important than that of outdoor pollution (Figure 6.1b). Indoor pollution problems differ in developed and developing countries. In developed countries, low ventilation rates and the presence of products and materials that emit a large variety of compounds are the cause of most problems; in developing countries, human activity, especially combustion processes, is the source of most pollution.

Epidemiological studies showed associations between health events (such as death and admission in hospitals) and daily average concentrations of particles, ozone, sulphur dioxide, airborne acidity, nitrogen dioxide and carbon monoxide. Although the associations for each of these pollutants were not significant in all studies, taking the body of evidence as a whole, the consistency is striking. For particles and ozone, it has been accepted by many that the studies provide no indication of any threshold of effect and an assumption of linearity was made when defining the exposure–response relationships (WHO, 2000).

Indoor air quality is related to outdoor air pollutant concentration through the rate of air change and reactivity of the pollutant. Façade air tightness, as an intrinsic characteristic of a building, represents a key factor in this relation because it is the main link between indoor and outdoor environments; it is also an important characteristic of the natural ventilation property of the building. When the airflow through the external openings is large, the indoor concentration of the outdoor pollutants is practically equal to the outdoor concentration. When the building is tight, experiments in the Natural Ventilation in the Urban Environment (URBVENT) project and in a related French programme showed that the indoor–outdoor pollutant ratio (I/O) depends upon the façade air tightness and the outdoor concentration. Experiments were conducted for ozone, nitrogen dioxide and particle matter. The most important reduction was noticed for ozone, with an I/O ratio of 0.05 to 0.33 (a higher I/O ratio was measured for higher outdoor ozone concentration). The I/O ratio for nitrogen dioxide was between 0.05 and 0.95, with lower values for higher outdoor concentration. For particle matter, the I/O ratio was between 0.2 and 0.7, with values depending upon the outdoor concentration and upon the size of the particles.

EXPERIMENTAL STUDY OF THE OUTDOOR–INDOOR POLLUTANT TRANSFER

The key outdoor pollutants (SO_2, NO_2, CO, O_3, suspended particle matter and lead) are usually monitored in large cities. Experiments showed that the mean indoor and outdoor concentration levels of sulphur dioxide and lead are equal. Ozone and nitrogen dioxide react with the building material, resulting in a lower indoor than outdoor concentration when the building is airtight. The particle matter transfer depends upon the particle size. The experimental

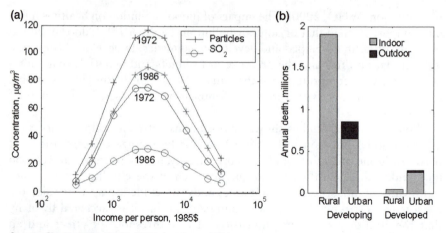

Source: Shafik, 1994; WHO, 1997; Lomborg, 2001

Figure 6.1 *Relationship between pollution and development: (a) particles and SO₂ pollution in relation to income; (b) estimated global annual deaths from indoor and outdoor pollution*

results show that the ratio between indoor and outdoor concentration (I/O) also depends upon the outdoor concentration of the pollutant.

The indoor–outdoor ratio was studied for ozone, nitrogen dioxide and particle matter in the framework of the URBVENT project and of the French programme PRIMEQUAL. A literature review shows that the ozone concentration is smaller indoors than outdoors and that the ratio increases with the airflow rate (see Figure 6.2a). In the case of closed windows (shown by CW in Figure 6.2a), the transfer is more complex. Our experimental results confirm that this complexity comes from the air tightness of the building façade. Other studies showed that the indoor–outdoor ratio also depends upon the outdoor concentration (see Figure 6.2b). These two parameters were considered as explanatory variables in the prediction of the I/O ratio.

Experimental procedure

Two types of measurements were performed: one-time measurement of the façade permeability and continuous measurement of the indoor and outdoor pollution levels. Nine schools were selected in order to cover a wide range of urban environments, façade characteristics and types of ventilation. The choice of the tested classrooms inside the schools was guided by practical reasons concerning the security of the pupils (Iordache, 2003). The wall-covering materials, furnishing and cleaning procedures are roughly the same, from one school to the other, so that these parameters should not be considered in the study. For each school, two week-campaigns were conducted, one during the summer and the other during winter.

Façade permeability was measured for every classroom and was calculated based on two permeability laws obtained by the false door method (Ribéron,

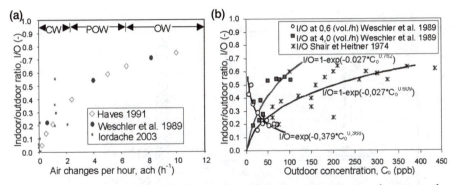

Figure 6.2 *The variation of indoor per outdoor ozone ratio as a function of (a) air changes per hour (CW = closed window; POW = partially opened window; OW = open window) and (b) outdoor concentration*

1991; ASTM, 1999): one for the normal room and another for the sealed room (see Figure 6.3a). In both situations, the classroom was pressurized and depressurized. The shift from the pressurized to the depressurized configuration occurred by inverting the ventilation system. The airflow that crosses the façade of the classroom is equal to the airflow introduced through the ventilation duct crossing the false door. The indoor–outdoor pressure difference was measured with a micro-manometer. Each series of experiments contains six or more simultaneous measurements of the airflow and the indoor–outdoor pressure difference between 3 and 60Pa. The permeability law of the classroom, relating the airflow rate, Q, to the pressure drop across the façade, Δp, was obtained by regression for normal operation (total permeability) and sealed room (when the façade was sealed by Scotch-taping all of the joints). The permeability laws of the façade were calculated as the difference between total permeability and the sealed room permeability (see Figure 6.3a).

The air tightness of the building façade, one of the two input parameters of the model, classifies the buildings in three groups: very permeable, permeable and airtight (see Figure 6.3b). The airflow through the façade was estimated based on the façade permeability law, and the pressure difference on the façade was measured continuously and simultaneously with the other parameters.

The following variables were measured continuously: the pressure difference across the façade; the outdoor and indoor concentration of ozone, nitrogen dioxide, carbon dioxide, indoor temperature and humidity; and the state of the window (open or closed).

The pressure difference between indoor and outdoor was measured by a differential micro-manometer. Two Teflon tubes were placed so that they would have no difference in height between the outdoor and indoor outlets (in isothermal conditions, 1m height difference represents 12Pa, and that is considerable compared to the order of the measured values). In order to take into consideration the wind effect, the outdoor tube outlet was placed perpendicular to the façade.

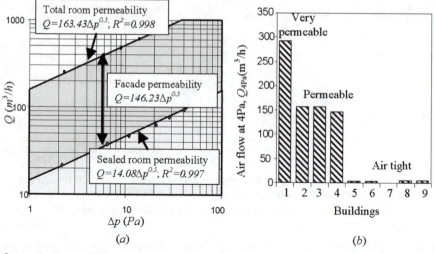

Source: Iordache, 2003

Figure 6.3 *Building classification according to permeability*

The O_3 and NO_2 concentrations were measured using the same device for both the indoor and the outdoor concentrations in order to avoid the error introduced by the use of two different devices. The indoor and outdoor air samples were taken by means of 6mm diameter Teflon tubes, which are chemically inert. The length of the tubes was less than 6m and the air sampling point was placed at more than 0.5m from the walls. The time step between two consecutive measurements was ten minutes; an electromagnetic valve switched every five minutes between indoor and outdoor measurements.

The concentration of the indoor and outdoor suspended particle matter (PM) was sampled every minute by two light diffraction analysers with 15 channels for 0.3, 0.4, 0.5, 0.65, 0.8, 1, 1.6, 2, 3, 4, 5, 7.5, 10, 15 and 20μm. For security reasons, the PM measurement device inside the classroom was placed on a shelf out of reach of the children and as far as possible from direct pollution sources such as the blackboard. The outdoor analyser was placed in a heated and ventilated metallic case fixed either on the exterior side of the façade or on the roof of the building.

The indoor temperature and the relative humidity were measured with sensors placed 1m beneath the ceiling of the classroom. The state of classroom windows (open or closed) was precisely recorded by means of magnetic sensors connected in series.

Modelling approach

The ratio of indoor–outdoor concentration (I/O) is a non-linear function of two variables: pollutant outdoor concentration and façade air tightness. Because the phenomena involved are continuous (e.g. no phase change), the

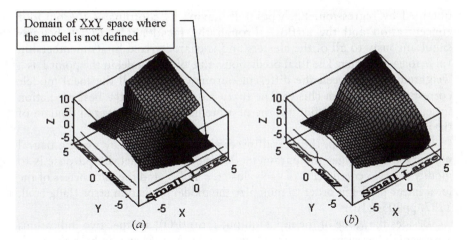

Figure 6.4 *Two types of multivariable models: (a) multiple regression;*
(b) fuzzy modelling

model should be continuous in values and in derivatives. The non-linearity may be dealt with by interpolating local models. If the local models were represented by linear functions defined on local regions obtained by multiple regression, two problems would arise (see Figure 6.4a). First, continuity would not be respected since the planes represented by the linear models cannot have all edges in common. Second, if experimental data is not available in a region, the regression model cannot be calculated. In order to alleviate this problem, the modelling technique adopted is fuzzy logic. This has the advantage that the local models are connected smoothly to one another and that a model can be obtained even if there is no data in a region (see Figure 6.4b). Besides the value of interest (ratio of input–output concentration), the fuzzy modelling gives information on model precision and degree of confidence.

The algorithm used to obtain the model consists in finding the initial zones for the local models; in determining the local models; in interpolating between the local models to obtain the overall mapping; and, finally, in adjusting the parameters in order to minimize the error of the overall model.

The first step of the algorithm is to group together the experimental data by means of the 'subtractive clustering' method (Jang et al, 1997, pp423–433). This is resumed at learning the two parameters, centre of the cluster, c, and standard deviation, σ, of the projection of the Gaussian distribution density function on the axes of the input variables.

The second step of the algorithm is to obtain the coefficients of the linear model that correspond to each cluster determined in the previous step by using the multiple regression method based on least square estimator.

The third step is to interpolate between the local models by using a Sugeno-type fuzzy model. This model is represented by fuzzy rules that have, in the antecedent, the clusters described by the centre, c, and the standard deviation, σ and, in consequence, the linear model characterized by the parameters obtained by regression. Each point P, having as coordinates the outdoor concentration and the airflow through the façade, (Co, Q_{4Pa}), belongs simultaneously to all of the clusters and is characterized by its membership value to each cluster. The final prediction value of the model in the point P is a weighted sum between the different output values of all the local models corresponding to each cluster. The fuzzy model provides the best prediction for each cluster centre, but not the best prediction for the overall domain of the input values.

In the fourth step, the overall prediction is improved by using a neural network that changes the parameters of the fuzzy model. Its purpose is to modify the two coefficients of each cluster, c and σ, and the parameters of the local linear model in order to minimize the model prediction error (Jang et al, 1997, pp205–210).

Besides the value of the input–output ratio (I/O), another two indications are given: the precision of result and the degree of confidence in both the result and the precision.

The precision relates to the dispersion of the I/O values for similar inputs due to parameters that influence the output, but were not considered in the model. Quantitatively, the precision is the distance from the centre of the distribution to the limit of the 95 per cent confidence interval of the I/O ratio. This distance is equal to the standard deviation of the dispersed points multiplied by 1.96 (Wonnacott and Wonnacott, 1990). The formula for standard deviation:

$$\sigma_{I/O-\overline{I/O}} = \sqrt{\frac{1}{n-1}\sum_{i=1}^{n}\left[\left(I/O-\overline{I/O}\right)^2\right]} \cong \sqrt{\sum_{i=1}^{n}\frac{1}{n}\left(I/O-\overline{I/O}\right)^2} \tag{6.1}$$

is applicable for clearly bordered clusters. Iordache (2003) changed the equation (6.1), which provides the standard deviation of a cluster, j, into a weighted mean in order to adapt it to the fuzzy logic, where the weights are equal to the membership value $(\mu_{i,j})$ of the point, i to the fuzzy cluster, Fj:

$$\sigma_{Fj(IJE-\overline{IJE})} \cong \sqrt{\sum_{i}\left[\frac{\mu_{i,j}}{\sum_{j}(\mu_{i,j})}(IJE-\overline{IJE})\right]^2} \tag{6.2}$$

The degree of confidence is a measure of the credibility of the value and of the precision. The confidence in the results is higher where there are more experimental data. It is measured by:

$$CR_i = \frac{\mu_i}{\max_i(\mu_i)} = \frac{\sum_j \mu_{i,j}}{\max_i\left(\sum_j \mu_{i,j}\right)} \tag{6.3}$$

where $\mu_{i,j}$ is the membership value.

Thus, the indoor–outdoor concentration ratio is characterized by three values: predicted I/O ratio, the distance from the predicted value to the limit of the 95 per cent confidence interval and the credibility in this prediction.

OUTDOOR–INDOOR TRANSFER MAPPING

The indoor–outdoor concentration ratio (I/O) is mapped on outdoor concentration, C_o, and the three main levels of air tightness of the façade: 'airtight' ($Q_{4Pa} \approx 0m^3/h$), 'permeable' ($Q_{4Pa} \approx 150m^3/h$) and 'very permeable' ($Q_{4Pa} \approx 300m^3/h$). The I/O ratio was determined for closed windows (measurements during the night). Since the room volume was about 150 cubic m^3, the maximum air change per hour was approximately two air changes per hour (ACH).

Ozone

The I/O ratio diminishes with the outdoor concentration for the airtight façades and increases for the other two types of façades (see Figure 6.5). Two clusters were found: the first is situated in the zone of the airtight façade ($c_{Q4Pa} \approx 5m^3/h$) and middle-ranged outdoor concentration ($c_{Co} \approx 28ppb$); the second one is placed in the zone of the 'most permeable' façades ($c_{Q4Pa} \approx 292m^3/h$) for middle-ranged outdoor concentration ($c_{Co} \approx 36ppb$). The two peaks of the model are placed in the zone of the 'airtight' façade with low outdoor O_3 concentration and the zone of the 'most permeable' façade with high outdoor O_3 concentration (see Figure 6.5a). The second map (see Figure 6.5b) presents the precision of the model expressed by the dispersion of the points in the database. The map shows that the smallest dispersion of the I/O value is 0.18, while the higher dispersion is 0.38, (see Figure 6.5b). The third map presents the credibility of the first two maps (see Figure 6.5c). It is higher in the zones where more measurement points were collected (i.e. in the proximity of the two clusters). The highest credibility zone ($CR > 0.5$) corresponds to the middle-ranged outdoor O_3 concentrations, between the

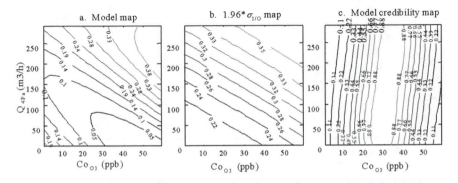

Figure 6.5 *Ozone outdoor–indoor transfer: (a) I/O ratio; (b) precision; (c) degree of confidence*

centres of the two clusters, while the lowest credibility zones ($CR < 0.25$) are for the 'most permeable' façade with low outdoor concentrations and an 'airtight' façade with high outdoor concentrations.

Nitrogen dioxide

The same three parameters – mean value, standard deviation and credibility – were calculated for nitrogen dioxide. The I/O ratio diminishes with the outdoor concentration regardless of the façade air tightness. The values of the I/O ratios corresponding to the airtight facades are slightly higher then those corresponding to 'permeable' or 'very permeable' façades (see Figure 6.6a). The model precision is almost the same for the whole domain (see Figure 6.6b). The credibility is higher in the zones where more measurements are available (i.e. in the proximity of the clusters). Two clusters were found for lower outdoor concentration ($Co_{NO_2} < 15ppb$): one cluster corresponds to the 'airtight' buildings and the second one corresponds to the 'very permeable' buildings. The credibility parameter diminishes with the rise of the outdoor concentration, with values of between 0 and 0.5 for outdoor concentrations higher than 20 parts per billion (ppb) (see Figure 6.6c).

Particle matter

The same three values are estimated for particle matter of three different sizes: 0.3–0.4μm, 0.8–1μm and 2–3μm. Similar conclusions can be drawn for all three particle sizes.

The I/O ratios diminish with the outdoor concentration regardless of the building façade air tightness or the size of the particles. For the size interval of 0.3–0.4μm (see Figure 6.7a), the model surface is relatively plane, so the I/O ratio diminishes linearly with the outdoor concentration. For the other two sizes, the model maps present a concavity in the model surfaces for the small values of the outdoor concentration and the 'permeable' façades (see Figure 6.7d and g). Contrary to the first two size intervals, the model surface of the class 2–3μm presents I/O ratios of 0.65, corresponding to high outdoor

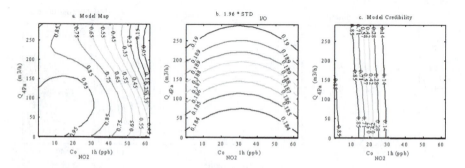

Figure 6.6 *NO$_2$ outdoor–indoor transfer: (a) I/O ratio; (b) precision; (c) degree of confidence*

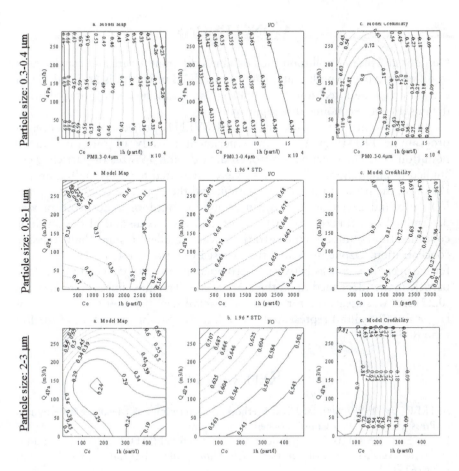

Notes: (a) I/O ratio for 0.3–0.4μm, (b) precision for 0.3–0.4μm, (c) degree of confidence for 0.3–0.4μm, (d) I/O ratio for 0.8–1μm, (e) precision for 0.8–1μm, (f) degree of confidence for 0.8–1μm, (g) I/O ratio for 2–3μm, (h) precision for 2–3μm, (i) degree of confidence for 2–3μm

Figure 6.7 *Particle matter outdoor–indoor transfer*

concentration and a 'very permeable' façade. However, the prediction credibility index is very small for that zone.

The dispersion of the I/O ratio presents almost constant values for all outdoor pollution range and façade permeability. The value of the index that characterizes this dispersion is about 0.33 for the first size interval (see Figure 6.7b), while it is twice as high for the last two size intervals (see Figure 6.7e and h). The prediction credibility presents the same diminishing trend with the outdoor concentration (see Figure 6.7c, f and i).

CONCLUSIONS

Outdoor and indoor pollution each exhibit a different nature and usually refer to different types of pollutants. After a threshold in wealth is attained, when the financial and technological means are available, outdoor pollution diminishes with economic development.

In the joint framework of the URBVENT project and the French programme PRIMEQUAL – an experimental study of outdoor–indoor pollution transfer of ozone – nitrogen dioxide and 15 sizes of particle were studied in nine schools. Three maps were calculated for every pollutant: the I/O ratio; the precision of this estimation; and the degree of confidence in the I/O ratio and precision. The ratio of indoor–outdoor concentration was determined as a function of airflow through the façade and of the outdoor concentration. Indoor concentration was smaller inside than outside concentration. Ozone presented the lowest I/O ratio (0.1–0.4). The I/O ratio for nitrogen dioxide was between approximately 0 and 0.95. The I/O ratio for particle matter depended upon the particle size. The most important variation (0.25–0.7) was measured for particles of small size (0.3–0.4μm); particles of larger size (0.8–3μm) represented lower, but comparable, variation of the I/O ratio (0.3–0.7).

REFERENCES

ASTM E 779 (1999) 'Standard Test Method for Determining Air Leakage Rate by Fan Pressurization', West Conshohocken, Pennsylvania

Hayes, S. R. (1991) 'Use of an indoor air quality model (IAQM) to estimate indoor ozone levels', *Journal* of *Air and Waste Management Association*, vol 41, no 2, pp161–170

Iordache, V. (2003) *Étude de l'Impact de la Pollution Atmosphérique sur l'Exposition des Enfants en Milieu Scolaire : Recherche de Moyens de Prédiction et de Protection*, PhD thesis, University of La Rochelle, France, pp138–139

Jang, J. S. R., Sun, C. T. and Mizutani, E. (1997) *Neuro-Fuzzy and Soft Computing: A Computational Approach to Learning and Machine Intelligence*, Prentice Hall, Upper Saddle River, New Jersey

Lee, I. Y., Shannon, J. D. and Park, H. M. (1994) 'Evaluation of parameterizations for pollutant transport and dispersion in an urban street canyon using a three-dimensional dynamic flow model', Proceedings of the 87th Annual Meeting and Exhibition, 19–24 June, Cincinnati, Ohio

Lomborg, B. (2001) *The Skeptical Environmentalist*, Cambridge University Press, Cambridge

Ribéron, J. (1991) 'Guide méthodologique pour la mesure de la perméabilité à l'air des enveloppes de bâtiments', *Cahiers du CSTB*, no 2493, Centre Scientifique et Technique du Bâtiment, Paris

Shafik, N. (1994) 'Economic development and environmental quality: An econometric analysis', *Oxford Economic Papers*, vol 46, pp757–773

Shair, F. H. and Heitner, K. L. (1974) 'Theoretical model for relating indoor pollutant concentrations to those outside', *Environmental Science and Technology Journal*, vol 8, no 5, p444

Weschler, C. J., Shields, H. C. and Naik, D. V. (1989) 'Indoor ozone exposures', *Journal of Air Pollution Control Association*, vol 39, pp1562–1568

WHO (World Health Organization) (1997) *Health and Environment in Sustainable Development: Five Years after the Earth Summit*, WHO, www.who.int/environmental_information/Information_resources/htmdocs/execsum.htm

WHO (2000) *Air Quality Guidelines*, WHO, Geneva

Wonnacott, T. H. and Wonnacott, R. J. (1990) *Introductory Statistics for Business and Economics*, Fourth edition, John Wiley and Sons, New York, pp142–148

World Health Organization, www.who.int/environmental_information/Air/Guidelines

Strategies for Natural Ventilation

Cristian Ghiaus and Claude-Alain Roulet

INTRODUCTION

Wind and buoyancy, the driving forces for natural ventilation, may be used for different ventilation strategies: wind variation-induced single-sided ventilation, wind pressure-driven cross-ventilation and buoyancy pressures-driven stack ventilation. Single-sided ventilation, the most localized of all strategies, may be used when ventilation is needed for individual rooms. Cross-ventilation allows fresh air to reach the floor of a building and depends upon building form and the urban environment. Stack ventilation systems circulate air through the whole building and depend upon building form and internal layout. Combinations of all of these strategies exploit their individual advantages.

WIND VARIATION-INDUCED SINGLE-SIDED VENTILATION

For the uninitiated, natural ventilation means opening a window to let fresh air into a room, which is otherwise airtight (see Figure 7.1a). The airflow through the opening is due to wind and buoyancy. The wind has a mean and a fluctuating component that may vary over the opening and produce a 'pumping effect'. When the indoor temperature is higher than outdoor, the buoyancy makes the cold air enter at the lower part and the hot air exit at the upper part of the opening. An empirical model of this complex phenomenon is (de Gidds and Phaff, 1982):

$$v_{eff} = (c_1 v_r^2 + c_2 H \cdot \Delta T + c_3)^{1/2} \tag{7.1}$$

where c_1 ($c_1 \approx 0.001$) is a dimensionless coefficient depending upon window opening, c_2, c_3 ($c_2 \approx 0.0035$, $c_3 = 0.01$) are buoyancy and wind constant,

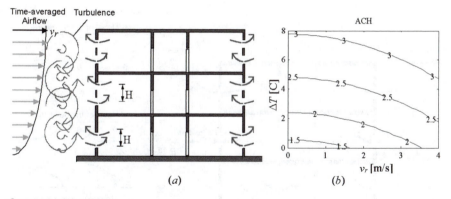

Source: (a) Axley (2001)

Figure 7.1 *(a) Single-sided wind-driven ventilation; (b) air changes per hour calculated for a room of 2.7m in height with windows of 1.5m in height and a window area of 1/20 of the floor area*

v_r [m/s] is the mean wind speed for the site, H [m] is the height of the opening, and ΔT [K] is the mean temperature difference between inside and outside.

The flow rate through the opening is:

$$\dot{V} = 0.5 A_w v_{eff} \tag{7.2}$$

where A_w is the effective area of the open window.

The UK Building Research Establishment (BRE) has proposed recommendations for single-sided ventilation: a window area of 1/20 of floor area, a height of approximately 1.5m, and a maximum room depth of 2.5 times the ceiling height (BRE, 1994).

Let us consider a typical office room with height $h = 2.75$m, window height $H = 1.5$m, and window area 1/20 flow area, $A_w = A/20$. The volume of this room would be $V = whl = h\,A$. The flow rate through the opening would be $\dot{V} = 0.5\,A_w v_{eff}$. Expressing this flow in air changes per hour, $\dot{V} = ACH/3600 \cdot V$, we obtain:

$$ACH = \frac{3600}{V} \cdot 0.5 A_w v_{eff} = \frac{3600}{h} \cdot \frac{0.5}{20} \cdot v_{eff} \tag{7.3}$$

The dependence of air changes per hour (ACH) as a function of v_r and ΔT is shown in Figure 7.1b. When the difference between indoor and outdoor temperature is minimal or when the wind velocity is low, the airflow rate is low. Single-sided ventilation is a solution that is not very effective for cooling by ventilation during warm weather periods.

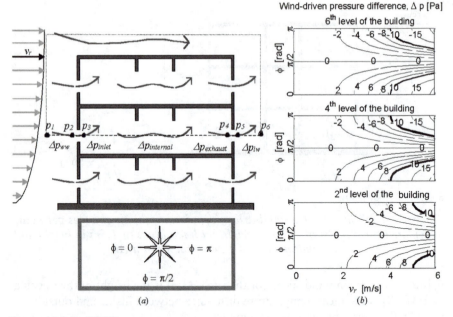

Source: (a) Axley (2001)

Figure 7.2 *Wind-driven cross-ventilation: (a) pressure drops associated with wind-driven cross-ventilation; (b) Wind pressure differences for a rectangular, isolated building*

WIND-DRIVEN CROSS-VENTILATION

Wind airflow over a building tends to induce positive (inward-acting) pressures on windward surfaces and negative (outward-acting) pressures on leeward surfaces, thereby creating a net pressure difference across the section of the building that drives *cross-ventilation* airflow. Cross-ventilation takes place when air enters the building on one side, sweeps the indoor space and leaves the building on another side (see Figure 7.2a).

The positive windward pressure Δp_{ww} and the negative leeward pressure Δp_{lw} are, in fact, pressure differences from the ambient air pressure of the free-field airflow. While these pressure differences often vary rapidly with time (due to turbulence in the wind airflow) and position (due to the aerodynamic effects of building form), on average, they may be related to a reference time-averaged approach wind velocity v_r:

$$p_{ww} = C_{p-ww} \left(\frac{\rho v_r^2}{2} \right) \tag{7.4}$$

$$p_{wl} = C_{p-lw} \left(\frac{\rho v_r^2}{2} \right)$$ (7.5)

where ρ is the density of the air, $\rho v_r^2/2$ is the kinetic energy per unit volume of the reference wind velocity, and $C_{p-ww} > 0$, $C_{p-lw} < 0$ are the so-called wind pressure coefficients of the windward and leeward surface locations under consideration. The reference wind velocity is most commonly (but not always) taken as the time-averaged wind velocity at 10m above the building height. The wind pressure difference between the façades is:

$$\Delta p_w = p_{ww} - p_{wl} = (C_{p-ww} - C_{p-lw}) \frac{\rho v_r^2}{2}$$ (7.6)

Considering, for example, the pressure changes along a given cross-ventilation airflow path in Figure 7.2a:

$$\Delta p_w = \Delta p_{\text{inlet}} + \Delta p_{\text{internal}} + \Delta p_{\text{exhaust}}$$ (7.7)

For typical design conditions, the reference wind velocity is approximately 4 m/s in open land, but less than 1m/s in a dense urban context. Windward wind pressure coefficients are typically around +0.5, leeward wind pressure coefficients −0.5, and the density of air approximately 1.2 kilograms per cubic metre (kg/m^3). Thus, we may expect the driving wind pressure for cross-ventilation to be approximately 10Pa in open land:

$$\Delta p_w = [+0.5 - (-0.5)] \frac{1.2 kg/m^2 \cdot (4 \ m/s)^2}{2} = 9.6 \ Pa$$ (7.8)

This pressure could be less than 1Pa in an urban context. Furthermore, a 10Pa driving pressure is small relative to typical fan-driven pressure differences that are of one or two orders of magnitude larger. Thus, in order to achieve similar ventilation rates, the resistance offered by the natural ventilation system will have to be small relative to ducted mechanical ventilation systems.

This simple natural ventilation scheme suffers from a critical shortcoming: it depends upon wind direction and intensity. As wind directions change, so do the wind pressure coefficients. Consequently, the driving wind pressure may drop to low values even when windy conditions prevail, causing the natural ventilation airflow rates to drop. When wind speeds drop to low values, the driving wind pressure will again diminish and ventilation airflow will subside regardless of wind direction. For example, Figure 7.2b shows the wind pressure difference calculated for a six-storey building. We can see that the estimated value for the pressure difference, $p \approx 10Pa$, occurs for a restricted range of wind direction. The variability of the pressure induced by the wind demands special measures, such as self-regulating vents for pressure reduction, wind catchers or a design that makes the building insensitive at wind variations (e.g. double-skin façades). The variability of wind-induced pressure puts forward the 'zero-wind' design condition as a critical case, although some limited studies indicate 'zero-wind' conditions are not only unlikely at many locations, but they may well be short lived (Skaret et al, 1997; Deaves and Lines, 1999; Axley, 2000).

Another shortcoming of the cross-ventilation strategy is the spread of pollutants through the building. For instance, the air entering the (non-smoking) room on the right of Figure 7.2 is not outdoor air, but transferred air from the room upwind, where, for instance, smoking is allowed.

In spite of these shortcomings, wind-driven cross-ventilation has been employed in some recently built non-residential buildings, although its use is uncommon. Examples include the machine shop wing of the Queen's Building of De Montfort University, Leicester, UK, designed by the architects Short Ford Associates architects (see Figure 7.8) and environmental engineers Max Fordham Associates, and a number of skyscrapers designed by architect Ken Yeang of TR Hamzah and Yeang Sdn Bhd, Malaysia.

Even within the time-averaged modelling assumptions, there are significant sources of uncertainty that should be kept in mind. Wind pressure coefficients, C_p, are seldom known with certainty – they vary from position to position over the building envelope and are sensitive to small details of form. They are altered significantly by the shelter offered by other buildings, vary with wind direction and are affected by building porosity. Wind characteristics are generally known with certainty only for regional airports where detailed records are maintained. Consequently, evaluation of the reference wind speed and direction for a given site is always problematic and subject to error. Finally, empirical coefficients associated with flow-resistance models introduce another source of uncertainty, although perhaps not as significant as that due to wind.

BUOYANCY-DRIVEN STACK VENTILATION

Warm and humid air is lighter than cold or dry air. In temperate climates and in the absence of artificial cooling, indoor air is often warmer than outdoor air and tends to leave the building through the upper openings. This air is replaced by colder air entering in the lower openings.

Any opening can be used for stack ventilation. However, stack pressure is often rather small, and large openings may be needed to guarantee large enough airflow rates. This is especially valid for ducts, which should be larger for natural ventilation than for mechanical ventilation, where pressure difference may be 10 or even 100 times larger.

Stack pressure is proportional to indoor–outdoor temperature difference and to the vertical distance to the neutral pressure level. Therefore, and for given opening areas, the airflow rates increase with temperature difference and vertical distance between openings.

The neutral pressure level (NPL) is a very important concept for the correct design of natural stack ventilation. This level sets itself so that the airflow rates that enter and leave the building are balanced. It depends not only upon size

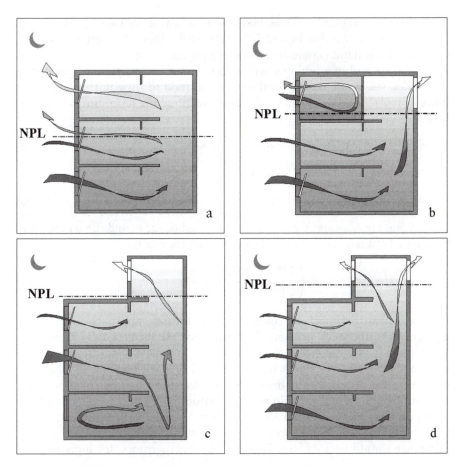

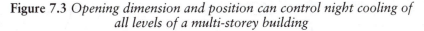

Notes: (a) poor cooling of upper level; (b)–(d) various ways of improving cooling of the upper level

Figure 7.3 *Opening dimension and position can control night cooling of all levels of a multi-storey building*

and location of openings, but also upon indoor and outdoor temperatures, wind and possibly fans. It tends to place itself closer to the largest openings. When purely stack-driven ventilation is used to cool high buildings, it is impossible to pass fresh air through the openings above the NPL. Opening a window in a high building implies a modification of NPL location, and the air path in the whole building can be radically changed with an inversion of the flow direction in some openings.

The top opening should be as large and as high as possible so that the NPL would be as high as possible in the building in order to provide fresh air to the largest possible part of the building. It should be placed in the low-pressure façade of the building so that wind and stack pressure work in the same direction.

If the stack pressure in the highest storeys is low, special arrangements may correct the situation (see Figure 7.3). If these arrangements are impossible, mechanical ventilation could be considered for these storeys.

Warm air within a building will tend to move up and flow out of upper-level exhausts, while cooler outdoor air will tend to flow in through lower inlets to replace it. For example, the pressure along the loop shown in Figure 7.4a is:

$$p_o g \cdot \Delta z - p_{inlet} - p_{internal} - \rho_i g \cdot \Delta z - \Delta p_{exhaust} = 0 \qquad (7.9)$$

The stack pressure, $p_s = (\rho_o - \rho_i) g \cdot \Delta z$, equals the pressure losses:

$$\Delta p_s = \Delta p_{inlet} + \Delta p_{internal} + \Delta p_{exhaust} \qquad (7.10)$$

The driving pressure stack varies with building height, h, and the temperature difference between the indoor and outdoor environment:

$$\Delta p_s = (p_0 - p_1) g \cdot \Delta z = \left(\frac{352.6}{T_0} - \frac{352.6}{T_i} t \right) g \cdot \Delta z \qquad (7.11)$$

During warm periods, as outdoor temperatures approach indoor air temperatures, the stack pressure differences for all but very tall multi-storey buildings may be expected to be small relative to typical wind-driven pressure differences. Figure 7.4b shows the dependence of stack pressure as a function of temperature difference and height. For a three-storey building of about 10m, the difference between indoor and outdoor temperatures should be approximately 23°C in order to obtain roughly a 10Pa pressure difference, typical for wind-driven pressure. For an eight-storey building, this temperature difference should be 10°C (see Figure 7.4a). Furthermore, for higher floors,

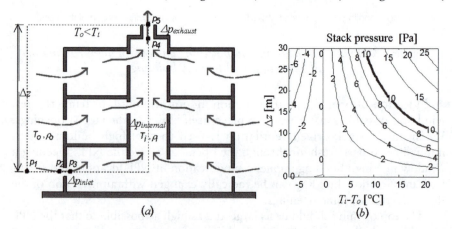

Source: (a) Axley (2001)

Figure 7.4 *Stack pressure-driven natural ventilation: (a) pressure drops associated with buoyancy-driven stack ventilation; (b) pressure stack variation as a function of temperature difference and building height*

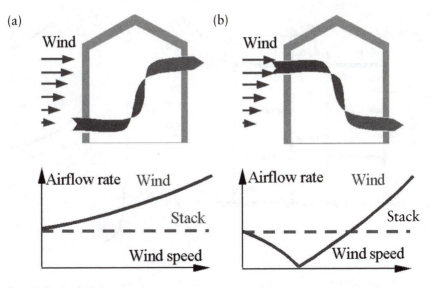

Source: Roulet (2004)

Figure 7.5 *Combined effects of wind and stack: (a) adding the effects of wind and stack; (b) opposite effects of wind and stack*

the stack pressure difference available to drive natural airflow will be proportionately smaller. For wintertime air-quality control, when large indoor–outdoor temperature differences may be expected, buoyancy-driven stack ventilation may be effective, although differences of air distribution with storey level must be accounted for by proper sizing of inlet vents. However, buoyancy-driven stack ventilation alone cannot be supposed to be a very effective strategy for cooling. In practice, stack configurations have often achieved acceptable ventilation rates – but due to wind forces that also drive flow in stack ventilation systems, thus complicating the system behaviour. Given that low wind conditions may be unlikely and short lived at most locations, simple buoyancy-driven stack flow is not likely to occur often, in practice. Thus, combined wind- plus buoyancy-driven stack ventilation should be considered instead.

COMBINED WIND- AND BUOYANCY-DRIVEN VENTILATION

In most cases, indoor air is warmer than outdoor air and the stack effect drives the airflow from bottom to top. The wind drives the airflow from the windward to the leeward side of the building. If the ventilation openings are located in an appropriate manner, the wind pressure is added to the stack effect and the ventilation is reinforced (see Figure 7.5a).

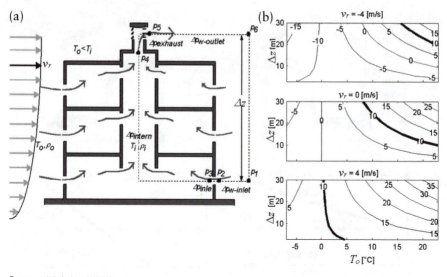

Source: (a) Axley (2001)

Figure 7.6 *Combined wind- and buoyancy-driven ventilation: (a) pressure drops; (b) total pressure as a function of wind velocity, temperature difference and building height*

On the contrary, if the top openings are on the windward side and the bottom openings on the leeward side, the wind thwarts the stack effect and the ventilation is reduced and even suppressed for a specific wind velocity (see Figure 7.5b).

It is therefore recommended to locate the ventilation openings in naturally ventilated buildings according to dominant winds.

When properly designed, stack ventilation uses both wind- and buoyancy-driven pressure differences. For example, let us consider a stack ventilation system under the combined influence of wind and buoyancy differences (see Figure 7.6a). This system is similar to that illustrated in Figure 7.4a, but with a stack terminal device added to respond to the prevailing wind direction in order to maximize the negative pressure induced by wind (e.g. operable louvers and rotating cowls).

A representative pressure loop (e.g. loop $p_1-p_2-p_3-p_4-p_5-p_6-p_1$) will now include both buoyancy-driven and wind-driven pressure differences that appear as a simple sum:

$$\Delta p_s + \Delta p_w = \Delta p_{inlet} + \Delta p_{internal} + \Delta p_{exhaust} \qquad (7.12)$$

where:

$$p_s = (\rho_0 - \rho_i)g \cdot \Delta z \qquad (7.13)$$

and:

$$\Delta p_w = (C_{p-inlet} - C_{p-exhaust}) \frac{\rho v_r^2}{2}$$ (7.14)

Pressure-loop equations for each of the additional five ventilation loops in Figure 7.6a will assume the same general form, although the values of the various parameters will change. For the pressure loop shown in Figure 7.6a, both the inlet wind pressure coefficient $C_{p-inlet}$ and the exhaust wind pressure coefficient $C_{p-exhaust}$ are likely to be negative as both are on the leeward side of the building. Consequently, the wind-driven pressure difference will act to cause flow in the direction indicated only if the absolute value of the exhaust is greater than that of the inlet. For this reason, driving wind pressure differences for the leeward rooms of stack ventilation systems tend to be smaller than those of the windward rooms. As a result, unless inlet vents are designed accordingly, ventilation rates may be expected to be lower in these rooms and may actually reverse under certain conditions. Figure 7.6b shows the pressure difference obtained by superposing the wind-induced pressure from Figure 7.2b and the stack pressure from Figure 7.4b. We can see that when stack ventilation is assisted by wind, the pressure difference may be easily achieved. Self-regulating vents can serve to maintain ventilation rates at the design level and thereby mitigate this problem, but cannot inhibit flow reversals or provide flow when the net driving pressure, $\Delta p_s + \Delta p_w$, drops to zero or becomes negative. The stack pressure contribution Δp_s will act to compensate for low or reverse wind pressures; but again this contribution must be expected to be smaller for the upper floors of the building. Consequently, upper leeward rooms tend to experience the lowest driving pressures and, thus, lower ventilation rates (see Figure 7.6b).

Ventilation stacks that extend above nearby roofs, especially when equipped with properly designed stack terminal devices, tend to create negative (suction) pressures that are relatively independent of wind direction. Thus, stack systems serve to overcome the major limitation of simple cross-ventilation systems identified above, while providing similar airflows in a building's individual rooms. As a result of these advantages, stack ventilation systems – perhaps most often using a central *slot* atria as a shared stack – have become the most popular natural ventilation solutions used in commercial buildings during recent years, and a number of manufacturers have developed specialized components.

COMBINATIONS OF FUNDAMENTAL STRATEGIES

Frequently, the three basic strategies (single-sided, cross- and buoyancy-driven ventilation) are used concurrently in single buildings to handle a variety of ventilation needs as illustrated in Figure 7.7. The most notable example of such an approach is found in the Queen's Building of De Montfort University in Leicester, UK (see Figure 7.8), a building that has proven to be the most influential of the first generation of the newer naturally ventilated buildings.

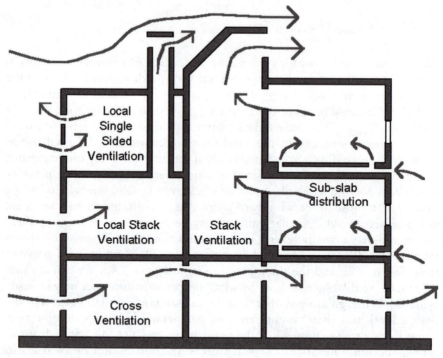

Source: Axley (2001)

Figure 7.7 *Mixed natural ventilation strategies in a single building in order to satisfy local and global ventilation needs*

In other instances, the elaboration resides in the details of inlet, exhaust and distribution. One common approach involves the use of in-slab or access-floor distribution of fresh air to provide greater control of air distribution across the building section and to temper incoming air to prevent cold drafts (see Figure 7.7). This type of fresh air distribution is similar to displacement ventilation, most commonly implemented mechanically, and offers similar benefits (e.g. the use of thermal plumes generated by equipment and occupants to assist the airflow and improved air quality in the occupied zone of rooms).

BALANCED STACK VENTILATION

A number of ancient Middle Eastern strategies using both roof-level inlets and exhausts – including the traditional Iranian wind towers, or *bagdir*, and the Arabian and Eastern Asian wind catchers, or *malkaf* – are being reconsidered for broader application and technical refinement.

In these *balanced* stack ventilation schemes, air is supplied in a cold stack (i.e. with air temperatures maintained close to outdoor conditions through proper insulation of the stack) and exhausted through a warm stack (see Figure 7.9).

Figure 7.8 *Queen's Building of De Montfort University, Leicester, UK*

Let us consider, for example, the loop through the second level of Figure 7.9. The pressure equation for this loop will be similar in form to the case of combined wind- and buoyancy-driven ventilation:

$$\Delta p_s + \Delta p_w = \Delta p_{inlet} + \Delta p_{internal} + \Delta p_{exhaust} \qquad (7.15)$$

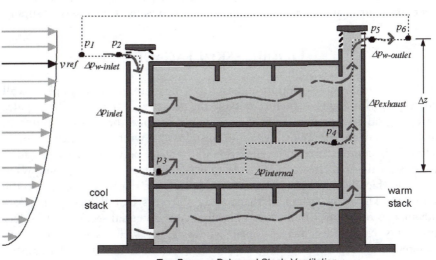

Top-Down or Balanced Stack Ventilation

Figure 7.9 *Top-down or balanced stack natural ventilation systems use high-level supply inlets to access less contaminated air and to place both inlet and outlets in higher wind velocity exposures*

If air temperatures within the cold stack can be maintained close to outdoor levels, the stack pressure is determined by the indoor-to-outdoor air density difference and the height difference from the stack exhaust and the floor-level inlet locations:

$$\Delta p_s = (\rho_0 - \rho_i)g \cdot \Delta z \tag{7.16}$$

Airflow through each floor level will, therefore, be identical to that expected in the simpler single-stack scheme if the airflow resistance of the supply stack (and its inlet and outlet devices) is similar to that provided by the air inlet devices of Figure 7.6. The driving wind pressure is determined by the difference between inlet and exhaust wind pressure coefficients and the kinetic energy content of the approach wind velocity:

$$\Delta p_w = (C_{p-\text{inlet}} - C_{p-\text{exhaust}}) \frac{\rho v_{\text{ref}}^2}{2} \tag{7.17}$$

However, in this case, the high location of the inlet ensures a higher inlet wind pressure and insensitivity to wind direction. This, combined with the potential of a wind-direction insensitive exhaust stack, makes this scheme particularly attractive for urban environments. Balanced stack systems have been commercially available in the UK for, apparently, over a century (Axley, 2001), although these commercially available systems have, until recently, been designed to serve single rooms rather than whole buildings.

Stack ducts and wind catchers are devices used for balanced stack ventilation (see Chapter 8). In cold conditions, it is possible to achieve ventilation air heat recovery with *top-down* schemes by using co-axial supply.

DOUBLE-SKIN FAÇADE

A double façade construction consists of a normal concrete or glass wall combined with a glass structure outside the actual wall. Double-skin façades offer several advantages. They can act as buffer zones between the internal and external environment, reducing heat loss in winter and heat gain in summer. In combination with ventilation of the space between the two façades, the passive thermal effects can be used to best advantage. Opening windows in the inner façade can draw natural ventilation from the buffer zone into the building. The stack effect of thermal air currents in tall buildings offers advantages over lower buildings. This eliminates potential security and safety problems caused by having open windows, as well as wind pressure differentials around the building. Double façades can be used for solar-assisted stack ventilation or balanced stack ventilation.

Practising appropriate openings in both inner and outer skins allows natural ventilation across the double skin. In this case, the acoustic insulation is reduced, but is still better than that of single-skin facade. In winter, this provides pre-heated air for the building. During the summer, this pre-heating is a disadvantage; but the advantage is that the double skin, if well designed, allows safe night cooling since the outer skin protects the inner one from wind and driving rain.

In order to avoid overheating during the summer, it is paramount to use either external solar protection, or, if they are, as usual, between the two skins, to install white or reflecting solar protection. In addition, the space between the two skins should be well ventilated, with an air inlet and air exhaust at each level or at each two levels. If the inlet is at the bottom of a high-rise building and the exhaust at the top, the air becomes too hot and the upper levels will not only get hot air, but so will the walls, even with closed windows.

In addition, special caution should be given to the respective locations of exhaust and inlet openings in the outer skin: the warm exhaust air should not enter, once again, the inter-skin space. Examples of application are given in Chapter 8.

PASSIVE EVAPORATIVE COOLING

An improvement of the *balanced stack* ventilation system, also based on ancient Middle Eastern and Eastern Asian solutions, consists in adding evaporative cooling to the supply stack. Traditionally, evaporative cooling was achieved through water-filled porous pots within the supply air stream or through the use of a pool of water at the base of the supply stack (Santamouris and Asimakopoulos, 1996; Allard, 1998). In more recent developments, water sprayed high into the supply air stream cools the air stream and increases the supply air density, thereby augmenting the buoyancy-induced pressure differences that drive airflow (Bowman et al, 2000). New developments in passive downdraught cooling are given in Francis and Ford (1999).

The loop analysis of this so-called *passive downdraught evaporative cooling* (PDEC) scheme is similar to that of the *balanced-stack* scheme; but here the buoyancy effects of the increased moisture content must be accounted for. Consider the representative diagram of such a system shown in Figure 7.10. Two height differences must now be distinguished: z_a (the height above the room inlet location of the moist air column in the supply stack) and z_b (the height of the exhaust above this moist column).

The air density in the moist air supply column, ρ_s, will approach the saturation density corresponding to the outdoor air wet bulb temperature – more specifically, experiments indicate that these supply air conditions will be within 2°C of the wet bulb temperature. Hence the loop equation describing the (time-averaged) ventilation airflow in this system becomes:

$$(\Delta p_{inlet} + \Delta p_{internal} + \Delta p_{exhaust}) = \Delta p_s + \Delta p_w \tag{7.18}$$

where:

$$\Delta p_s = [\rho_0 z_b + \rho_s z_a - \rho_i(z_a + z_b)]g \tag{7.19}$$

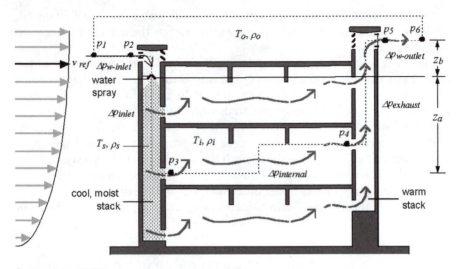

Source: Axley (2001)

Figure 7.10 *Passive downdraught evaporative cooling stack ventilation*

$$\Delta p_w = (C_{p\text{-inlet}} - C_{p\text{-exhaust}}) \frac{\rho v_r^2}{2} \tag{7.20}$$

For a quantitative measure of the impact of this strategy, let us consider a case similar to the one discussed above for wind- and buoyancy-induced natural ventilation, but with a cool moist column height that equals the stack height of 10m (i.e. $z_a \approx 10\text{m}$ and $z_b \approx 0\text{m}$). If the outdoor air, with a temperatures of 25°C and a humidity of 20 per cent relative humidity (i.e. with a density of approximately 1.18kg/m³) is evaporatively cooled to within 2°C of its wet bulb temperature (12.5°C), its dry bulb temperature will drop to 14.5°C, while its density will increase to approximately 1.21kg/m³ and relative humidity (RH) to 77 per cent. If internal conditions are kept just within the thermal comfort zone for these outdoor conditions (i.e. 28°C and 60 per cent RH), using an appropriate ventilation flow rate given internal gains, then internal air density will be approximately 1.15kg/m³. Consequently, the buoyancy pressure difference that will result will be:

$$\Delta p_s = \left(1.18\frac{\text{kg}}{\text{m}^3}(0\text{m}) + 1.21\frac{\text{kg}}{\text{m}^3}(10\text{m}) - 1.15\frac{\text{kg}}{\text{m}^3}(0+10\text{m}) \right) 9.8\frac{\text{m}}{\text{s}^2} = 6.4\text{Pa} \tag{7.21}$$

Without the evaporative cooling (i.e. with $z_a \approx 0\text{m}$ and $z_b \approx 10\text{m}$):

$$\Delta p_s = \left(1.18\frac{\text{kg}}{\text{m}^3}(10\text{m}) + 1.21\frac{\text{kg}}{\text{m}^3}(0\text{m}) - 1.15\frac{\text{kg}}{\text{m}^3}(10+0\text{m}) \right) 9.8\frac{\text{m}}{\text{s}^2} = 2.9\text{Pa} \tag{7.22}$$

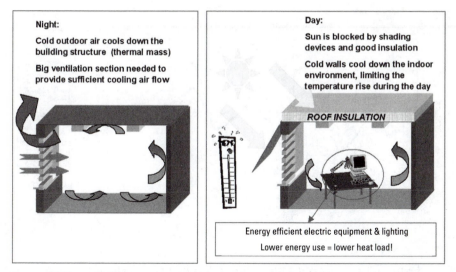

Source: BBRI and PROBE (2002)

Figure 7.11 *Strategy for intensive night cooling*

Thus, in this representative example, evaporative cooling more than doubles the buoyancy pressure difference while, at the same time, providing adiabatic cooling.

PASSIVE COOLING

Principles of passive cooling

Passive cooling through night-time ventilation is a comfortable, cheap and energy-efficient way of keeping the indoor environment within a comfortable temperature range in most European climates, particularly on the continent. In well-adapted buildings, it can ensure a comfortable indoor climate during the summer without artificial cooling.

The principles of passive cooling are as follows:

- As far as possible, avoid internal heat gains.
- Avoid external heat gains.
- Store the remaining heat gains in the building structure.
- Cool the building structure with a large ventilation rate when the external temperature is lower than the internal temperature. Large ventilation rates are easily obtained by natural ventilation through windows and doors.

Such a strategy can be applied only in climates where the daily average outdoor temperature is within comfort limits, and where there is a significant temperature swing between night and day. Fortunately, this is the case in most European climates.

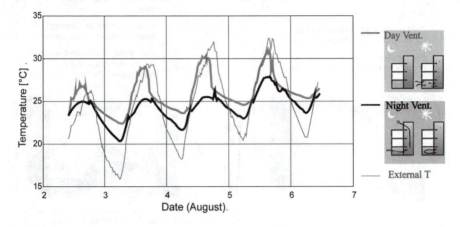

Source: Roulet (2004)

Figure 7.12 *Effect of passive cooling through night ventilation on the LESO building, Switzerland*

Figure 7.12 shows the evolution of internal and external temperatures in two identical office spaces (of 40m³) at floor level of the LESO office building of the École Polytechnique Fédérale de Lausanne, Switzerland, which have been ventilated following two different strategies:

1   the usual strategy in office buildings, ventilating during the day but not at night; and
2   the passive cooling strategy with natural ventilation at night.

The office spaces have considerable thermal inertia and external solar blinds. The night ventilation rate corresponds to 10 to 12 air changes per hour. One person occupies the offices during eight hours per day, often with a personal computer running.

Design guidelines for passive cooling

Climate
To use outdoor air for cooling at night, the temperature swing should be rather large, with a mean temperature and humidity within the comfort range. In addition, the dew point of the outdoor air should be below the internal temperature. Otherwise, there is a risk that outdoor air, entering the building, raises its relative humidity above 80 per cent, leading to mould growth or water vapour condensation hazards.

Thermal insulation
The basic requirement for making passive cooling work is to keep heat from entering the building. This implies, in the first place, that the building should

have a good thermal insulation and an efficient solar protection strategy. Provisions should be made to avoid hot air from entering the building by reducing the ventilation rate during the day. When these conditions are met, the amount of heat extracted by night ventilation can be assessed (Van der Maas et al, 1994; Roulet et al, 1996). Whether this cooling energy is sufficient depends upon the amount of heat stored during the day.

Solar protection

It should first be emphasized that efficient solar protections are external. Indeed, any type of solar protection absorbs a part of the incident solar radiation, and transforms it into heat, which can be evacuated only if the protection is outdoors. In order to be efficient at all times of the day and allow for enough day lighting, solar protections should be movable. They should preferably be automated (with regard to users' preferences), as users are not always present to move the solar protection down (e.g. during the weekends in office buildings). Huge improvement in comfort conditions can be obtained with appropriate automatic control of solar protections (Guillemin and Molteni, 2002; Guillemin, 2003).

Limit internal gains

Install efficient electrical appliances and automatic control (presence and luminance sensitive) on artificial lighting. Computers and other appliances should be turned off when not in use. Until now, the most efficient (the largest lumen per watt ratio) white light source is still the sun. Therefore, and for many other reasons, day lighting should be promoted. It should, however, be controlled since it varies constantly. Movable solar protections and electro-chromic glazing can perform this control.

Thermal inertia

Assuming that the zone is not ventilated, its thermal inertia limits the indoor temperature rise due to internal heat gain during daytime. If the rise in temperature can be made acceptably small by increasing the thermal inertia and by lowering the allowed heat gain, night ventilation is a viable cooling option. The time constant of the building (i.e. the building thermal capacity divided by the heat transfer coefficient, including transmission and minimum hygienic ventilation) is a good measure of the thermal inertia of the whole building. It should be a few days at least.

Another simple parameter characterizes the thermal response of a building zone to a step or sinusoidal change in heat gain (Van der Maas and Maldonaldo, 1997). It is the product of the total wall surface area A and the mean thermal effusivity b. The thermal effusivity of a homogeneous material is defined as the square root of the product of thermal conductivity λ, density ρ, and specific heat c:

$$b = \sqrt{\lambda \rho c} \qquad (7.23)$$

Its value (units in $Ws^{1/2}/(m^2K)$) varies over two orders of magnitude (from $b = 2000$ for heavy concrete to $b = 20$ for light fibreglass). The parameter b is calculated as the area-weighted average of the b-values of the exposed wall surface materials. Note that, since heat needs time to penetrate the materials, only the first few centimetres are relevant.

Ventilation

Only when the thermal inertia is sufficiently large, does it make sense to investigate the ventilation requirements. In the worst case (no wind), the stack ventilation or the airflow rate of the air handling unit at night should be able to remove all of the heat stored in the walls during daytime. Note that it is much easier to get the large airflow rates required for cooling (ten air changes per hour) by natural ventilation through large openings than with mechanical ventilation. It is recommended to size and place the ventilation openings so that all of the cooled spaces are below the neutral pressure level (see 'Buoyancy-driven stack ventilation').

SOLAR-ASSISTED VENTILATION

Heating the exhaust air in stack ducts increases the stack pressure differential. For this purpose, solar energy can be used by transforming the stack ducts, or part of them, into hot air solar collectors.

There is usually little difficulty in providing required airflow rate to a building when wind assists the stack effect (see Figure 7.6b). But since wind speed is reduced in the urban environment, natural ventilation in an urban area is usually designed based on buoyancy-driven flow. When buoyancy pressure resulting from the difference between the internal and the external temperature is insufficient, solar-induced ventilation can be an alternative. The principle is to increase the stack pressure by heating the air in the ventilation stack, resulting in a greater temperature difference than in conventional systems.

The pressure losses for a solar collector are:

$$\Delta p_s = \Delta p_{inlet} + \Delta p_{internal} + \Delta p_{exhaust} \tag{7.24}$$

Depending upon the position of the control damper, Δp_{inlet} or $\Delta p_{exhaust}$ include the control damper pressure losses.

The stack pressure is:

$$\Delta p_s = \rho_0 T_0 [1/T_e - 1/T_i] g \Delta z \tag{7.25}$$

where T_i is the inlet air temperature of the collector, usually equal to the indoor temperature, and T_e is the exit temperature of the collector:

$$\Delta T_e = A/B + (T_i - A/B) \exp[-BwH/(\rho_e c_p Q)] \tag{7.26}$$

Figure 7.13 *Views of the Building Research Establishment's Environmental Office of the Future building, showing the solar-assisted stack air ducts*

with, $A = h_1 T_{w1} + h_2 T_{w2}$, $B = h_1 + h_2$, where h_1, h_2 (W/m²K) are surface heat transfer coefficients for internal surfaces of the collector; T_{w1}, T_{w2} (°C) are surface temperatures of internal surfaces of the collector; w (m) is the collector width; H (m) is the height between inlet and outlet openings; ρ_e (kg/m³) is the air density at exit; c_p (J/(kg.K)) is the specific heat of air; and Q (m³/s) is the volumetric air flow rate.

The principle of the solar collector may be used for different types of devices: Trombe walls, double façades, solar chimneys or solar roofs. A Trombe wall is a wall of moderate thickness covered by a pane of glass separated by the wall by a gap of 50 to 100mm. It may be used for ventilation or for heating (see Figure 7.14). A solar chimney is a chimney with a gap of about 200mm placed on the south or south-west façade of the building. Solar roofs are used when solar altitude is large. In this case, a roof has a larger surface area for collecting the solar radiation than a vertical wall or chimney.

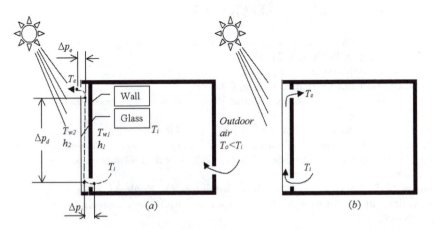

Figure 7.14 *Solar collector used as (a) ventilator and (b) heater*

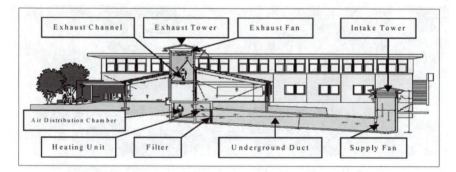

Source: Heiselberg (2002)

Figure 7.15 *Mediå school: fan-assisted natural ventilation*

FAN-ASSISTED NATURAL VENTILATION

In some cases, natural ventilation cannot alone provide the required airflow rate. This could be the case when the ventilation openings are too small for the wind and temperature conditions present on the site, or in rooms not directly connected to the outdoor environment. Where or when the natural ventilation can no more be ensured by either stack effect or wind, fans may be installed and switched on to ensure the necessary ventilation flow rate. Such fans may be installed either on stack ducts, or in walls or windows. What is important is that, when the fans are off, their openings are either tightly closed or part of the natural ventilation design.

A few buildings using this technique were monitored during the European HybVent and ResHyVent projects (see www.hybvent.civil.auc.dk/ and www.reshyvent.com).

REFERENCES

Allard, F. (ed) (1998) *Natural Ventilation in Buildings: A Design Handbook*, James and James Science Publishers, London

Axley, J. W. (2000) *Residential Passive Ventilation Systems: Evaluation and Design*, Air Infiltration and Ventilation Centre, Coventry, UK

Axley, J. W. (2001) *Application of Natural Ventilation for US Commercial Buildings*, NIST, Washington, DC.

Belgian Building Research Institute (BBRI) and PROBE (2002) *Pistes pour la Rénovation des Immeubles de Bureaux – un Meilleur Confort avec Moins d'Énergie*, Rapport CSTC no 6, Centre Scientifique et Technique de la Construction, Limelette, Belgium

Bowman, N. T., Eppel, H., Lomans, K. J., Robinson, D., Cook, M. J. (2000) 'Passive downdraught evaporative cooling', *Indoor and Built Environment*, vol 9, no 5, pp284–290

BRE (Building Research Establishment) (1994) 'Natural ventilation in non-domestic buildings, BRE Garston (UK)', *BRE Digest*, BRE, vol 399

de Gidds, W. and Phaff, H. (1982) 'Ventilation rates and energy consumption due to open windows: A brief overview of research in The Netherlands', *Air Infiltration Review*, vol 4, pp4–5

Deaves, D. M. and Lines, I. G. (1999) 'On persistence of low speed conditions', *Air Infiltration Review*, vol 20, no 1, pp6–8

Francis, E. and Ford, B. (eds) (1999) *Recent Developments in Passive Downdraught Cooling: An Architectural Perspective*, James and James Science Publishers, London

Guillemin, A. (2003) *Using Genetic Algorithms to Take into Account User Wishes in an Advanced Building Control System*, PhD thesis no 185, ENAC, Lausanne, Switzerland

Guillemin, A. and Molteni, S. (2002) 'An energy-efficient controller for shading devices self-adapting to the user wishes', *Building and Environment*, vol 37, no 11, pp1091–1097

Heiselberg, P. (ed) (2002) *Principles of Hybrid Ventilation*, IEA ECBCS HybVent project, ECBCS ExCo Support Services Unit (ESSU), Birmingham, UK

Roulet, C.-A.(2004) *Santé et qualité de l'environnement dans les Bâtiments*, Presse Polytechniques et Universitaire Romandes, Lausanne, Switzerland

Roulet, C.-A., Van der Maas, J. and Flourentzou, F. (1996) *A Planning Tool for Passive Cooling of Buildings*, vol 3 Indoor Air 1996, Nagoya

Santamouris, M. and Asimakopoulos, D. (eds) (1996) *Passive Cooling of Buildings*, James and James Science Publishers, London

Skaret, E., Blom, P. and Brunsell, J. T. (1997) *Energy Recovery Possibilities in Natural Ventilation of Office Buildings*, 18th AIVC Conference: Ventilation and Cooling, Athens, Greece, pp311–321

Van der Maas, J., Flourentzou, F. Rodriguez, J.-A. and Jaboyedoff, P. (1994) *Passive Cooling by Night Ventilation*, vol 2, EPIC, Lyon

Van der Maas, J. and Maldonaldo, E. (1997) 'A new thermal inertia model based on effusivity', *International Journal of Solar Energy*, vol 19, pp131–160

8

Specific Devices for Natural Ventilation

Claude-Alain Roulet and Cristian Ghiaus

INTRODUCTION

The most common device for natural ventilation is the operable window for which the mechanism involved is primarily wind-driven ventilation, although buoyancy may have a non-negligible effect. For automatic control of the airflow, the operable window may be mechanically actuated. For low flow rate, self-regulating vents may be used. These vents, used in wind-driven ventilation, provide a constant airflow rate for a large range of wind velocities. Stacks and chimneys are used for buoyancy-driven ventilation; when designed to take advantage of the wind, stacks become wind catchers. Double-skin façades allow natural ventilation and ensure noise insulation and security.

OPERABLE WINDOWS

Operable windows are often used to control natural ventilation. They are well adapted to deliver the very large airflow rates needed to evacuate pollutants generated by a short activity, such as cooking, smoking and painting, or to evacuate heat, particularly for passive cooling. They are, however, not well adapted to deliver small but continuous and controlled airflow rates, and protection against rain, dust, insects and burglary may be insufficient. Operable windows are, therefore, a complement to other natural ventilation devices.

There are many types of operable windows (see Figure 8.1). These are sorted according to the way they open. Each type presents advantages and inconveniences, mentioned below.

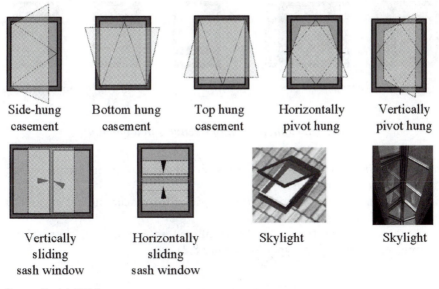

| Side-hung casement | Bottom hung casement | Top hung casement | Horizontally pivot hung | Vertically pivot hung |

| Vertically sliding sash window | Horizontally sliding sash window | Skylight | Skylight |

Source: Roulet (2004)

Figure 8.1 *Various types of operable windows*

The *side-hung casement window* rotates around a vertical axis, often indoors (as in France) but also outdoors (as in The Netherlands). This allows a complete opening, but offers poor protection against rain.

The *hinged window* may be either top or bottom hung. In order to offer some protection against the driving rain, the bottom-hung window opens indoors, while the top-hung window opens outdoors. The bottom-hung window offers good ventilation potential for evacuating hot air since the largest opening is high, close to the ceiling. Care should be taken not to place such windows too close to the ceiling, since the effective opening is strongly reduced in this case.

Some windows can be open on either the vertical or horizontal axis, taking advantage of these two types. These three types of window openings can have good air tightness when closed, provided that a convenient seal is installed.

Pivot-hung windows may also have their pivoting axis either horizontal or vertical. Such windows can be completely turned, thus facilitating the cleaning. Some of these windows are equipped with Venetian blinds that can then be put either on the outer face, for summer solar protection, or on the inner face, to protect the occupant against glare in winter without loosing solar heat gains. Horizontal pivot-hung windows offer good ventilation potential through the stack effect. These windows, however, cannot be airtight and, when open, may start autorotation in strong winds.

Sash windows may slide in a horizontal or vertical direction. These allow both small and large airflow rates. It is, however, not easy to make them airtight since this requires flattening the sash against the frame in a parallel

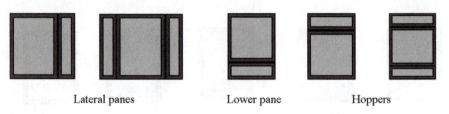

Lateral panes   Lower pane   Hoppers

Source: Roulet (2004)

Figure 8.2 *Combination of openings in a window*

movement. The main advantage of sash windows is their small overall thickness, even when open.

Operable *skylights* or *roof lights* are useful for evacuating hot air and to pull the neutral level up.

Several opening types can be combined in a window, thus taking advantages of the various types (see Figure 8.2).

LOUVERS

Neither the operable windows, nor the vents described in the following section are well suited for large airflow rates when protection against rain, insects and burglary is required (e.g. for intensive night ventilation in order to control thermal comfort). In such cases, the building can be equipped with large ventilation louvers. Figure 8.3 presents two buildings equipped with such louvers.

The first example in Figure 8.3 is a renovated building; the louvers were installed in an existing frame, in front of an operable window. As they reduced the outdoor view of the occupants and the available daylight, it was decided to remove them during the winter. The second building in Figure 8.3 is a new

Source: Belgian Building Research Institute (BBRI) and PROBE (2002); Heiselberg (2002)

Figure 8.3 *Louvers in a new building and in a renovated building*

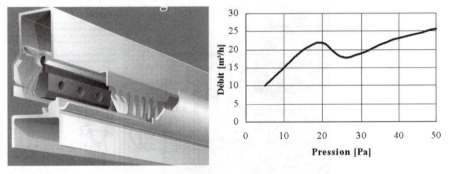

Source: Renson

Figure 8.4 *'Constant airflow' vent to be installed in a window frame*

building; the louvers were installed in the wall. Behind the louvers, there is a valve that can be automatically opened. These louvers are equipped with a mosquito net and are designed not to let water enter the building or to increase the risk of burglary.

VENTS

There are many appropriate air inlets on the market which provide controlled airflow rate and avoid the penetration of rain, dust and insects, or attenuate external noise. Most are controlled by hand, but some are self-regulating.

The 'constant airflow rate' inlet, shown in Figure 8.4, changes its permeability as a function of the pressure difference between the indoor and outdoor environment in order to keep the airflow rate at an approximately constant value. The nominal airflow of such vents is related to the pressure difference, which may vary from country to country.

In the hygrostatic air inlet shown in Figure 8.5, a moisture-sensitive ribbon closes the passage of air when the indoor air is too dry and opens it when the indoor air is too humid. A similar system can control the air exhaust. Such hygrostatic air grilles are most appropriate to control indoor air quality in dwellings where air humidity is, in most cases, the main contaminant.

One of the reasons for replacing natural ventilation with mechanical ventilation is the external noise, often disturbing in the urban environment.

Source: Aereco and Aldes (2003)

Figure 8.5 *Moisture-controlled air inlets and outlets*

Source: Renson (2004)

Figure 8.6 *Vent with acoustic attenuation*

Therefore, several providers developed vents equipped with acoustical attenuation (see Figure 8.6). A compromise should be found between acoustic attenuation, which ideally requires airtightness, and high air permeability that decreases sound attenuation.

STACK DUCTS

Stack ducts have long been used to either introduce outdoor air in buildings or to extract vitiated air from rooms. The stack effect, which moves the air in such ducts, could be enhanced by the use of wind catchers or fans.

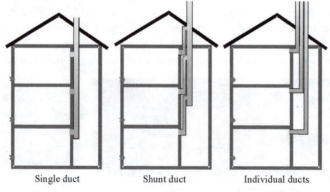

Single duct   Shunt duct   Individual ducts

Source: Roulet (2004)

Figure 8.7 *Three ways of installing stack ventilation ducts*

There are three main ways of installing such ducts (see Figure 8.7). The single duct should be avoided, since noise, pollution (odours) and even fire are easily propagated from one floor to the other. Individual ducts are preferred since they do not present such inconveniences or hazards. They are, however, much more expensive and use more building space. Therefore, the compromise of the shunt ducts is often used.

WIND CATCHERS

In windy areas, wind catchers tower on top of buildings to take advantage of higher wind velocity. Their role is to ensure a depressurization that does not depend upon wind direction, together with protecting the ventilation duct against rain. They have long been used (see Figure 8.8); but modern versions are available on the market. Wind catchers can also be installed in areas without wind, on the top of stack ducts in order to protect them from rain.

Source: http://www.babyloniangal.com/files/tours/yazd.html

Figure 8.8 *The Yazd wind catcher in Iran*

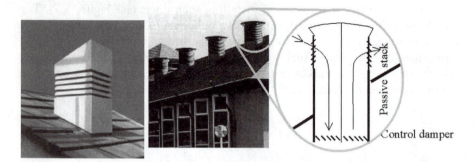

Source: Monodraught Ltd (2003)

Figure 8.9 *Windcatcher natural ventilation systems*

The Windcatcher natural ventilation systems, distributed by Monodraught Ltd in the UK (see Figure 8.9), offer air change rates as high as five air changes per hour under relatively low wind conditions – 3 metres per second (m/s) measured 10m above the building.[1] These systems may also be supplied with co-axial fans to provide mechanical assistance during extreme weather conditions.

CHIMNEYS

Some buildings are equipped with chimneys for natural exhaust. These chimneys increase the exhaust ventilation rate since they increase the thermal effect and usually have a large area. Figure 8.10 presents a building with two chimneys, equipped with ventilation louvers (see previous section on 'Louvers').

DOUBLE-SKIN FAÇADES

Double-skin façades are used for several reasons – to:

- protect the indoor environment from outdoor noise;
- protect shading devices from rain and wind;
- allow for safe natural ventilation and passive night cooling; and
- renovate the building skin without perturbing the occupants.

In most cases, solar shading devices are installed in the space between the two skins. This space must, therefore, be ventilated in order to avoid overheating, and the air pathway should not be higher than two levels. This means that the air inlets and outlets should be placed at each level or, at most, at each of the two levels.

Source: N. Hijmans, BBRI

Figure 8.10 *Chimneys on the roof of the IVEG building in Hoboken (Belgium)*

As an example, the façade of the main postal office in Lausanne was renovated in 1997 (see Figure 8.11). Instead of installing air conditioning, it was decided, after a preliminary study, to use night passive cooling to avoid overheating during the summer. A double-skin façade was designed to renovate without disturbing the occupants and to allow for safe night ventilation. Transparent sluice valves are placed in front of each window so that windows could be kept open for night cooling. These blades prevent driving rain from entering the building and also protect the blinds, which are cooled by the surrounding air.

Source: LESO.PB, EPFL (2001)

Figure 8.11 *The glazed blades in the outer skin protect the Lausanne postal office from driving rain and allow large airflow rates*

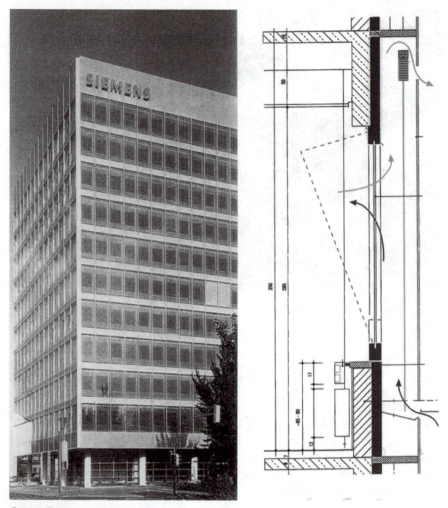

Source: Pasquay (2004)

Figure 8.12 *The double-skin façade of the Siemens building, Dortmund*

The Siemens building in Dortmund was renovated with a double-skin façade after a fire in 1996 (see Figure 8.12). The mechanical ventilation system was then replaced by natural ventilation. Figure 8.12 shows the façade section. The inner façade has operable windows; the ventilated façade space houses the louvers. The outdoor air can pass through 10cm wide slots at the bottom and the top of the outer glazed screens.

The results of over 50 tracer gas measurements show that a supply of fresh air of 30 cubic metres per hour (m^3/h) for each person can always be achieved with only tilted windows and without cross-ventilation (Pasquay, 2004).

CONCLUSIONS

The driving forces of natural ventilation vary in amplitude with time. Therefore, the natural ventilation rate should be controlled with appropriate devices. In addition to operable windows, through which not only air but also rain, insects, noise and dust may enter the buildings, several type of dedicated ventilation devices are found in buildings, these include: louvers, which providing large ventilation rate with protection against rain; vents, which ensure a good control of ventilation rate and protect well against most nuisances; wind catchers; and chimneys, which increase airflow rate.

Double-skin façades are well suited to noisy or polluted areas, and protect against driving rain. However, the ventilation rate through the windows or vents is reduced, and care should be taken to avoid overheating problems between the two skins.

NOTE

1   See www.monodraught.com/WindCatcher.

REFERENCES

BBRI and PROBE (2002) *Pistes pour la Rénovation des Immeubles de Bureaux – un Meilleur Confort avec Moins d'Énergie*, Rapport CSTC no 6, BBRI, Limelette, Belgium

Heiselberg, P. (ed) (2002) *Principles of Hybrid Ventilation*, IEA ECBCS HybVent project, 76 p. ECBCS ExCo Support Services Unit (ESSU) or http://hybvent.civil.auc.dk/

Pasquay, T. (2004) 'Natural ventilation in high-rise buildings with double facades, saving or waste of energy?' *Energy and Buildings*, vol 36, no 4, pp381–390

Roulet, C. A. (2004) *Santé et Qualité de l'environnement dans les Bâtiments*, PPUR, Lausanne

9

The Design of Optimal Openings

Manuela Almeida, Eduardo Maldonado,
Matheos Santamouris and Gérard Guarracino

INTRODUCTION

The air exchange rates in naturally ventilated buildings depend upon the internal and external geometry of the building and upon the local weather characteristics. In urban canyons, where the local wind speed is reduced, the geometry of a building's façade and of its openings plays an increased role. Design decisions for the use of natural ventilation in buildings need an estimation of the appropriate size of the openings and of their location in the façade. However, tools that are currently available require precisely these parameters (size and location of the openings and wind speed and direction) as inputs to calculate the air change rates. Thus, these tools can be used to verify the design when the openings are already known; but they are not very practical in helping designers to select a suitable solution. Indeed, designers need to solve an inverse problem (i.e. to specify the opening (size and location) and the façade in order to obtain a required airflow rate in a straightforward way, without a trial and error procedure).

The main objective of this chapter is to present a methodology and performance criteria for the best practice design of naturally ventilated buildings. The aim is to optimize the façade of urban buildings in order to better exploit the driving forces of natural ventilation and to maximize its performance, promoting energy conservation, improved indoor air quality and the better use of renewable energy sources.

The problem of inversing the model for calculating airflow rate is not trivial because the governing equations are not explicit; consequently, a direct solution to the problem is not possible and an indirect solution is required. One possible way to obtain the optimal dimensions of the openings is to develop a database of air change rates obtained through simulations using a validated tool, and to search systematically for the best solution to a particular problem. This methodology thus consists of the three following steps:

1   Define the typologies of buildings in urban canyons and of the corresponding architectural scenarios for naturally ventilated buildings.
2   Calculate the natural ventilation potential for all of the defined architectural scenarios. This consists of simulating the airflows through the openings and air change rates inside buildings for a large number of possible cases in order to create a database.
3   Search the database using suitable database management software. An alternative is to develop a neural network that is trained on the database in order to find the openings that correspond to the required airflow in the given weather conditions.

Weather conditions, especially wind speed, depend upon the form and orientation of the canyon (see Chapter 4) and are not addressed in this chapter. This model simply treats them as required inputs or boundary conditions.

ARCHITECTURAL SCENARIOS

In an urban environment, natural ventilation inside buildings is affected by three main geometrical parameters:

1   the canyon geometry, consisting of the ratios of geometric variables such as the height of the buildings (H), as well as the length (L) and the width (W) of the canyon: H/W, L/W and H/L;
2   the building configuration regarding potential ventilation paths: single-sided ventilation or cross-ventilation;
3   the types of façade geometry and characteristics of the openings (size and location).

The canyon geometries can be defined in terms of the following geometric parameters (see Figure 9.1):

* H, the mean height of the buildings in the canyon;
* W, the canyon width;
* L, the canyon length.

Given these parameters, the geometrical descriptors are limited to three measures:

*   the aspect ratios H/W and H/L;
*   and the building density $j = A_r/A_1$, where A_r is the plan of the roof area of the average building and A_1 is the 'lot' area or unit ground area occupied by each building.

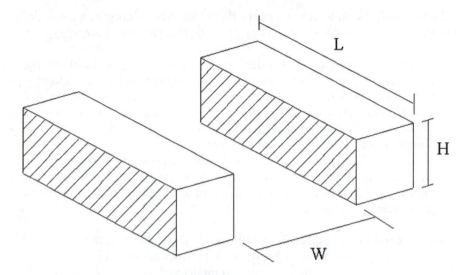

Figure 9.1 *The geometry of canyons*

In terms of building geometries, three main types can be considered:

1 small offices and apartments, typically behaving as single-sided ventilation cases;
2 the same as above, but with a chimney linking them to the roof of the building;
3 larger sized apartments and offices, typically allowing for cross-ventilation (openings in more than one façade).

For each case, two types of façades are possible:

1 flat façades, such as those shown in Figure 9.2; and
2 façades with obstacles, such as balconies, overhangs or other elements such as those shown in Figures 9.3 to 9.6, creating complex wind patterns and pressure distributions on the openings.

The wind flow around façades with obstacles is very complex and strongly depends upon the façade geometry. Only the flat façades are addressed here because the findings can be generalized to apply to all buildings of this type. Other types of façades cause complex pressure patterns and must be studied individually.

The airflow through an external opening is strongly dependent upon the wind-induced pressure difference across it. This wind-induced pressure depends upon the detailed knowledge of pressure coefficients (C_p) on each building surface. Although there are several tools for predicting C_p values in simplified geometries (IEA, 1984; Knoll et al, 1995; Santamouris and

Figure 9.2 *Flat façades*

Figure 9.3 *Façade with obstacles (solar shading)*

Figure 9.4 *Non-flat façades*

Figure 9.5 *Façades with balconies*

Figure 9.6 *Façades with obstacles*

Asimakopolous, 1995; Santamouris and Boonstra, 1997; Allard et al, 1998; Orme et al, 1998; Orme, 1999; Jiang and Chen, 2001), their use is mostly limited to flat façades subjected to undisturbed wind incidence, such as buildings placed in an open terrain, not in complex urban environments. Reliable C_p values for complex urban layouts and/or complex façades can only be obtained through wind tunnel studies for each specific case (Allen, 1984; Sharag-Eldin, 1998).

The modelling of cross-ventilation suffers from the same limitations as pointed out above. C_p values are strongly dependent upon the complex wind patterns; as a result, they are not known with sufficient accuracy for all but the simplest geometries. Wind-tunnel studies are also required and their usefulness is questionable due to their limited applicability to the specific geometry under study.

General studies can thus be done only for cases that do not depend upon C_p; these comprise:

- single-sided ventilation; and
- cross-ventilation of buildings with openings in a single façade, including a chimney linking them to the roof, in the absence of wind (stack-induced flow only).

These two situations are described and elaborated upon in the following sections.

Single-sided ventilation scenarios

Single-sided ventilation scenarios in buildings can be studied with very simple geometries such as the one shown in Figure 9.7, a small room with only one external opening located on one façade. For this scenario, ventilation rates have been calculated with a validated simulation model: AIOLOS (Descalaki et al, 1998).

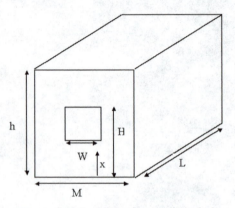

Figure 9.7 *Scenario for single-sided ventilation*

Stack-induced ventilation scenarios

Stack-induced ventilation can be simulated with the same model of a single room shown in Figure 9.7, but by considering it inserted within a multi-storey building. The stack effect is induced by a single external opening in the façade and a chimney linking the room to the roof of the building, as shown in Figures 9.8 to 9.10. Air change data has been produced for an apartment located in each floor of a building with five stories with the COMIS software (Feustel and Smith, 2001; Warren, 2001). Different chimney heights and diameters using commercially available smooth tubing were simulated.

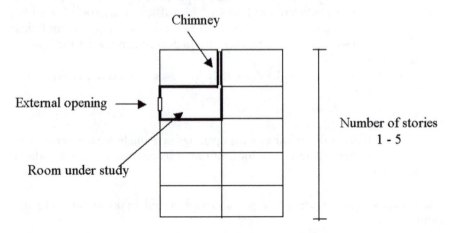

Figure 9.8 *Scenario for stack-induced situations*

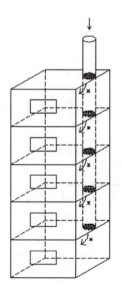

* only one inlet at a time

Figure 9.9 *Building envelope and stack*

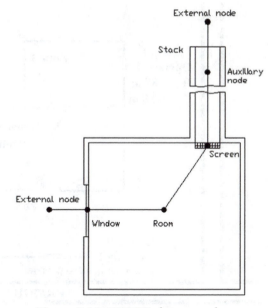

Figure 9.10 *COMIS chimney scheme*

Limitations of the single-sided ventilation case

It should be clearly noted that, in situations of single-sided ventilation, even small cracks in closed windows or doors will cause some natural cross-ventilation potential and the situation will no longer be a simple case of single-sided ventilation.

This can be easily demonstrated with a few parametric and sensitivity studies for a real case. Experiments concerning the airflow rates in an apartment located in Ermou Street in Athens were conducted during the project, Natural ventilation in the Urban Environment (URBVENT). The azimuth of the axis of the Ermou canyon is approximately 92 degrees from north. The apartment is located in the corner of the building and consists of two separate rooms (zones 1 and 3), separated by a hallway (zone 2), as represented in Figure 9.11. It is a small office, with a useful floor area of 20 square metres (m^2). The apartment has two external openings (a door in zone 3 and a window in zone 1) with the dimensions shown in Figure 9.11. The apartment also has two internal openings: two doors ($1.90m^2 \times 0.70m^2$) between zones 1 and 2, and 2 and 3, respectively. Figure 9.12 shows a view of this apartment building (Georgakis and Santamouris, 2004).

The influence of cracks has been studied with the help of the AIOLOS software by varying the crack dimensions while maintaining the respective opening completely closed. For example, it has been assumed that there were cracks around the opening in zone 1, which is always closed, while the door in zone 3 is open. The crack width has been changed from 0m to 0.10m, the limiting values allowed by AIOLOS.

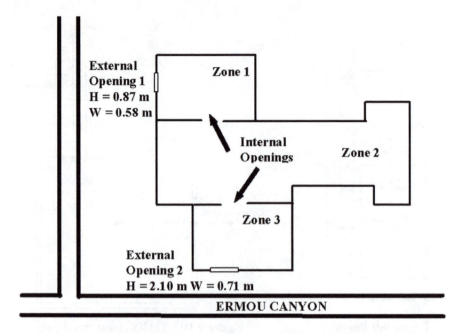

Figure 9.11 *Plan of the Ermou apartment, Athens*

The following base scenario was arbitrarily chosen, assuming typical values for some variables in order to illustrate the situation:

- The discharge coefficient of opening 1 is 0.
- The cracks in zone 1 have a variable width (from 0–0.10m) and a length equal to the perimeter of the opening 1.
- The discharge coefficient of the internal openings is 0.2.
- The discharge coefficient of opening 3 is 0.7.
- The cracks in zone 3 have a length equal to the perimeter of the opening 3 and a width of 0.001m.
- The wind is such that the Cp values for openings 1 and 3 are 0 and 1, respectively.

Figures 9.13 through 9.15 show the variation of the average air change rate in zones 3, 2 and 1, respectively. It can be seen that the air exchange in zone 3, where the main opening occurs, increases as the cracks in the other rooms increase. It should be noticed that, without cracks (crack width = 0), the same air exchange is observed as in the case of pure single-sided ventilation. But, as the cracks increase and are accounted for, it is now possible to achieve some air exchange – approximately 1 air change per hour (*ACH*) – in zones 1 and 2 by cross-ventilation, which is very important for indoor air quality in those spaces.

It is also important to note that it takes only a few small cracks to achieve enough air exchange in zones 1 and 2. As the cracks grow larger, there is little

Figure 9.12 *Ermou office apartment building, Athens*

additional effect upon the air exchange rates. Cracks in excess of 0.5cm have no practical effect upon increasing the air exchange rate.

The air change rates estimated for single-sided ventilation must therefore be considered with care: whenever there is a possibility for cracks to exist in other façades, this could create a clear potential for cross-ventilation, and the corresponding air change rate would be higher.

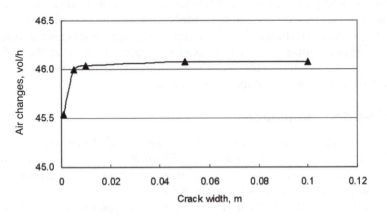

Figure 9.13 *Air exchange in zone 3 with cracks in opening 1*

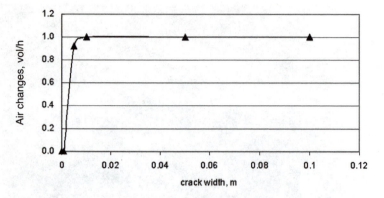

Figure 9.14 *Air exchange in zone 2 with cracks in opening 1*

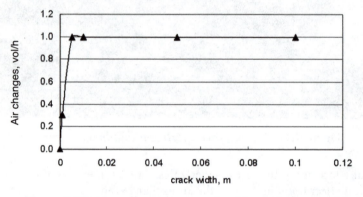

Figure 9.15 *Air exchange in zone 1 with cracks in opening 1*

DATABASE FOR NATURAL VENTILATION POTENTIAL

For the previously defined architectural scenarios, the air change rates can be calculated by using existing software tools such as AIOLOS and COMIS in order to produce databases. Two such databases have been created, one for single-sided and another for stack-induced ventilation, by varying the size and location of the openings, the wind speed and the temperature difference between the indoor and outdoor environment.

Single-sided ventilation

Airflow and air change rates for cases of single-sided ventilation can be calculated for the small room described in Figure 9.7 by using typical climatic conditions. In all of the studies, only summer conditions have been simulated. It is assumed that in winter, when outdoor temperatures are cool, occupants will always limit natural ventilation to minimum hygienic rates in order to reduce their heating bills. Therefore, the interior temperature of the simulated room was kept constant at 25°C.

Table 9.1 *Exterior climatic conditions considered in the simulations*

Temperature (T)	Wind velocity (u)
26–41°C	0–10m/s

Table 9.2 *Variations of the dimensions considered in the simulations*

Width of the room (M)	Length of the room (L)	Height of the room (h)	Height of the opening bottom (x)	Height of top of window (H)	Width of window (W)
3–5m	3–5m	2.8–5m	0.1–2.4m	0.6–3m	0.2–4m

For the exterior environment, the climatic data that were used are listed in Table 9.1, which covers a wide range of external temperatures (*T*) and wind velocities (*u*) (normal component relative to the window, the only one of interest for single-sided ventilation).

For the simulations, six geometric variables related to room and opening dimensions were considered. All variables were changed, allowing for different combinations. This creates thousands of different architectural scenarios that can provide a deep insight into the magnitude of airflows under different circumstances. Table 9.2 lists the range of variations of the dimensions used in the simulations.

Figures 9.16 and 9.17 show just two examples of the results that can be obtained from the simulations. They highlight how the temperature difference between the outside and the inside environment (DT) and the wind velocity influence the air exchange rate.

What is visible in Figures 9.16 and 9.17 is that as the temperature difference increases, the air changes inside the room also increase (see Chapter

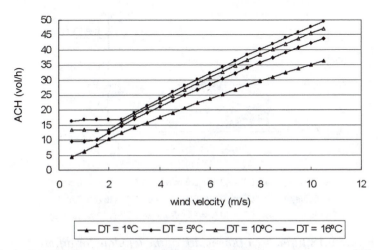

Figure 9.16 *Influence of wind velocity for different temperature differences*

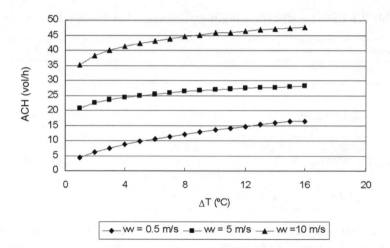

Figure 9.17 *Influence of temperature difference for different wind velocities*

3 for more detail on this subject). However, the impact of the temperature difference on the exchange rate is lower as the temperature difference becomes larger, or (stated the other way around) the influence of the temperature difference is larger when the wind velocity is lower. As was expected, wind velocity has a stronger impact on the air change rate than does the temperature difference.

Figures 9.18 to 9.20 show the influence of the geometric characteristics and the location of the window for different wind velocities and temperature differences.

Figure 9.18 shows a linear variation of the air change values (*ACH*) with the width of the window (*W*), which is clearly in line with the expected behaviour.

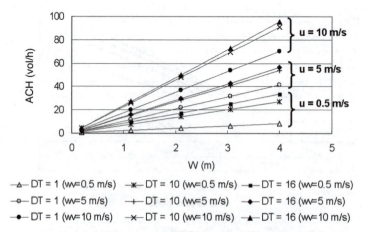

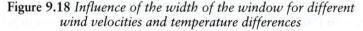

Figure 9.18 *Influence of the width of the window for different wind velocities and temperature differences*

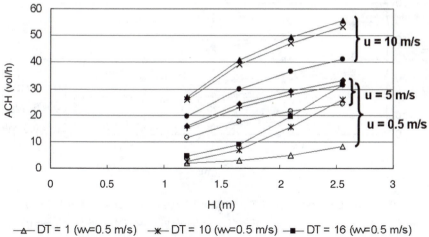

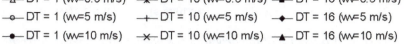

Figure 9.19 *Influence of the height of the window for different wind velocities and temperature differences*

Figure 9.19 shows the influence of the height of the top of the window (*H*) on the air exchange rate for different wind velocities and temperature differences. As the height increases and, with it, the window area, *ACH* values also increase and the stack effect becomes more intense. However, in this case the variation is no longer linear since stack effect has an important role to play in the process.

Figure 9.20 shows the influence of the height of the opening bottom (*x*) on the air exchange rate for different wind velocities and temperature differences. Here, the tendency is the opposite of what is seen in the previous figure: as *x* increases, the air exchange values become lower, which is precisely in line with the same arguments indicated in the previous case.

Stack-induced ventilation

The values of the airflow rates and the air changes corresponding to the different architectural stack-induced natural ventilation scenarios previously described (see Figures 9.8 to 9.10) were calculated with the COMIS software. For these stack-effect simulations, as in the previous parametric study, only situations during the summer were of interest. The temperatures that have been used were exactly the same as in the single-sided ventilation simulations.

Due to the already stated lack of reliable C_p values, no wind values have been considered in this study. In all simulations, the wind velocity was set equal to zero. In this situation, the simulations were carried out by varying the room's dimensions, as well as the dimensions of the external openings, although with less amplitude. The range of the variations that have been studied is listed in Tables 9.3 and 9.4.

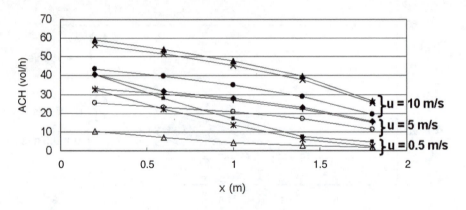

Figure 9.20 *Influence of the height of the opening bottom for different wind velocities and temperature differences*

The following figures show some of the results obtained with these simulations in order to illustrate trends. The results are also in line with the expected behaviour.

For instance, Figure 9.21 shows the influence of the useful area of the chimney (screen as defined in Figure 9.10) on the air change rate (ACH) for two chimney diameters: 0.10m and 0.50m. These results were obtained for a temperature difference between the outside and inside environment of 10°C and when the room was located on the first floor of the building (maximum chimney height). For the same conditions, Figure 9.22 shows the influence of the chimney diameter for two useful areas of the outlet (screen = 10 per cent and screen = 100 per cent).

It is possible to see that, as expected, as the useful area or the duct diameter increase, the air changes inside the room also increase. However, for small chimney diameters, this effect is quite small.

Table 9.3 *Variations of the chimney characteristics considered in the simulations*

Diameter (metres)	Useful area (percentage)	Floor
0.1–0.5m	10–100%	1–5

Table 9.4 *Variations of the room dimensions considered in the simulations*

Width of the room (M)	Length of the room (L)	Height of the room (h)	Height of the opening bottom (x)	Height of top of window (H)	Width of window (W)
5m	3–5m	2.8–5m	0.1–1.8m	2–2.3m	1–2m

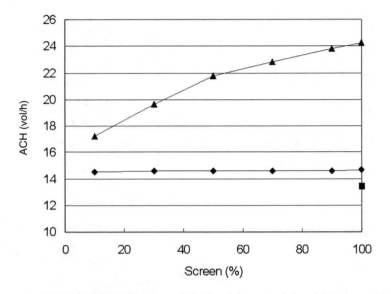

Figure 9.21 *Influence of the useful area of the chimney*

Figure 9.21 also shows the air change for the same room but for single-sided ventilation. It is evident that the presence of the chimney clearly improves the air change rate.

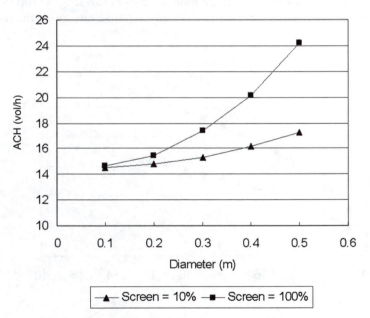

Figure 9.22 *Influence of the chimney diameter*

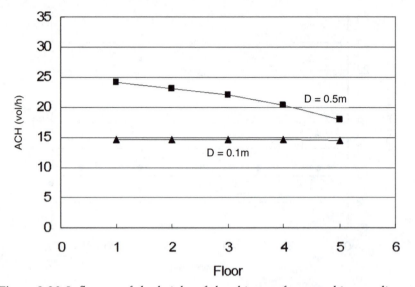

Figure 9.23 *Influence of the height of the chimney for two chimney diameters*

Figure 9.23 shows the influence of the chimney height (i.e. on which floor the apartment is located in the building) for two different chimney diameters. Figure 9.24 shows the influence of the temperature difference for the same two chimney diameters, in perfect accordance with the expected behaviour.

As the location of the room in the building moves towards the top floor, the chimney height becomes smaller and the air exchange rate inside the room

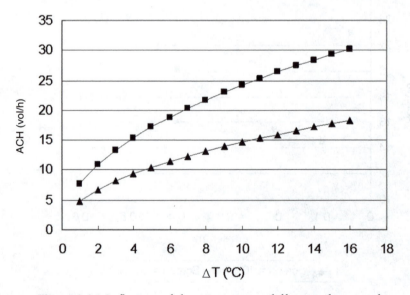

Figure 9.24 *Influence of the temperature difference for two chimney diameters*

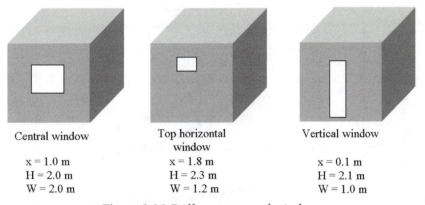

Central window	Top horizontal window	Vertical window
x = 1.0 m	x = 1.8 m	x = 0.1 m
H = 2.0 m	H = 2.3 m	H = 2.1 m
W = 2.0 m	W = 1.2 m	W = 1.0 m

Figure 9.25 *Different types of windows*

also decreases. This trend is not as evident when the chimney diameter is reduced as the duct resistance is too important and controls the flow.

The influences of the height of the room and of the geometric characteristics of the window are also important. Figure 9.25 shows three different types of windows that can be used in buildings, each with different impacts upon the natural ventilation rates that they allow.

Figure 9.26 shows that, for the same floor area, the air exchange decreases when the room height increases (and as the volume of the room also becomes correspondingly higher). Figure 9.27 shows the results obtained for the three types of windows depicted in Figure 9.25. The strong influence of the window characteristics on the air exchange rate is evident. During the summer, the openings on the top of the wall are less effective than in other seasons.

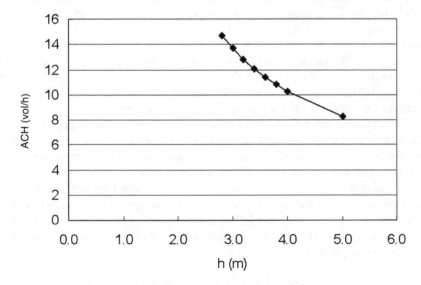

Figure 9.26 *Influence of the height of the room*

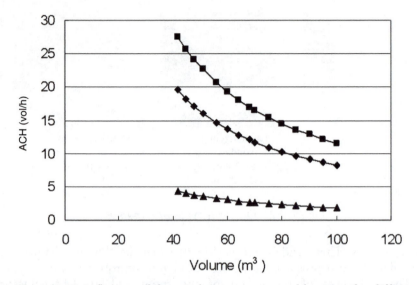

Figure 9.27 *Influence of the window geometry and location for different volumes of the room*

A METHODOLOGY TO CALCULATE THE OPTIMUM OPENINGS FOR NATURALLY VENTILATED BUILDINGS LOCATED IN URBAN CANYONS

For design purposes, it is necessary to size the openings for naturally ventilated buildings. The use of available tools for sizing requires iterative procedures in which the building geometry (including the opening) and the weather conditions are specified, and in which the tools calculate the airflow rate. Based on the results, the designer can then try different openings until the desired air exchange rate is reached. An alternative to the iterative procedure is to obtain a large database of flow rates for building configurations and climatic conditions that can be encountered in practice, and to search the database for openings that correspond to a desired airflow rate.

The database can be searched by interrogation; but, in this case, the results that will be found are limited to the values in the database that were obtained by simulation. A better alternative is to have the tools for simultaneously searching and making an interpolation of the results.

The search in the database of both the direct result (the airflow rate) and the inverse result (the opening dimension) can be accomplished with a recurrent neural network model. The direct neural network model calculates the air flow in naturally ventilated apartments in buildings located in an urban canyon under specific:

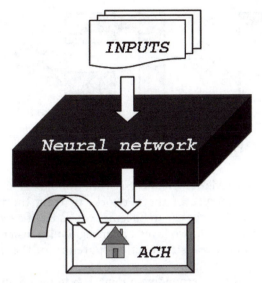

Figure 9.28 *General outline of the model*

- climatic conditions;
- canyon characteristics;
- building openings;
- building geometrical and operational characteristics.

The inverse model calculates the suitable characteristics of the openings when the requested ventilated performance is specified. These models are based on the same geometries previously described in 'Single-sided ventilation scenarios' and 'Stack-induced ventilation scenarios'. They have been derived from a database of more than 2 million values simulated with the methodologies discussed in the same sections.

Methodology for developing the model

The neural network model is based on establishing empirical laws obtained from the database of simulated air exchange values. In practice, this model can be seen as a black box that establishes the link between input variables which influence the studied phenomenon and an output variable corresponding to the value that the designer seeks to define.

Development of neural networks

Neural networks are models that take into account all of the variables (inputs and outputs) and find the parameters of functions which can be used to correctly reproduce the same input–output relation. An implementation of the neural networks can be achieved, for example, in standard software

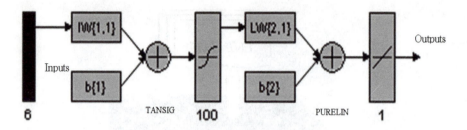

Figure 9.29 *Feed-forward neural network*

packages such as the Matlab Neural Network Toolbox. This toolbox is used to define the architecture of the network, to train the network and to stimulate new data. The chosen architecture consisted of a feed-forward back propagation network with two layers, a tan-sigmoid transfer function for the first layer and a linear transfer function (purelin) for the second layer (see Figure 9.29).

The input and the corresponding output data in the database were used to train a network until the approximation of a function which associates the input vector with specific output vectors was accurate enough. Four neural network models have been built, two treating the single-sided ventilation case, and the other two treating the stack-induced ventilation case.

The neural networks were used to obtain tools for calculating the airflow rate (direct simulation) and the openings (inverse model).

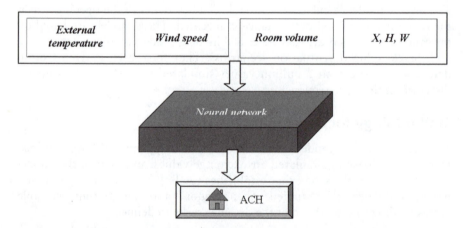

Figure 9.30 *Architecture of the model of calculating ACH for single-sided ventilation*

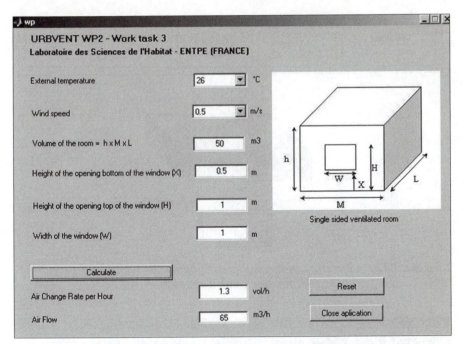

Figure 9.31 *Graphical interface to calculate ACH*

Tool for a single-sided ventilated room

Calculation of ACH

Each network is a feed-forward back propagation network that has, as inputs, the values of external temperature, the wind velocity, the room volume, the height of the opening top of the window, the height of the opening bottom of the window and the width of the window. After being trained according to corresponding values of air change per hour for the rooms, the network can simulate new inputs and predict the value of the air change rate per hour for the single-sided ventilated room, as shown in Figure 9.30. A graphical interface is best suited to help users to use the model (see Figure 9.31).

Calculating the optimal opening

The same procedure was used for obtaining the optimal openings. Each network has as inputs the values of external temperature, wind velocity, room volume, height of the opening bottom of the window, height of the opening top of the window and the value of the air change rate per hour. After being trained, the network can predict the width of the window for the single-sided ventilated room (see Figures 9.32 and 9.33).

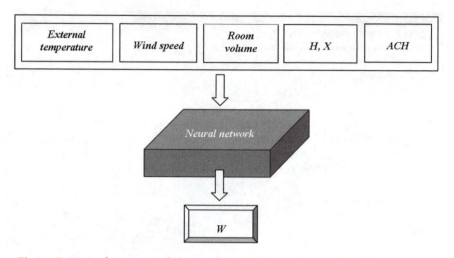

Figure 9.32 *Architecture of the model calculating the width of the window (W) for single-sided ventilation*

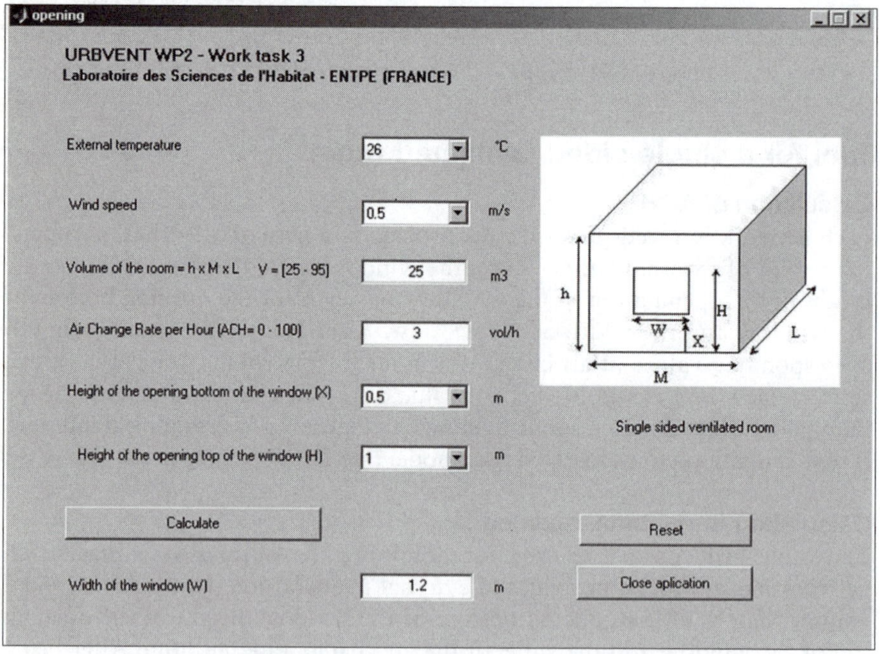

Figure 9.33 *Graphical interface to optimize the opening*

Tool for a ventilated room with stack effect

The techniques used for this situation are identical to those previously described for single-sided ventilated rooms.

Each network has as inputs the values of external temperature, the room volume, the height of the opening top, the height of the opening bottom of the window and the width of the window, the diameter of the chimney, the useful area and the floor level of the room in the building. All networks can predict the value of the air change rate per hour for the natural ventilated room with stack effect.

For calculating the optimal opening, each network has as inputs the values of external temperature, wind velocity, room volume, the height of the opening bottom, the height of the opening top of the window, the value of the air change rate per hour, the diameter of the chimney, the useful area and the floor level of the room in the building. Each network can predict the width of the window for the naturally ventilated room with stack effect.

Global model

The four models were gathered in one global tool developed with Matlab. It allows the user to choose the desired calculation (i.e. whether the output is the calculation of airflow or the opening width for each of the studied scenarios). In order to use this software, Matlab must be installed on the computer. The interface shown in Figure 9.34 makes the connection to the four models.

This model is included in the CD that is part of this handbook.

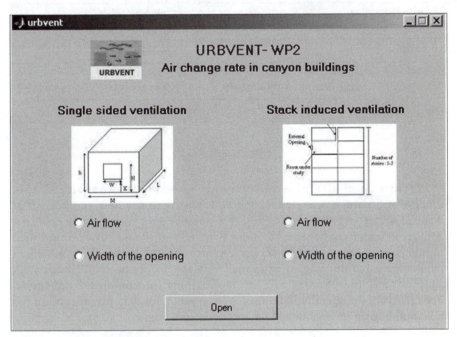

Figure 9.34 *Graphical interface to start the program*

EXPERIMENTAL VALIDATION OF THE DESIGN OF OPTIMAL OPENINGS FOR THE USE OF NATURAL VENTILATION

The airflow rates predicted by the model described in 'Database for natural ventilation potential' were compared with corresponding experimental data in order to assess their accuracy.

Detailed experiments have been carried out in five urban canyons in Athens where the ambient conditions were measured in the street within the canyon and above the top of the buildings (Santamouris et al, 1999; Santamouris and Georgakis, 2003; Georgakis and Santamouris, 2004). In parallel, tracer gas experiments have been carried out in buildings located in each canyon where the air flow rate has been measured for both single-sided and cross-flow configurations. The experimental data have been analysed and the exact air flow rate has been calculated for each case.

The predictions of the model developed to calculate the air flow rate in naturally ventilated buildings located in urban canyons have been compared with the experimental data. The comparison has shown that there is a good agreement between the experimental and the theoretical data for both studied configurations (see Table 9.5).

Table 9.5 *Comparison between experimental and theoretical ACH for single ventilation in the five measured canyons*

Single-sided ventilation		Experimental air changes per hour (ACH)		
Ermou	Miltiadou	Voukourestiou	Kaniggos	Dervenion
0.2–0.8	0.4–1.1	0.8–1.2	0.2–1	0.4–1.5
Single-sided ventilation		Mean theoretical ACH		
Ermou	Miltiadou	Voukourestiou	Kaniggos	Dervenion
0.65	1.5	1	1.3	1.35

CONCLUSIONS

The estimation of natural ventilation rates in buildings is not an easy task under any circumstances. In isolated buildings with a simple geometry (flat façades) located in an open terrain, it is possible to obtain estimates with a certain degree of confidence: the fluid dynamics of the air flow around such buildings has been studied by several researchers and models are available in the literature. For buildings in urban canyons, the flow patterns are much more complex and few studies are available, short of complex wind-tunnel arrangements for specific locations. This type of study is not an option for most building designers due to cost and time constraints.

This chapter describes a model, based on neural network methodologies, that allows designers to obtain quick estimates of the size of the openings needed to provide the desired levels of natural ventilation rates in buildings located in urban canyons for single-sided and stack-effect situations. These results have been confirmed by comparison with real data and are shown to be reliable. Designers can use this tool to size openings in building façades to obtain a certain level of air exchange rate, or to predict the ventilation rate for existing openings and building geometries.

REFERENCES

Allard, F., Santamouris, M., Alvarez, S., Descalaki, E., Guarracino, G., Maldonado, E., Sciuto, S. and Vandaele, L. (1998) *Natural Ventilation in Buildings: A Design Handbook*, James and James Science Publishers, London.

Allen C., (1984) *Wind Pressure Data Requirements for Air Infiltration Calculations*, Technical Report TN 13, AIVC (Air Infiltration and Ventilation Center), Brussels, Belgium

Descalaki, E., Klitsikas, N., Geros, V., Santamouris, M., Alvarez, S. and Grosso, M. (1998) *AIOLOS Software*, European Commission, DG XVII for Energy, Altener Programme, Aiolos Project, Brussels, Belgium

Feustel, H. E. and Smith, B. V. (2001) *COMIS 3.1 User's Guide*, LBNL, Berkeley, California

Georgakis, C. and Santamouris, M. (2004) 'On the Airflow in Urban Canyons for Ventilation Purposes', *The International Journal of Ventilation*, vol 3, no 1, pp53–66

International Energy Agency (IEA) (1984) *Wind Pressure Workshop Proceedings*, Technical Note 13.1, AIVC, Brussels, Belgium

Jiang, Y. and Chen, Q. Y. (2001) *Using Large Eddy Simulation to Study the Effects of Turbulence Scale on the Pressure Distribution around a Building*, Building Technology Program, Massachusetts Institute of Technology, Clima 2000 World Congress, Naples

Knoll B., Phaff, J. C. and de Gids, W. F (1995) *Pressure Simulation Program*, Proceedings of the 16th AIVC Conference on Implementing the Results of Ventilation Research, AIVC (Air Infiltration and Ventilation Center), Palm Springs, California

Orme, M., Liddament, M. and Wilson, A. (1998) *An Analysis and Data Summary of the AIVC's Numerical Database*, Technical Report 44, AIVC, Brussels, Belgium

Orme, M. (1999) *Applicable Models for Air Infiltration and Ventilation Calculations*, Technical Report 51, AIVC, Brussels, Belgium

Santamouris, M. and Asimakopoulos, D. (1995) *Passive Cooling of Buildings*, James and James Science Publishers, London.

Santamouris, M. and Boonstra, C. (1997) *Natural Ventilation*, Brochure prepared by EC 2000 Project, European Commission, Directorate General for Energy and Transport, Brussels, Belgium

Santamouris, M., Papanikolaou, N., Koronakis, I., Livada, I. and Asimakopoulos D. (1999) 'Thermal and air flow characteristics in a deep pedestrian canyon under hot weather conditions', *Atmospheric Environment*, vol 33, pp 4503–4521.

Santamouris, M. and Georgakis C. (2003) 'Energy and Indoor Climate in Urban Environments: recent trends', *Journal of Buildings Services Engineering Research and Technology*, vol 24, no 2, pp69–81

Sharag-Eldin, A. (1998) *Predicting Natural Ventilation in Residential Buildings in the Context of Urban Environments*, University of California, Berkeley

Warren, P. (2000) *Multizone Air Flow Modeling (COMIS): Technical Synthesis Report*, IEA ECBCS Annex 23, Faber Maunsell Ltd, ESSU, Air Infiltration and Ventilation Centre, Coventry

10

Natural Ventilation Potential

*Mario Germano, Cristian Ghiaus and
Claude-Alain Roulet*

INTRODUCTION

Natural ventilation potential (NVP) may be defined as the possibility of ensuring an acceptable indoor air quality through natural ventilation only. *Passive cooling potential* (PCP) can also be defined as the possibility of ensuring an acceptable indoor thermal comfort in summer by solely using natural ventilation.

The three objectives of natural ventilation in buildings are indoor air quality, thermal comfort and energy savings. The methodology proposed in this chapter provides an assessment of the natural ventilation potential for indoor air quality, while taking into consideration the other objectives. More precisely, 'comfort' requirements impose the appropriate ventilation strategies to be used for each given meteorological situation. On the basis of these strategies, the methodology evaluates the appropriateness of a given location to natural ventilation.

Ensuring an acceptable indoor air quality or cooling down the building structure by natural ventilation is subject to many conditions that depend upon the site (e.g. outdoor air quality, outdoor air temperature and moisture, outdoor noise, local winds or global wind, and urban structure) or upon the building (e.g. indoor pollutant sources, indoor heat sources and stored heat, indoor air quality requirements, position and size of ventilation openings, indoor temperature, orientation of building, and internal air-path distribution).

Since the details of the building needed for airflow estimation cannot be known until the project is well advanced, it is interesting to assess the natural ventilation potential of the site itself, regardless of the building. In this way, an analysis of the results can provide the type of ventilation to which a given site is suited, as well as the type of building that should be built or how to refurbish an existing one.

DRIVING FORCES OF NATURAL VENTILATION

Wind pressure

As mentioned in Chapter 3, one of the driving forces of natural ventilation for a building exposed to wind is the wind pressure, given by:

$$\Delta p_w = \frac{1}{2} C_p \rho v^2 \tag{10.1}$$

where C_p is a pressure coefficient depending upon the wind direction and upon the considered surface of the building envelope, ρ is the air density expressed in kilograms per cubic metre (kg/m^3) and v is the wind speed expressed in metres per second (m/s). Pressure coefficients are determined either experimentally, in wind tunnels, or numerically, using computational fluid dynamics.

It is important to mention that Δp_w from equation (10.1) is the pressure due to the impingement of the airflow on a surface, not due to the pressure drop through a hole. If there is an opening through which air may flow, the pressure strongly drops, and the pressure coefficient no longer has a meaning.

Moreover, these coefficients are strongly influenced by the wind direction and the surroundings of the building. They can take any value between −1 and +1 (Orme et al, 1994), depending upon the shape, dimension and location of surrounding buildings. In addition, their value may depend upon details that are not modelled in the scale model placed in the wind tunnel or in the computer model.

These considerations on pressure coefficients, together with other points mentioned hereafter, justify the resort to qualitative modelling. One of the assumptions made in the current methodology is that, given two city locations with different *local* wind speeds, natural ventilation will be more effective at the location having the highest wind speed (local wind speed includes the influence of the building's surroundings). In particular, such comparisons will be made with so-called base sites, as is explained in 'Procedure for evaluating a site'.

Surface wind

One problem in the assessment of natural ventilation potential is the weather data. Measurements are available only at met stations and at airports. An alternative is to use data obtained from weather models that are used for forecasting. These models give good results and have the advantage that values are available for relatively high resolution (of the order of kilometres). The inaccuracy introduced by the model is smaller than the inaccuracy introduced by data transfer in a homogeneous site (see 'Data transfer in a homogeneous site' in Chapter 3). The wind data used in the Natural Ventilation in the Urban Environment (URBVENT) project come from the archive of the Swiss Federal Office of Meteorology and Climatology, hereafter referred to as MeteoSwiss. These data provide the wind speed and direction at an altitude of 10m above

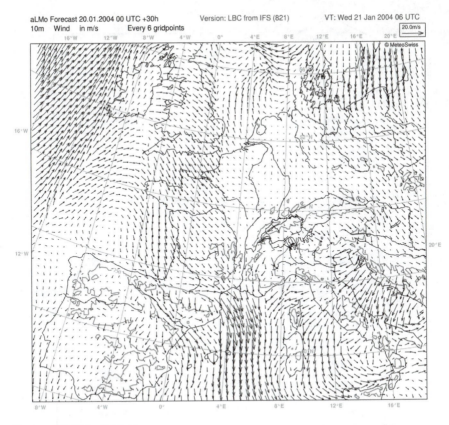

Source: www.MeteoSwiss.ch

Figure 10.1 *Wind field at 10m calculated by the LM model*

the ground for 125,125 points across Europe with a spatial resolution of 7km and a temporal resolution of four times per day. The model that the data come from, called the Lokal-Modell (LM) model, is a prediction model that solves the primitive hydro-thermodynamical equations describing compressible non-hydrostatic flow in a moist atmosphere by using the finite difference method (Steppeler et al, 2002). The predictions, which have proved to fit the measurements well, use continuously new initial conditions and have been archived for several years, making it possible to carry out a statistical analysis of the data.

Influence of the urban environment on the local wind speed
The LM model takes into account the variation of altitude, but not the presence of buildings, by considering the roughness of the terrain. The wind speed estimated at 10m above the surface should be transformed when the site of interest is located in an urban canyon. The local wind speed v^{local} is influenced by the following parameters: the speed $v^{undisturbed}$ of the undisturbed

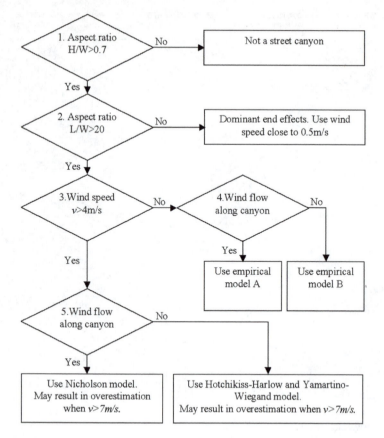

Source: Mat Santamouris and Chrissa Georgakis, Athens University

Figure 10.2 *Algorithm for assessing wind speed inside the canyon*

(surface) wind, the orientation θ of the undisturbed wind compared with the canyon orientation, the width W, the height H and the length L of the canyon (see Chapter 4).

The algorithm proposed in Chapter 4 and described in Figure 10.2 is applied to assess the wind speed within a canyon.

In other cases (i.e. when the site of interest is located outside a canyon; see 'Not a street canyon' in Figure 10.2), a simple rule of thumb can be applied:

$$v^{local} = TCF \times v^{undisturbed} \qquad (10.2)$$

where *TCF* is a terrain correction factor whose values are given in Table 10.1 (Chandra et al, 1983).

The models used in the algorithm (see Figure 10.2) are described in Chapter 4. The resulting local wind speeds, v^{local}, are used in the subsequent equations (10.12) and (10.31).

Table 10.1 *Terrain correction factor for wind speed*

Terrain type	TCF
Rural or suburban	0.85
Urban	0.67
City centre	0.47

Stack pressure

The other driving force of natural ventilation is stack pressure, or pressure due to buoyancy. It is induced by density differences between the indoor and outdoor air. The Bernoulli equation, combined with the ideal gas equation of state, leads to the stack pressure difference between two openings separated by a vertical distance h:

$$\Delta p_s = \rho_i g \, h \, \frac{T_i - T_e}{T_i + T_e} \tag{10.3}$$

where ρ_i is the internal air density, g is the acceleration of gravity, and T_i and T_e are the internal and external air temperatures. In the absence of wind, when $T_i > T_e$, the air enters through the lower openings and goes out through the upper ones (upward flow). A downward flow takes place when $T_i < T_e$. If both openings have the same area, A, then the airflow is given by:

$$\dot{m} = \rho_i A \, D_d \sqrt{2 \, g \, h \, \frac{T_i - T_e}{T_i + T_e}} \tag{10.4}$$

where C_d is a discharge coefficient for each of the openings.

CONSTRAINTS TO NATURAL VENTILATION

The two constraints to natural ventilation retained here are noise and pollution. Others exist, such as compromising the safety of the building while leaving windows open, or the fact that the occupants do not interact in a proper way; but they are only briefly mentioned.

Noise

Noise is a constraint to natural ventilation especially when the building is occupied. The definition of the acceptability of noise used in the current methodology is inspired by the Swiss federal regulation, which resorts to degrees of sensitivity:

- *high*: zones requiring an increased protection against noise, such as relaxation areas;

Table 10.2 *Equivalent sound pressure levels (L$_{eq}$) expressed in dB(A): Table of correspondence between qualitative and quantitative levels*

	Silent		Acceptable		Unacceptable	
	Daytime	Night time	Daytime	Night time	Daytime	Night time
Degree of sensitivity						
High	[0, 50 [	[0, 40 [	[50, 65 [	[40, 60 [	[65, ∞ [	[60, ∞ [
Medium	[0, 55 [	[0, 45 [	[55, 70 [	[45, 65 [	[70, ∞ [	[65, ∞ [
Low	[0, 60 [	[0, 50 [	[60, 70 [	[50, 65 [	[70, ∞ [	[65, ∞ [

- *medium*: zones where no disturbing company is allowed, such as residential areas and areas restricted to public facilities;
- *low*: zones where disturbing companies are allowed, such as industrial, agricultural and craft areas.

Table 10.2 supplies a correspondence between qualitative levels – used in the current methodology – and quantitative levels in function of the degrees of sensitivity. These levels are inspired by the Swiss noise regulation (OPB, 1986).

Pollution

In order to assess outdoor air quality, the following pollutants are usually considered:

- nitrogen dioxide (NO_2);
- sulphur dioxide (SO_2);
- carbon monoxide (CO);
- ozone (O_3); and
- volatile organic components (VOCs).

These pollutants each have long-term and short-term limiting values, or both. For instance, the Swiss environment protection law (*loi sur la protection de l'environnement, LPE*) imposes for nitrogen dioxide a daily limiting value of $80\mu g/m^3$, whereas the annual limiting value is $30\mu g/m^3$.

ASSUMPTIONS OF THE METHODOLOGY

The first assumption is that the building is built or will be built in a way that gets the most out of the potential for natural ventilation. The same applies in the case of refurbishment.

The second assumption is that the building's occupants are aware of natural ventilation and open the windows or ad hoc openings accordingly. Indeed, it does not make sense to assess the potential for natural ventilation if the occupants make the building airtight anyway. We suppose here that they apply the best ventilation strategy.

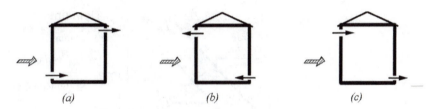

Source: Li and Delsante, 2001

Figure 10.3 *Situations when* $T_i > T_e$: *(a) assisting wind force; (b) opposing wind force with upward flow; (c) opposing wind force with downward flow*

In addition, we assume that the contributions to ventilation due to wind and to stack pressure are never opposed. As mentioned in Chapter 5, this opposition was shown to occur (Li and Delsante, 2001), but can always be avoided by designing the building and by opening the apertures correctly.

As mentioned earlier, we suppose that the airflow rate is a monotonic increasing function of the wind speed. This is generally fulfilled if wind and stack have no opposed effects (this condition is met in accordance with the previous assumption) and if the wind direction is constant.

CLIMATIC SUITABILITY

Climatic suitability of a heating, ventilation and air conditioning (HVAC) system is a measure of the energy needed for heating and for mechanical cooling, as well as a measure of the energy saved for cooling when ventilation is used. The climate should be taken into account in relation to the building's thermal behaviour and the anticipated thermal comfort. Constraints on comfort are important because they impose the ventilation strategy to be used.

Indoor temperature of a free-running building

The free-running temperature is defined as the indoor temperature of the building in thermal balance with the outdoor environment when neither heating nor cooling is used. Furthermore, it is assumed that the free-running temperature is defined for the minimum ventilation rate required for indoor air quality, which implies that the building is almost airtight. With these assumptions, it may be accepted that, for a given month of the year, the indoor temperature of the free-running building is a function of the hour of the day. This temperature is calculated in the current project by means of a thermal simulation program.

Adaptive comfort

The thermal comfort exhibits a neutral zone. In Figure 10.4, this zone is delimited by a lower comfort limit, T_{cl}, and an upper comfort limit, T_{cu}. These

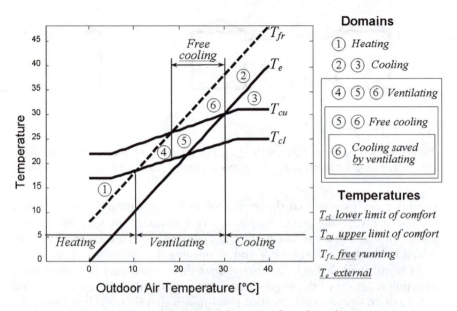

Figure 10.4 *Heating, ventilation and cooling domains*

limits vary with the mean outdoor temperature, resulting in an adaptation of the comfort criteria to the season. It is argued that thermal comfort in naturally ventilated buildings has larger seasonal differences than assumed by ISO 7730 and ASHRAE 55 Standards (Fountain et al, 1996; Brager and de Dear, 1998; Sayigh and Marafia, 1998; de Dear, 1999; Nicol, 2001).

Domains for heating, cooling and ventilation

Using the indoor temperature of the free-running building, the outdoor temperature and the comfort zone, the domains for heating, cooling and ventilation can be expressed by binary value functions (δ). Heating is needed when the free-running temperature is below the lower limit of comfort zone:

$$\delta_h = \begin{cases} 1, \text{ when } T_{fr} < T_{cl} \\ 0, \text{ otherwise} \end{cases} \quad (10.5)$$

Mechanical cooling is required when both outdoor temperature and free-running temperature are larger than the upper limit of the comfort zone:

$$\delta_c = \begin{cases} 1, \text{ when } T_{fr} > T_{cl} \text{ and } T_e > T_{cu} \\ 0, \text{ otherwise} \end{cases} \quad (10.6)$$

Ventilation may be used between heating and cooling. When mechanical or natural ventilation supply larger airflow rates than the minimum needed for indoor air quality, the indoor temperature may be varied from T_{fr} to max(T_e, T_{cl}). This solution may be applied in situations corresponding to zones 3 to 5 in

Figure 10.4. In zone 5, if the building were maintained airtight, then mechanical cooling would be needed. But, by using ventilation, the indoor temperature may be decreased by increasing the airflow, approaching the outdoor air temperature if the air exchange becomes very large. By controlling the airflow rate, the indoor temperature may be varied in the interval defined by the temperature for a free-running building (that corresponds to the situation when the building is airtight) and the outdoor temperature. Zone 5, defined by:

$$\delta_{fc} = \begin{cases} 1, \text{ when } T_e \leq T_{cu} \text{ and } T_{fr} > T_{cu} \\ 0, \text{ otherwise} \end{cases} \tag{10.7}$$

corresponds to mechanical cooling saved by ventilation (or free cooling).

Degree hours

Degree hours are a representative indication of the energy consumption for heating and cooling, as well as an indication of the energy saved for cooling by natural ventilation. For heating, they are defined as the sum of the differences between the lower limit of comfort temperature and the free-running temperature, when $T_{fr} < T_{cu}$:

$$DH_h = \frac{1}{N} \sum_{i=1}^{N} (T_{cl_i} - T_{fr_i}) \delta_{h_i} \tag{10.8}$$

where δ_h is defined in (10.5) and N is the number of moments in the considered period. In our case, we considered four daily instants during two years; thus $N = 4 \times 2 \times 365 = 2920$ instants. If the degree days have to be considered for one given month j, then the summation is done exclusively on the instants belonging to that month:

$$DH_{hj} = \frac{1}{N} \sum_{i=1}^{N} (T_{cl_i} - T_{fr_i}) \delta_{h_i} \tag{10.9}$$

where E_j is the set of instants i belonging to month j.

Similarly, the degree hours for cooling represent the sum of the differences between the free-running temperature and the upper limit of comfort, when $T_{fr} > T_{cu}$ and $T_e > T_{cu}$:

$$DH_c = \frac{1}{N} \sum_{i=1}^{N} (T_{fr_i} - T_{cu_i}) \delta_{c_i} \tag{10.10}$$

where δ_c is defined in (10.6).

Finally, the degree days of energy saved by natural ventilation for cooling is the same sum, when $T_e \leq T_{cu}$ and $T_{fr} > T_{cu}$:

$$DH_{fc} = \frac{1}{N} \sum_{i=1}^{N} (T_{fr_i} - T_{cu_i}) \delta_{fc_i} \qquad (10.11)$$

where δ_{fc} is defined in (10.7). In other words, a contribution is brought to the sum only if it is too warm inside when the building is airtight and if it is cool enough outside.

Usually, the factor $1/N$ does not appear in these definitions. It has been included here to make degree hours independent of the number of instants considered.

Criteria for natural ventilation

Criteria for natural ventilation can be defined similarly to the degree hours.

Criterion related to wind

For the criterion related to wind pressure, the following definition is proposed:

$$WT = \frac{1}{N} \sum_{i=1}^{N} v_i^{local} \qquad (10.12)$$

where v^{local} is the local wind speed; WT stands for *wind time*.

Criterion related to stack effect

The criterion related to stack effect is defined as:

$$ST = \frac{1}{N} \sum_{i=1}^{N} \left| \frac{T_{i_i} - T_{e_i}}{T_{e_i}} \right| \qquad (10.13)$$

where T_i and T_e are the internal and external air temperatures, respectively; ST stands for *stack time*.

According to the cases of Figure 10.4, the internal temperature can be written as:

$$T_i = \begin{cases} T_{cl} \text{ if } T_{fr} < T_{cl} \\ T_{fr} \text{ if } T_{cl} \leq T_{fr} \leq T_{cu} \\ T_{cu} \text{ if } T_e \leq T_{cu} \text{ and } T_{fr} > T_{cu} \\ \frac{1}{2}(T_{fr} + T_e) \text{ if } T_{fr} > T_{cu} \text{ and } T_e > T_{cu} \end{cases} \qquad (10.14)$$

The following assumptions have been made here:

- If $T_{fr} < T_{cl}$: the heating system ensures that the indoor temperature never falls below the lower limit of the comfort temperature.
- If $T_{cl} \leq T_{fr} \leq T_{cu}$: the internal temperature can be anything between T_{cl} and T_{cu} depending upon the airflow rate. If the flow rate is zero, then $T_i = T_{fr}$.

In any case, the flow should not exceed a critical value in order to prevent the internal temperature from falling below the lower limit of comfort.

- If $T_e \leq T_{cu}$ and $T_{fr} > T_{cu}$: free cooling is used to make sure that the internal temperature is, at the most, at the upper limit of the comfort temperature.
- If $T_{fr} > T_{cu}$ and $T_e > T_{cu}$: the assumption is made that no air-conditioning system is used. The internal temperature can be anything between T_e and T_{fr} depending upon the airflow rate. If wind is absent, an equilibrium temperature between both of these values will be reached because, on the one hand, if the airflow drops, T_i will tend towards T_{fr} and the stack effect will then induce a flow due to the difference between T_i and T_e. On the other hand, an increasing flow will bring T_i closer to T_e, decreasing the stack-induced flow. Both trends balance each other out towards an equilibrium temperature well approximated by $1/2(T_{fr} + T_e)$.

By defining δ_v as:

$$\delta_v = \begin{cases} 1, \text{ when } T_{cl} \leq T_{fr} \leq T_{cu} \\ 0, \text{ otherwise} \end{cases} \tag{10.15}$$

and by considering (10.14), the internal temperature can be written as follows:

$$T_i = T_{cl}\delta_h + T_{fr}\delta_v + T_{cu}\delta_{fc} + \frac{1}{2}(T_{fr} + T_e)\delta_c \tag{10.16}$$

This expression can be inserted in (10.13) in order to calculate *ST*.

Criterion related to noise

The criterion related to noise is defined as:

$$NT = \frac{1}{N}\sum_{i=1}^{N} NL_i \tag{10.17}$$

where NL_i is the noise level; *NT* stands for *noise time*.

Criterion related to pollution

The criterion related to pollution is defined as:

$$PT = \frac{1}{N}\sum_{i=1}^{N} PL_i \tag{10.18}$$

where PL_i is the pollution level; *PT* stands for *noise time*.

Frequency distributions

Degree hours can be calculated as soon as we know the monthly variation of daily mean temperature (time series). However, this approach has two disadvantages: the data are not easily available and, if accessible, they should be available for numerous years (typically 5 to 20 years) in order to be statistically significant. An alternative to using time series of daily mean temperature is to use the probability distribution of daily mean temperature. The probability distribution is obtained on measurements achieved during long periods of time. The same goes for wind speed distributions.

Let us suppose that the probability density function, $pdf(x)$, of a random variable x is known. Then, the average, $\bar{f}$, of a function, $f(x)$, is given by:

$$\bar{f} = \lim_{N \to \infty} \frac{1}{N} \sum_{i=1}^{N} f_i = \int_{-\infty}^{\infty} pdf(x)\, f(x)\, dx \qquad (10.19)$$

Let us now suppose that the probability density function, $pdf_{jk}(x)$, depends upon the month j of the year and on the hour k of the day. In this case, the average $\bar{f}_{jk}$ for month j and hour k is given by:

$$\bar{f}_{jk} = \lim_{N \to \infty} \frac{1}{N} \sum_{\substack{i=1 \\ i \in E_{ji}}}^{N} f_{jk_i} = \int_{-\infty}^{\infty} pdf_{jk}(x)\, f_{jk}(x)\, dx \qquad (10.20)$$

where E_{jk} is the set of instants i belonging to month j and to hour k.

The monthly average $\bar{f}_j$ for month j and the hourly average $\bar{f}_k$ for hour k are given by:

$$\bar{f}_j = \frac{1}{H} \sum_{k=1}^{H} \bar{f}_{jk} \qquad (10.21)$$

$$\bar{f}_k = \frac{1}{M} \sum_{j=1}^{M} \bar{f}_{jk} \qquad (10.22)$$

where H is the number of hours considered in a day, in our case four, and M is the number of months considered in a year, usually 12. The yearly average can be written as:

$$\bar{f} = \frac{1}{H\,M} \sum_{j=1}^{M} \sum_{k=1}^{H} \bar{f}_{jk} \qquad (10.23)$$

Degree hours

For a function $f_{jk}(T)$ of the external temperature, the average $\bar{f}_{jk}$ is given by:

$$\bar{f}_{jk} \cong \int_{-\infty}^{\infty} N_{jk}(T_e)\, f_{jk}(T_e)\, dT_e \qquad (10.24)$$

with $N_{jk}(T_e)$ the normal probability density function for external temperatures:

$$N(x) = \frac{1}{\sigma\sqrt{2\pi}} \exp\left(-\frac{1}{2} \left(\frac{x-\mu}{\sigma}\right)^2 \right) \qquad (10.25)$$

where μ is the mean and σ^2 is the variance of variable x.

By replacing $f_{jk}(x)$ by $[(T_{cl}(x) - T_{fr_{jk}}(x)]\delta_{h_{jk}}(x)$ in (10.24), the degree hours for heating related to month j and to hour k can be rewritten as (see equation (10.8)):

$$\overline{DH}_{hjk} = \int_{-\infty}^{\infty} N_{jk}(T_e) \, (T_{cl}(T_e) - T_{fr_{ji}}(T_e)) \, \delta_{h_{ji}}(T_e) \, dT_e \qquad (10.26)$$

In fact, the right-hand side of this equation is the limit when N goes to infinity of the right-hand side of equation (10.8), whose summation is restricted to values of i belonging to set E_{jk}.

Similarly, degree hours for cooling and degrees hours of energy saved for cooling by natural ventilation can be rewritten, respectively, as:

$$\overline{DH}_{cjk} = \int_{-\infty}^{\infty} N_{jk}(T_e) \, (T_{fr_{ji}}(T_e) - T_{cu}(T_e)) \, \delta_{c_{ji}}(T_e) \, dT_e \qquad (10.27)$$

$$\overline{DH}_{fcjk} = \int_{-\infty}^{\infty} N_{jk}(T_e) \, (T_{fr_{ji}}(T_e) - T_{cu}(T_e)) \, \delta_{fc_{ji}}(T_e) \, dT_e \qquad (10.28)$$

Criterion related to wind

For a function $f_{jk}(v)$ of the wind speed, the average $\overline{f}_{jk}$ is given by:

$$\overline{f}_{jk} \cong \int_{-\infty}^{\infty} W_{jk}(v) \, f_{jk}(v) \, dv \qquad (10.29)$$

with $W_{jk}(v)$ the Weibull probability density function for wind speed:

$$W(x) = \begin{cases} a \, b \, x^{b-1} \exp(-ax^b) & \text{if } x > 0 \\ 0 & \text{if } x \leq 0 \end{cases} \qquad (10.30)$$

where a and b are two strictly positive parameters.

If $f(v)$ is replaced by the squared local wind speed, it comes out that *wind time* for month j and for hour k can be written as:

$$\overline{WT}_{jk} = \int_{-\infty}^{\infty} W_{jk}(v) \, v^{local}(v) \, dv \qquad (10.31)$$

The local wind speed is, indeed, a function of the undisturbed wind speed as explained in 'Influence of the urban environment on the local wind speed'.

Criterion related to stack effect

If $f_{jk}(T_e)$ is replaced by $\left| \dfrac{T_{i_{jk}} - T_e}{T_e} \right|$ in (10.29), *stack time* for month j and for hour k can be written as:

$$\overline{ST}_{jk} = \int_{-\infty}^{\infty} N_{jk}(T_e) \left| \frac{T_{i_{jk}}(T_e) - T_e}{T_e} \right| dT_e \qquad (10.32)$$

Criterion related to noise

As solely one value is assigned for the noise level for daytime and one for night time throughout the year, equation (10.17) can simply be written as:

$$NT = \frac{1}{2}(NL_{\text{daytime}} + NL_{\text{night-time}}) \qquad (10.33)$$

Criterion related to pollution

For the same reasons, equation (10.18) can simply be written as:

$$PT = \frac{1}{2}(PL_{\text{daytime}} + PL_{\text{night-time}}) \qquad (10.34)$$

MULTI-CRITERIA ANALYSIS

Multi-criteria analysis is a technique devoted to simplifying a decision problem and to solving it. The problem is made up of several possibly conflicting objectives, translated into criteria. An example is given in 'Principles of the multi-criteria analysis method Qualiflex' below. The expected result of a multi-criteria evaluation is an action or a group of actions to be taken (Schärlig, 1990a, 1990b). In our case, the actions are 'to build in a given place' and the decision is 'where to build.' This is why *action* and *location* have the same meaning in the following text.

Why multi-criteria analysis ...

Two main reasons led to the choice of multi-criteria analysis as a tool for evaluating the potential for natural ventilation. First, the driving forces and constraints mentioned above make up several criteria that are not commensurable (Schärlig, 1990a, p37). In other words, except, perhaps, wind and stack pressure translated into airflow rates, they cannot be reduced to a single criterion. Second, the intention is to be exhaustive and thus to take into account the entire set of criteria involved in natural ventilation – namely, in our case, wind and stack pressure, noise and pollution.

Moreover, the airflow due to wind depends upon numerous parameters seldom known with sufficient precision (see, for instance, the remark on pressure coefficients in 'Wind pressure'). In fact, one of the advantages of multi-criteria analysis applied here is that the airflow does not need to be known precisely: stating that a higher wind speed (and, thus, a larger wind-induced airflow) will be present in a given location will suffice. This, of course, is valid only under the assumption that the airflow rate is an increasing function of the wind speed.

... rather than traditional models?

This way of reasoning suits the philosophy according to which *approximately correct* results are preferable to *exactly wrong* ones. Traditional 'exact' modelling, such as computational fluid dynamics (CFD) and zonal models (e.g. Feustel and Dieris, 1992), give results that are very sensitive to input data (Fürbringer, 1994). Moreover, these data are not readily available with sufficient accuracy. The models present the following additional drawbacks:

- They do not process qualitative knowledge.
- The results depend strongly upon the user, who should be an expert in the field.
- They do not provide directly and automatically the uncertainty of the outcomes.

Moreover, each of these models has a restricted field of application and none of them allows for a global and systemic approach. For example, none of them is able to completely model natural ventilation as the combined effect of wind and temperature gradients in a multi-zone building with large openings.

One of the reasons to use multi-criteria analysis is to obtain a pre-design tool. Computational fluid dynamics, zonal models and so on are design tools which can be used during the advanced stages of designing a building; they are not suitable for the first steps of pre-designing a building.

Procedure for evaluating a site

In order to evaluate a site from the natural ventilation potential point of view, the intention is to avoid simply giving a 'mark' to it. The results of the evaluation will be a ranking of the site in comparison with other well-known sites, referred to as *base sites*. The potential for natural ventilation of these sites is known, so that the ranking amongst them of the site to be assessed will provide its potential. In a sense, the base sites supply a scale of values.

The base sites are to be entered by an expert user, leaving the assessment (strictly speaking) to the 'normal' user. In addition, meaningful results will be provided together with this ranking.

Procedure for choosing base sites

The whole evaluation process relies on a set of well-known base sites. Several such sites are delivered with the tool; but the user may like to add some more – for example, in order to make the ranking more accurate, or to compare the assessed site with others that are well known to the user. The criteria such sites should fulfil are defined below.

The following characteristics will be available:

- NVP for this site, known from experience or from indoor air quality (IAQ) in existing, naturally ventilated buildings;

Table 10.3 *Example of the characteristics of a minimal but optimal set of base sites*

Building	1	2	3	4	5	6
Natural ventilation potential (NVP)	Low	Low	Good	Good	Low	Low
Urban fabric	Suburban	Urban	Urban	Suburban	Suburban	Urban
Exposed to wind	Yes	No	Yes	No	No	No
Outdoor temperature	Cold	Warm	Cold	Cold	Warm	Cold
Noise	Noisy	Noisy	Silent	Silent	Silent	Noisy
Pollution	Polluted	Clean	Clean	Clean	Polluted	Polluted

- location (climatic data is provided by the program from this location);
- urban fabric typology (e.g. open field, suburb, dense buildings, canyon, etc.);
- noise environment (silent, acceptable, unacceptable) during the day and night;
- outdoor air quality (clean, acceptable, unacceptable) – i.e. if pollution hinders natural ventilation or not.

The set of base sites should be distributed within the whole five-dimension volume defined by the five variables mentioned above. An evaluation could be performed with only two base sites (e.g. a rather good and a rather poor site from the NVP point of view); but the evaluation will be more accurate if more buildings are included. Ideally, between 20 and 40 base cases will be useful for each climatic zone: two different NVPs, four urban typologies, and two noise and two pollution levels. However, a set of few sites could be defined using an optimal design, provided that such specified sites exist. Table 10.3 shows an example of such a minimum set of sites.

Selected multi-criteria analysis method

Since some criteria are qualitative, particularly pollution (see 'Pollution'), the selected multi-criteria analysis method must be qualitative. The method Qualiflex was chosen. This method ranks locations as a function of their ranking in each single criterion. This method has been adapted for its use in the current methodology with regard to weights (see 'Adaptive weights').

Principles of the multi-criteria analysis method Qualiflex

The principles of Qualiflex (Paelinck, 1976, 1978, 1979) are explained hereafter in a simplified way as a result of an example made up of three actions a_1, a_2, a_3 (three sites in our case) and three criteria c_1, c_2, c_3.

Table 10.4 *Input table*

	c_1	c_2	c_3
Weight	5	4	1
a_1	*1*	*2*	*3*
a_2	*2*	*1*	*3*
a_3	*2*	*3*	*2*

Note: The ranking matrix elements are represented by figures in italics.

Let us assume that each action (each site in our case) is assigned a rank for each criterion and that each criterion is assigned a weight. Figures in italics in Table 10.4 represent the *ranking matrix* elements.

In this example, for the first criterion (whose weight is 5), a_1 is better placed than a_2 and a_3, which, in turn, are equally placed.

The next step consists in considering all of the possible action rankings R_i, for $i = 1, \dots (3!)$.

- R_1: a_1, a_2, a_3;
- R_2: a_2, a_1, a_3;
- R_3: a_3, a_1, a_2;
- R_4: a_3, a_2, a_1;
- R_5: a_2, a_3, a_1;
- R_6: a_1, a_3, a_2.

For each ranking R_i and for each criterion, the concordance with the ranking matrix must be checked by comparing every couple of actions. Each time the relative position is the same in the ranking matrix of the problem data and in the ranking R_i, a so-called concordance index is incremented by one; when the relative position is different, the concordance index is decremented by one.

In our example, let us consider ranking R_4 and criterion c_2. For each couple of actions:

1 R_4 causes a_2 to be better placed than a_1; so does the matrix for criterion c_2. As a result, the concordance index is incremented.
2 R_4 causes a_3 to be better placed than a_1. The matrix causes a_1 to be better placed than a_3 for criterion c_2. The concordance index is thus decremented.
3 R_4 causes a_3 to be better placed than a_2. The matrix causes a_2 to be better placed than a_3 for criterion c_2. The concordance index is thus decremented.

Therefore, the value of the concordance index for R_4 and c_2 is $1 - 1 - 1 = -1$. By repeating this operation for every couple (R_i, c_j), the concordance indices take the values given in Table 10.5.

A so-called global concordance index is then calculated for every ranking by adding the concordance indices of the ranking beforehand, multiplied by

Table 10.5 *Matrix of concordance indices*

	c_1	c_2	c_3
Weight	5	4	1
R_1	2	1	-2
R_2	0	3	-2
R_3	-2	1	0
R_4	-2	-1	2
R_5	0	-3	2
R_6	2	-1	0

the corresponding weight. For example, the global concordance index of R_4 is: $-2 \times 5 - 1 \times 4 + 2 \times 1 = -12$. The resulted rankings are given in Table 10.6.

If these indices are considered, the first ranking R_1 accords best with the data of the problem. Therefore, the ranking R_1, which causes a_1 to be better placed than a_2, and a_3 to be better placed than a_2, will be chosen.

Table 10.6 *Global concordance indices*

	Global concordance index
R_1	12
R_2	10
R_3	-6
R_4	-12
R_5	-10
R_6	6

Adaptive weights

The weights that appear in a multi-criteria analysis method represent, in a way, the importance of the related criterion. Usually, when a set of weights has to be drawn up, a committee of experts is brought together and comes to an agreement. Occasionally, an agreement is not even found and several multi-criteria analyses are carried out with the various sets of weights (hoping that the outcome is the same).

Frequently, weights are subjective and can depend upon the value system of the decision-maker(s), especially when the decision is of a political nature. In our case, some inhabitants may be more tolerant of noise in a given country than in another, and will assign a lower weight to this criterion.

With regard to the wind and stack effect criteria, the weights should not be subjective at all since physical phenomena are involved.

This weight problem has been solved in the current methodology by considering things in a reverse way: the set of weights results from the ranking of the locations and from the ranking matrix. Put another way, all of the weights contained between two chosen values are enumerated until one set is compatible with the mentioned ranking. The compatibility is checked by running Qualiflex each time. The sites ranked in this way are referred to as *base sites*. Clearly, an infinite number of sets are possible. The first encountered can be arbitrarily selected.

The ranking has to be worked out by an expert user who knows the base sites from a natural ventilation potential point of view and can create new base sites. If the case arises, the expert will rank a new site against the other base sites and launch a new search for weights. Base sites may also be removed, if required. Once the set of weights is fixed, it can be used for the initial purpose of the method – namely, to assess a new site.

Let us consider the example given above in which we try to find a set of weights and suppose that the expert proposes the following ranking: a_1, a_3, a_2. By enumerating all of the weights from 5 down to 0, we start with $w_1 = 5$, $w_2 = 5$ and $w_3 = 5$. With this set and with the ranking matrix given in Table 10.1, Qualiflex provides the following ranking: a_1, a_2, a_3.

Since this is not the ranking chosen by expert, the set of weights ($w_1 = 5$, $w_2 = 5$, $w_3 = 5$) has to be discarded. The same ranking comes out with the subsequently enumerated sets:

- $w_1 = 5, w_2 = 5, w_3 = 4$;
- $w_1 = 5, w_2 = 5, w_3 = 3$;
- $w_1 = 5, w_2 = 5, w_3 = 2$;
- $w_1 = 5, w_2 = 5, w_3 = 1$.

These must thus be discarded, as well. With the subsequent set ($w_1 = 5, w_2 = 4, w_3 = 5$), Qualiflex provides the ranking a_1, a_3, a_2. Since this is the ranking chosen by the expert, the following weights are retained: $w_1 = 5, w_2 = 4, w_3 = 5$. These can then be used in a 'normal' multi-criteria analysis, as presented in 'Principles of the multi-criteria analysis method Qualiflex' for evaluating a fourth action, a_4.

SOFTWARE TOOL

This section is not meant to be a user's guide for the software included in the accompanying CD (the reader will find such a guide in the CD). Instead, it describes the purpose of the steps encountered during the execution of the program.

The user has two possibilities at the beginning of the execution: he can either *add a new base site* or *assess the potential for natural ventilation of a new site*. In both cases, a new row of the ranking matrix (see 'Principles of the multi-criteria analysis method Qualiflex') has to be filled for the new site.

In the first case, once the new row of the ranking matrix is filled out, the user must provide a ranking of the base sites and start a search for a set of weights, which has to be compatible with both the matrix and the ranking. The base sites and the weights are stored in a database.

In the second case, once the ranking matrix is filled, the program supplies a ranking drawn up with the previously established weights.

Filling out the ranking matrix

Several frames (questionnaires) appear during the program execution in order to collect information from the user.

The user is asked to enter the location of interest. The coordinates are then used to determine the undisturbed wind speed and direction through time.

The user is then asked to enter the environment of the place of interest and the characteristics of the canyon located there, if any. These inputs, along with the undisturbed wind features, assess the local wind speed and direction. Outdoor temperatures are retrieved from the weather database due to the location entered by the user.

The user then enters qualitative daytime and night-time noise levels in accordance with Table 10.2. Finally, the user is asked to enter qualitative pollution levels. Pollution levels can be selected only qualitatively. The reason is that quantitative pollution levels would require substantial numbers of measurements from the user. Moreover, long-term *and* short-term limiting values exist for the pollutants of interest: nitrogen dioxide, sulphur dioxide, carbon monoxide, ozone and volatile organic components, amongst other pollutants. Finally, the transport and transformation of pollutants is complex (Clappier et al, 2000). However, pollution maps may be used, although these do not yet cover Europe.

Example

Let us consider the example given in the user's guide on the accompanying CD. The following base sites are entered in the database according to the ranking given in Table 10.7, with the same convention as in Table 10.4. Every criterion is found to have a weight of 5.

Table 10.7 *Ranking matrix before Lausanne's entry*

	WT	ST	PT	NT
Weight	5	5	5	5
La Rochelle	1	3	2	1
Brussels	2	1	2	3
London	3	2	1	3
Porto	4	4	2	2

In the example, a new site (Lausanne) is assessed and ranked by the multi-criteria analysis in third position (see Table 10.8).

Table 10.8 *Ranking matrix after Lausanne's entry*

	WT	ST	PT	NT
Weight	5	5	5	5
La Rochelle	1	3	2	1
Brussels	3	1	2	3
Lausanne	4	2	1	3
London	2	4	2	3
Porto	5	5	2	2

Rather than assign a mark to the new site, the user can state that it is better than London and not as good as Brussels from the natural ventilation potential point of view.

The program also provides a set of graphs.

Natural ventilation potential graphs

Three graphs have been retained for this topic:

1 the average squared wind speed;
2 the average stack temperature difference;
3 the fraction of time when free (passive) cooling is possible.

The first two graphs correspond to the first two criteria used in the multi-criteria analysis and are strictly associated with (hygienic) ventilation potential and not with any passive cooling potential. Indoor temperatures have been determined on the basis of the ventilation strategy to be applied, in accordance with equation (10.16).

The third graph provides the *fraction of time when free cooling is possible*, given by:

$$\frac{1}{N} \sum_{i=1}^{N} \delta_{fc_i} \qquad (10.35)$$

with:

$$\delta_{fc} = \begin{cases} 1, \text{ when } T_{fr} > T_{cu} \text{ and } T_e \leq T_{cu} \\ 0, \text{ otherwise} \end{cases} \qquad (10.36)$$

The summation counts, amongst N instants, the occurrences when free cooling is possible – that is, when both the following conditions are met:

- the air is too warm indoors ($T_{fr} > T_{cu}$);
- the outside air is cool enough to cool down the building ($T_e \leq T_{cu}$).

This kind of situation is particularly encountered during the night-time hours of summer if the building has a large thermal inertia.

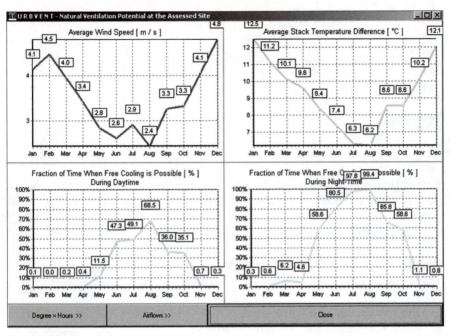

Source: Natural ventilation potential software

Figure 10.5 *Natural ventilation potential graphs (Lausanne, Switzerland)*

Remark

Criteria related to a *passive cooling potential* (PCP) could be defined by weighting the terms of the summation in equation (10.35) by the terms encountered in the criteria related to wind in equation (10.12), to stack effect in equation (10.13), to noise in equation (10.17) and to pollution in equation (10.18). These criteria would take the following form:

$$WT_{\text{PCP}} = \frac{1}{N} \sum_{i=1}^{N} v_i^{\text{local}} \delta_{fc_i} \tag{10.37}$$

$$ST_{\text{PCP}} = \frac{1}{N} \sum_{i=1}^{N} \left| \frac{T_{i} - T_{e_i}}{T_{e_i}} \right| \delta_{fc_i} \tag{10.38}$$

$$NT_{\text{PCP}} = \frac{1}{N} \sum_{i=1}^{N} NL_i \, \delta_{fc_i} \tag{10.39}$$

$$PT_{\text{PCP}} = \frac{1}{N} \sum_{i=1}^{N} PL_i \, \delta_{fc_i} \tag{10.40}$$

However, this passive cooling potential will not be addressed here.

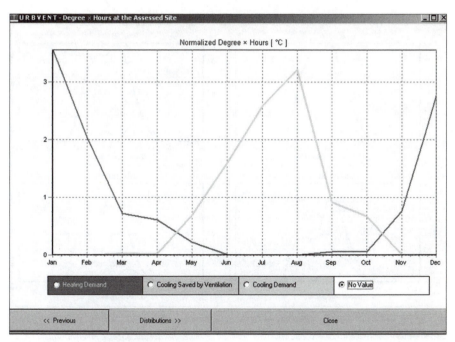

Source: Natural ventilation potential software

Figure 10.6 *Degree-hours graphs (Lausanne, Switzerland)*

Graphs of degree hours

These graphs (see Figure 10.6) represent the degree hours associated with:

- the heating demand;
- the cooling saved by ventilation; and
- the cooling demand.

These degree hours can also be obtained in a distribution form, as shown in Figure 10.7. This is very useful for sizing heating or cooling systems.

Airflow graph

Only airflow due to stack effect is displayed (see Figure 10.8), without accounting for the effect of wind pressure. This graph presents airflow in a very simple example, comprising a room with two openings, as sketched in the top left corner. This is a monthly averaged value, which does not guarantee that the airflow is always sufficient. Both apertures have the same area *A* and have a vertical distance of *H*. This airflow is calculated by means of equation (10.4).

Analysing the graphs: An example

The aim of this section is to explain how to interpret the graphical results and to stress the difference between months and between different locations in the

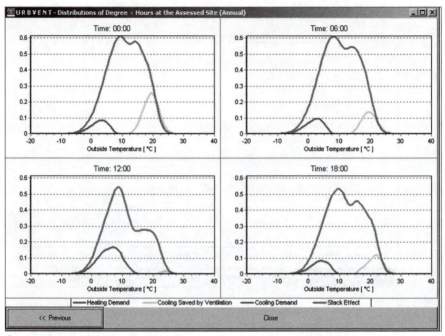

Source: Natural ventilation potential software

Figure 10.7 *Degree-hour distributions and inside–outside temperature difference ('stack effect') distributions*

example of Lausanne, Switzerland (see above) and Seville, Spain. Two distant sites have been selected for this case study in order to emphasize the differences encountered in the graphs. However, according to the situation, the user may need to compare different sites in the same city. In this case, local factors, such as local street geometry or local noise conditions, prevail in the ranking process.

Natural ventilation potential graphs

Figure 10.5 emphasizes the fact that stack effect is primarily due to temperature differences induced by the heating system. As one can see, the average stack temperature difference is higher during the heating season. Moreover, the assumption has been made that no cooling system is used, creating few stack effects during the 'cooling season'. If air conditioning were used, the outside–inside temperature difference would induce buoyancy; but this would be useless for ventilation purposes anyway since air conditioning already provides ventilation.

On the other hand, when considering the situation in Lausanne, Switzerland (see Figure 10.5), free (passive) cooling is almost only possible during summer. In fact, free cooling is possible only if the inside temperature is higher than the upper limit of comfort *and* if the outside temperature is lower

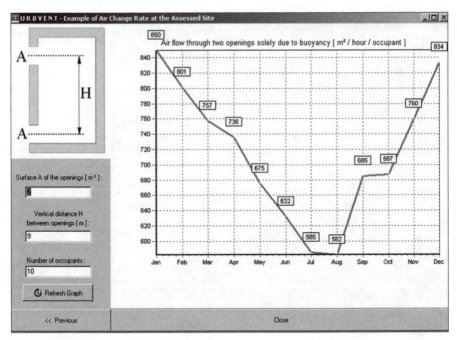

Source: Natural ventilation potential software

Figure 10.8 *Airflow graph (Lausanne, Switzerland)*

than this limit. This configuration is met especially during summer night-time hours in Lausanne. The situation in Seville, Spain (see Figure 10.9) is quite different in the sense that free cooling is also possible during spring and autumn.

Graphs of degree hours

When comparing the situations in Lausanne (see Figure 10.6) and Seville (see Figure 10.10), it is evident that the heating demand is higher in Lausanne and that the cooling demand is higher in Seville. Regarding the cooling demand, it should be stressed that it concerns a *cooling requirement when free cooling is not possible*, as opposed to cooling saved by ventilation. Thus, at a given time, the cooling may be achieved by ventilation (indicated in the 'cooling saved by ventilation' graph) or by mechanical cooling (indicated in the 'cooling demand' graph).

Expressed another way, in the case of Seville, the cooling demand can only be fulfilled by air conditioning. However, the decision can be made to avoid air conditioning and to tolerate higher temperatures in the building (or to adapt oneself to them). According to Figure 10.6, this situation is never encountered in Lausanne and this is corroborated by the fact that air conditioning is very seldom used in that city.

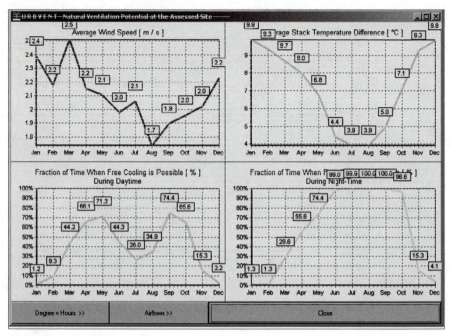

Figure 10.9 *Natural ventilation potential graphs (Seville, Spain)*

Airflow graph

The minimal airflow requirements are fulfilled as soon as pollutant concentrations in the room are acceptable. Frequently, the larger airflow needs come from odours and carbon dioxide evacuation and range from approximately 10 cubic metres (m^3) to $30m^3$ per hour and per occupant. As shown in Figure 10.8, these rates are largely exceeded.

SOFTWARE VALIDATION

This validation concerns only the part of the software that *ranks* the sites from the natural ventilation potential point of view, regardless of the graphs. It is important to mention that this piece of software is almost impossible to validate because it assesses a potential (i.e. something pre-existing the building and that has to be capitalized by the building's architecture). This is seldom entirely the case. In other words, the suppositions made in 'Assumptions of the methodology' are hardly ever fulfilled. However, a validation has been carried out, bearing in mind that one should keep an open mind about its results.

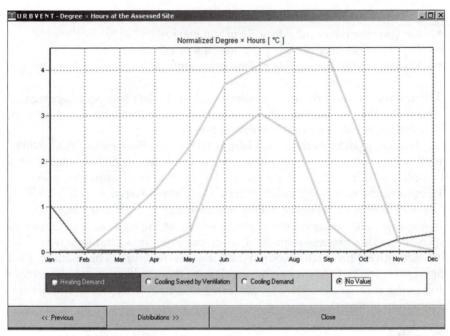

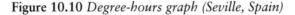

Source: Natural ventilation potential software

Figure 10.10 *Degree-hours graph (Seville, Spain)*

Method

The method chosen for the validation was based on a survey carried out within the frame of the European project HOPE (Health Optimization Protocol for Energy-Efficient Buildings) (Bluyssen et al, 2003), whose aim, amongst others, is to solve the conflict between strategies to reduce energy use and strategies to create healthy buildings. A substantial number of questionnaires have been distributed and perused. Amongst the questions, several have been considered relevant for the present validation. Some questions were related to indoor air quality and have been used here to describe the extent of the natural ventilation driving forces. These included the following:

- In winter, do you experience bad smells coming from furnishings, the kitchen or the stairway?
- In summer, do you experience bad smells coming from furnishings, the kitchen or the stairway?
- Is air odourless in winter?
- Is air odourless in summer?

Other questions, on external noise and external pollution, have been retained to describe the extent of the constraints. These were:

- Do you experience outside noise in winter?
- Do you experience outside noise in summer?
- Do you experience outside pollution in winter?
- Do you experience outside pollution in summer?

The answers to the first four questions and to the last four were aggregated separately. The two ensuing aggregation results were then aggregated, in turn, in order to provide a natural ventilation potential.

The aggregation method used here is Hermione (Flourentzou et al, 2003). It allows several levels of aggregation (such as the ones just mentioned) and is completely independent of the method Qualiflex used until this point. In Hermione, the user assigns each criterion to a class: Green + (best); Green o; Green –; Yellow +; Yellow o; Yellow –; Red +; Red o; Red –; or Black (worst). In our case, each criterion corresponds to one of the eight above-mentioned questions. This process requires a strict correspondence table between the answers given for each question and a class (colour). The method then aggregates the criteria and assigns a class to the newly aggregated criterion following democratic rules. In our case, this final criterion is the natural ventilation potential.

Results

Nine sites across Europe with naturally ventilated homes were selected to validate the software (see Table 10.9). Among them, four were chosen as base sites in order to provide a 'representative scale' of classes. These sites are written between square brackets in Table 10.9, along with their respective Hermione-assigned class according to the answers in the questionnaires.

The four base sites were introduced in the software database and the following set of weights was found: (5, 3, 5, 5) (see 'Adaptive weights'). These weights show that all of the criteria have roughly the same importance and that they are all relevant since none is equal to zero. Keeping these weights, the program finds the rankings for the five remaining sites; the results are given in Table 10.10.

Table 10.9 *HOPE sites and Hermione classes*

Site	Hermione class
[Switzerland 1] Switzerland 2	Green +
Germany 1 [Switzerland 3]	Green o
Switzerland 4	Green –
[Switzerland 5] Portugal 1 [Germany 2]	Yellow +
Italy 1	Yellow –

Table 10.10 *Ranking of Switzerland 2 compared with base sites (in square brackets)*

Site
[Switzerland 1]
Switzerland 2
[Switzerland 3]
[Switzerland 5]
[Germany 2]

Table 10.11 *Ranking of Germany 1 compared with base sites (in square brackets)*

Site
[Switzerland 1]
Germany 1
[Switzerland 3]
[Switzerland 5]
[Germany 2]

Table 10.12 *Ranking of Switzerland 4 compared with base sites (in square brackets)*

Site
[Switzerland 1]
[Switzerland 3]
Switzerland 4
[Switzerland 5]
[Germany 2]

Table 10.13 *Ranking of Portugal 1 compared with base sites (in square brackets)*

Site
[Switzerland 1]
[Switzerland 3]
[Switzerland 5]
Portugal 1
[Germany 2]

Table 10.14 *Ranking of Italy 1 compared with base sites (in square brackets)*

Site
[Switzerland 1]
[Switzerland 3]
[Switzerland 5]
[Germany 2]
Italy 1

It can be noticed that each of the five rankings provided by the software tool is in full agreement with the ranking of Table 10.9. For each of them, the probability that this agreement is due to pure luck is $^1/_5$. The probability that this agreement is due to chance for the entire set of rankings is $(\frac{1}{5})^5 = \frac{1}{3125} = 0.032\%$.

SENSITIVITY ANALYSIS

A sensitivity analysis has been conducted on the last ranking (see Table 10.14) to check the effect of small variations of the weight values on the ranking itself. For this purpose, a Plackett–Burman design (Plackett and Burman, 1943) has been carried out by varying the weights by −1 or +1. In order to lighten the notation, 'Switzerland 1', 'Switzerland 3', 'Switzerland 5', 'Germany 2' and 'Italy 1' have been assigned numbers 1, 2, 3, 4 and 5, respectively, so that the ranking of Table 10.14 can be written as (1, 2, 3, 4, 5).

Table 10.15 shows a Plackett–Burman design in eight runs. The weight variations are given in columns 2 to 5 and the resulting ranking is in column 6. For instance, in the first run, weights 6, 4, 6 and 4 are assigned to the four criteria, since the initial weights were 5, 3, 5 and 5.

Table 10.15 *Plackett–Burman design*

Run	Wind time	Stack time	Noise time	Pollution time	Ranking
1	+1	+1	+1	−1	(1, 2, 3, 4, 5)
2	+1	+1	−1	+1	(1, 4, 3, 2, 5)
3	+1	−1	+1	−1	(1, 2, 3, 4, 5)
4	−1	+1	−1	−1	(1, 4, 3, 2, 5)
5	+1	−1	−1	+1	(1, 3, 4, 2, 5)
6	−1	−1	+1	+1	(1, 2, 4, 3, 5)
7	−1	+1	+1	+1	(1, 2, 4, 3, 5)
8	−1	−1	−1	−1	(1, 2, 3, 4, 5)

The results show that the initial ranking (1, 2, 3, 4, 5) appears three times out of eight. A permanent feature is that site 1 (Switzerland 1) and site 5 (Italy 1) are always ranked in first and in last position, respectively.

CONCLUSIONS

It is important to conclude by emphasizing that the assessed natural ventilation potential is the potential of the *site*. Once a site with a good potential is found, the designer's task is to construct a building or to refurbish an existing one in a way that makes the most out of this potential. This is in accordance with the first assumption made is this chapter. In other words, both an appropriate site and an appropriate building are necessary conditions if natural ventilation is to be applied.

This is why this methodology is so difficult to validate: a proper validation would imply that buildings erected on the assessed site do take advantage of the best potential of those sites.

REFERENCES

Bluyssen, P. M., Cox, C., Maroni, M., Boschi, N., Raw, G., Roulet, C.-A. et al (2003) *European Project HOPE (Health Optimization Protocol For Energy-Efficient Buildings)*, Healthy Buildings, Singapore

Brager, G. and de Dear, R. (1998) 'Thermal adaptation in the built environment: A literature review', *Energy and Buildings*, vol 27, pp83–96

Chandra, S., Fairey, P. and Houston, M. (1983) *A Handbook for Designing Ventilated Buildings*, Florida Solar Energy Center, Final Report FSEC-CR-93-83, Florida.

Clappier, A., Martilli, A., Grossi, P., Thunis, P., Pasi, F., Krueger, B. C. et al (2000) 'Effect of sea breeze on air pollution in the Greater Athens Area. Part I: Numerical simulations and field observations', *Journal of Applied Meteorology*, vol 39, pp546–562

de Dear, R. (1999) *Adaptive Thermal Comfort in Natural and Hybrid Ventilation, Annex 35: Energy Conservation in Buildings and Community Systems*, International Energy Agency, Sydney, Australia

Feustel, H. E. and Dieris, J. (1992) 'A survey on air flow models for multizone structures', *Energy and Buildings*, vol 18, pp72–100

Flourentzou, F., Greuter, G. and Roulet, C.-A. (2003) *Hermione, une Nouvelle Méthode d'Agrégation Qualitative Basée sur des Règles*, 58èmes Journées du Groupe de Travail Européen d'Aide Multicritère à la Décision, Moscou, 9–11 Octobre 2003

Fountain, M., Brager, G. and de Dear, R. (1996) 'Expectations of indoor climate control', *Energy and Buildings*, vol 24, pp179–182

Fürbringer, J. M. (1994) *Sensibilité de modèles et de mesures en aéraulique du bâtiment à l'aide de plans d'expériences*, Thèse no 1217, Présentée au Département de Physique, École Polytechnique Fédérale de Lausanne, Suisse

Li, Y. and Delsante, A. (2001) 'Natural ventilation induced by combined wind and thermal forces', *Building and Environment*, vol 36, pp59–71

Nicol, F. J. (2001) *Characterizing Occupant Behaviour in Buildings: Towards a Stochastic Model Occupant Use of Windows, Lights, Blinds, Heaters and Fans*, Seventh International IBPSA Conference, Rio de Janeiro, Brazil

OPB (1986) 'Ordonnance sur la protection contre le bruit du 15 décembre 1986', *Etat* 3 juillet 2001

Orme, M. S., Liddament, M. and Wilson, A. (1994) *An Analysis and Data Summary of the AIVC's Numerical Database*. Technical Note AIVC 44, Air Infiltration and Ventilation Centre, University of Warwick, Coventry; Oscar Faber Partnership, St Albans

Paelinck, J. (1976) 'Qualitative multiple criteria analysis, environmental protection and multiregional development', *Papers of the Regional Science Association*, vol 36, pp59–74

Paelinck, J. (1978) 'Qualiflex, a flexible multiple-criteria method', *Economic Letters*, vol 3, pp193–197

Paelinck, J. (1979) 'The multicriteria method Qualiflex: Past experiences and recent developments', Working paper 1979/15, The Netherlands Economic Institute, Rotterdam

Plackett, R. L. and Burman, J. P. (1943) 'Design of optimum multifactoral experiments', *Biometrika*, vol 33, pp305–325

Sayigh, A. and Marafia, A. H. (1998) 'Thermal comfort and the development of bioclimatic concept in building design', *Renewable and Sustainable Energy Reviews*, vol 2 (1/2), pp3–24

Schärlig, A. (1990a) *Décider sur Plusieurs Critères*, Collection Diriger l'Entreprise, Presses Polytechniques et Universitaires Romandes, Lausanne

Schärlig, A. (1990b) *Pratiquer Électre et Prométhée*, Collection Diriger l'Entreprise, Presses Polytechniques et Universitaires Romandes, Lausanne

Steppeler, J., Bitzer, H.-W., Minotte, M. and Bonaventura, L. (2002) 'Nonhydrostatic atmospheric modeling using a z-coordinate representation', *Monthly Weather Review*, vol 130, no 8, pp2143–2149

11

Whole Life Costing of Ventilation Options

Cristian Ghiaus and Liam Roche

INTRODUCTION

Buildings are one of the biggest energy-consuming sectors. In Europe, approximately 30 per cent of energy is consumed in buildings, a large amount being used for heating (see Figure 11.1a). The main primary energy source is fossil (coal, oil and gas), with a small share of nuclear and renewable sources (see Figure 11.1b). Energy consumption increases constantly in the European Union, and it is estimated that by 2020 the import of energy will be larger than production (see Figure 11.1c). Two important solutions are discussed in this chapter: the development of energy production and demand management.

RENEWABLE ENERGY SOURCES

The development of renewable sources is hindered by financial and structural aspects. Although the price of energy obtained from renewable sources decreased considerably and is expected to decrease further (see Figure 11.2b), it will be 50 per cent more expensive than the electricity generated by gas burners (EC, 2001). Further development of renewable sources requires important financial efforts and aid through subsidies (EC, 2001). In addition, the structure of energy production is centralized around conventional sources (coal, oil and gas) and nuclear plants. In the short and medium term, it is estimated that conventional fuels will dominate energy sources.

The ease of use and the high energy value of oil explains its extensive consumption in Western economies after World War II (see Figure 11.2a). Despite the exponential growth in production and consumption, known

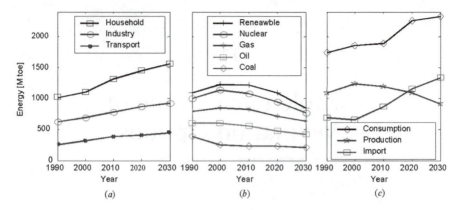

Source: EC, 2001

Figure 11.1 *Use of energy in Europe: (a) final energy consumption; (b) energy production by fuel; (c) total energy*

reserves also increased exponentially. Meanwhile, the price increased only linearly, except during the oil crises of the 1970s. The price per barrel is expected to exceed 20 Euros after 2000 (see Figure 11.2a).

The use of renewable sources on a larger scale is hindered by the price of the energy obtained from these sources and by the oil-centred organization of the economy. The price of the electricity obtained from renewable sources has decreased considerably and is expected to decrease further (see Figure 11.2b); however, it will still be 50 per cent higher than the price of the electricity generated by gas burners (EC, 2001). Generally, renewable sources need subsidies in order to be economically competitive with conventional solutions (EC, 2001). In addition to costs, the structure of energy production, which is centralized around conventional sources (coal, oil and gas) and nuclear plants, impedes the progress of the market of renewable sources. It is estimated that conventional fuels will dominate energy sources in the short and medium term. But the intensive use of fossil fuels seems to have negative effects on climate change due to greenhouse gas emissions. The Kyoto Protocol aims to reduce the carbon dioxide (CO_2) emissions of the developed countries specified in Annex 1 of the protocol. However, since the CO_2 emissions of developing countries will increase considerably during the following decades, the relative contribution of the developed countries will diminish (see Figure 11.2c). Due to the problems raised by the development of energy supply, demand management is considered to be the only way of meeting the challenges of climate change in the short term (EC, 2001).

The building sector is believed to be a major source for reducing energy consumption. In Europe, this reduction can be at least 20 per cent, which will represent 40 million tonnes oil equivalent (toe) per year, or the equivalent of 10 per cent of the oil consumption and 20 per cent of greenhouse gas emissions of the year 2000 (EC, 2001). The use of natural forces for controlling indoor

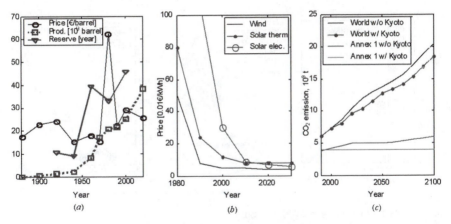

Source: DeMeo and Galdo, 1997; Lee et al, 1994; Lomborg, 2001

Figure 11.2 *Energy and CO_2 emissions: (a) oil price in US\$ per barrel (2000 figures) and oil production in millions of barrels and reserves in years; (b) price per kWh for renewable energy; (c) projected global CO_2 emissions*

comfort has the obvious advantage of negligible fossil-fuel consumption and greenhouse gas emissions.

The use of ventilation for cooling has an important potential in Western countries. We may estimate the energy savings for air conditioning if ventilation is used instead by assuming that, due to the thermal mass, the temperature differences between outdoors and indoors may be considered as daily means. If we then assume that the daily mean value of the free-running temperature is approximately 5°C higher than the mean outdoor temperature, the percentage of energy saved for mechanical cooling by using ventilation is as shown in Figure 11.3.

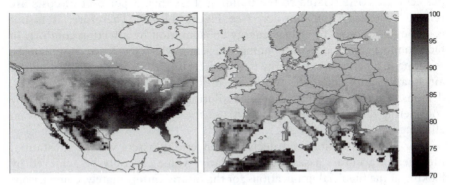

Figure 11.3 *Estimation of the percentage of energy saved for air conditioning when ventilation is used instead*

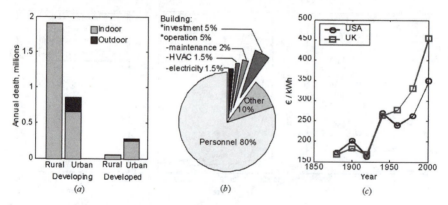

Source: WHO, 1997; Hanssen, 2000; Lomborg, 2001

Figure 11.4 *Socio-economic impact of energy in buildings: (a) estimated annual death from indoor and outdoor air pollution; (b) relative costs in office buildings; (c) economic efficiency of energy use*

In analysing the potential reduction of energy consumption in buildings, the two roles of buildings should be considered: providing a healthy indoor climate and comfort for its occupants. These issues are presented in more detail in Chapter 2. Health problems related to indoor air pollution differ between the developing and the developed world (see Figure 11.4a). In developing countries, the number of deaths due to indoor air pollution is higher in rural areas than in urban areas, while the situation is reversed in developed countries. Comfort is a very important factor, especially in the tertiary sector where it significantly influences productivity and contributes to the image of organizations. It is estimated that in office buildings in Western countries, approximately 80 per cent of expenses involve personnel costs and about 10 per cent are costs related to the building. Less then 3 per cent of costs are related to energy consumption (see Figure 11.4b). Therefore, it is not economically sound to reduce energy consumption by affecting comfort. In fact, comfort contributes to economic efficiency, which increased continuously, resulting in a better use of energy (see Figure 11.4c). The importance of indoor air quality and comfort, and their influence on health and efficiency, demonstrate that the effectiveness of solutions should be judged globally by considering the whole life cost analysis of the system and its implications on efficiency.

For any major financial decision concerning assets with a substantial lifetime, an accurate assessment of relative value can only be achieved by looking at the financial implications for the future. Unfortunately, comparisons are often incomplete, which may lead to increased financial burdens for companies at a later date. A crucial example is where there are two options available for a ventilation system. One is more economical than the other in terms of total capital and installation costs, but has higher maintenance and running costs. How are these to be fairly compared?

A widely accepted methodology for comparing such scenarios is to perform a life cycle cost–return calculation, which represents the current discounted cost corresponding to all of the costs (and benefits) associated with the choice over its lifetime. This calculation is described in the standard pr EN 13779. Other relevant standards include BS 5760-23 and ISO 15686. All initial and future costs and financial benefits associated with a choice are listed and estimated on a chronological scale; a discounting calculation is applied to determine what the equivalent current cost is for each item; then all of the discounted costs (negative values) and benefits (positive values) are combined into a single value: the whole life cost of the option. In the case where benefits have been fully accounted for, a choice that is worthwhile compared with the option of doing nothing is indicated by a positive return representing the financial benefit of a choice compared with doing nothing.

When comparing options that are for some essential functionality, obvious benefits that are common to all options are omitted. In the case of ventilation in buildings, the building could not operate at all without some sort of ventilation; but a simple calculation will ignore the assumed financial benefits associated with the normal operation of the building and look only at the incremental costs and benefits associated with each method of providing this essential service (BS ISO 15686). A highly significant possibility is the quantification of benefits associated with the normal operation of the building. Typically, salary-related costs dominate all other costs associated with the operation of most types of building, and may exceed by 100 times the energy bill in a modern office (see Figure 11.4b). Therefore, even small changes in productivity may dominate other financial implications. The difficulty is that productivity gains are difficult to quantify and to predict, and are subject to significant uncertainty. However, a number of quantitative studies exist, most of them indicating productivity gains from the use of natural ventilation (Fisk and Rosenfeld, 1997; Wargocki et al, 1999; Brightman and Moss, 2001; Fisk, 2001; Wargocki et al, 2003). In a range of studies, productivity gains between 0.4 per cent and 15 per cent were associated with providing local control of natural ventilation through the simple mechanism of an openable window.

Typically, the second most significant cost item associated with the choice of natural ventilation is the initial capital cost, which includes installation and commissioning costs. One guidance note (Martin and Fitzsimmons, 2000) suggests that a natural ventilation system will usually cost 10 to 15 per cent less than a mechanically ventilated alternative; but more exact figures should be used for the specific systems being examined, where information is available.

Other ongoing costs to be included are the energy consumption and the maintenance of the system over its lifetime. If possible, the indirect effect of the choice of system on costs associated with other systems should be taken into account, although this may sometimes be too complex to attempt. For example, the choice of a ventilation system may affect ventilation rates in winter, which has an effect on heating energy consumption (pr EN 13779, 2003).

It is possible to include the replacement and disposal costs of systems in calculations, as well. This is particularly relevant when dealing with systems that have relatively short lifetimes. In such a case, the full replacement and disposal costs may be included as a cost repeated at intervals equal to the expected life of the system. For systems with longer lifetimes, these costs are often ignored; but, in principle, it is better to include them. Of course, on a long time scale, there may be the option of adopting a different type of system, which makes assumed costs after this point of lesser importance.

The calculation

The calculation requires three types of data (BS 5760-23):

1   all costs and returns associated with a design choice;
2   a chosen time, the 'study period', beyond which all events will be ignored (ideally, this will be the operational life of the building; but in any case this needs to be long enough so that what happens afterwards is of little relevance to the current design decision);
3   discount rates (interest rates corrected for inflation) for the study period, representing the borrowing costs and investment returns that are affected by the choice made.

The real interest rate is related to nominal interest rates (rates actually charged or paid) by:

$$1+I_r = (1+I_n)/(1+F) \tag{11.1}$$

where I_r, I_n and F are the real and nominal interest rates and the rate of inflation expressed as fractions. For small values, the real interest rate is very close to the difference between the nominal interest rate and the inflation rate.

For example, if the interest rate is 5 per cent and the inflation rate is 2 per cent, then the appropriate discount rate is just under 3 per cent (in fact, $(1.05)/(1.02) - 1 = 0.0294 = 2.94$ per cent). Real interest rates tend to vary less with time than inflation or nominal interest rates, which commonly tend to go up and down together.

The calculation is most easily implemented in a spreadsheet containing each cost for each time interval (often a year) of the study period, and a column that contains the total costs for each time interval multiplied by the discounting factor, $1/(1 + I_r)^n$, where n is the year from the start (n can be fractional if shorter time intervals are used).

Example calculation for a two-storey office building

Suppose there are two design choices available, a mechanical ventilation system which has a capital cost of 117,000 Euros, with electricity costs of 6500 Euros per year and maintenance costs estimated at 5000 Euros every three years, and a natural ventilation system based on wind-driven roof vents with

Table 11.1 *Whole life cost/return of mechanical ventilation option*

Year	Discount factor (Euros)	Capital (Euros)	Maintenance (Euros)	Energy (Euros)	Discounted cost (Euros)
0	1.000	−117,000		−6500	−123,500.00
1	0.971			−6500	−6310.68
2	0.943			−6500	−6126.87
3	0.915		−5000	−6500	−10,524.13
4	0.888			−6500	−5775.17
5	0.863			−6500	−5606.96
6	0.837		−5000	−6500	−9631.07
7	0.813			−6500	−5285.09
8	0.789			−6500	−5131.16
9	0.766		−5000	−6500	−8813.79
10	0.744			−6500	−4836.61
11	0.722			−6500	−4695.74
12	0.701		−5000	−6500	−8065.87
13	0.681			−6500	−4426.18
14	0.661			−6500	−4297.27
15	0.642		−5000	−6500	−7381.41
16	0.623			−6500	−4050.59
17	0.605			−6500	−3932.61
18	0.587		−5000	−6500	−6755.04
19	0.570			−6500	−3706.86
20	0.554			−6500	−3598.89
				Total	−242,451.99

initial costs of 102,000 Euros, zero electricity costs and maintenance costs estimated at 500 Euros per year. In comparison with other similar buildings, it is estimated that a 2 per cent productivity improvement on a salary-related cost of 1 million Euros per year will be achieved with the naturally ventilated building.

Suppose the study period is set at 20 years and the real interest rate is assumed to be 3 per cent. The cost calculation is illustrated in Tables 11.1 and 11.2.

Note that these tables are intended only to exemplify the calculation method, using example data that has costs that are related in a typical way, and should not be used to justify any specific design. Every new ventilation design requires a similar calculation based on the best data available in order to assess it economically.

With the assumptions made, the mechanical ventilation system has a whole life cost of 242,000 Euros, whereas the natural ventilation system provides a positive return of 208,000 Euros. The natural ventilation system therefore saves 450,000 Euros compared to the mechanical ventilation system when capital, maintenance, energy and productivity costs are taken into account. It is notable that the effect on productivity dominates the calculation; but it can be seen that even if this factor is omitted, the natural ventilation option is found to be the better financial decision.

Table 11.2 *Whole life cost/return of natural ventilation option*

Year	Discount factor (Euros)	Capital (Euros)	Maintenance (Euros)	Energy (Euros)	Discounted cost (Euros)
0	1.000	−102,000	−500	20,000	−82,500.00
1	0.971		−500	20,000	18,932.04
2	0.943		−500	20,000	18,380.62
3	0.915		−500	20,000	17,845.26
4	0.888		−500	20,000	17,325.50
5	0.863		−500	20,000	16,820.87
6	0.837		−500	20,000	16,330.94
7	0.813		−500	20,000	15,855.28
8	0.789		−500	20,000	15,393.48
9	0.766		−500	20,000	14,945.13
10	0.744		−500	20,000	14,509.83
11	0.722		−500	20,000	14,087.21
12	0.701		−500	20,000	13,676.91
13	0.681		−500	20,000	13,278.55
14	0.661		−500	20,000	12,891.80
15	0.642		−500	20,000	12,516.31
16	0.623		−500	20,000	12,151.76
17	0.605		−500	20,000	11,797.82
18	0.587		−500	20.000	11,454.19
19	0.570		−500	20.000	11,120.58
20	0.554		−500	20/000	10,796.68
				Total:	207,610.76

CONCLUSIONS

It is considered that global warming due to excessive use of fossil fuels is one of the most important environmental issues that should be tackled in the short and medium term. The emission reduction of greenhouse gases can be brought about by changing the source of energy and by reducing consumption levels. Energy management represents the cheapest and the most direct way to address greenhouse gas emissions in the short term. The building sector offers large opportunities for this; it is thought that energy consumption could be reduced by 20 per cent in this sector. Heating needs may be reduced by improving thermal insulation and by reducing air infiltration. But these measures may result in discomfort during the hot season. Ventilation is the cheapest and the most convenient way to cool. Free cooling by ventilation has a very high potential for cooling, especially in temperate and northern regions. The use of natural forces for ventilation results in larger airflow rates and in the reduction of space occupied by ventilation gains. But the random variation of weather conditions imposes the automatic control of airflow and the support of mechanical systems when the natural forces are not available.

The cost of ventilation solutions should be judged over the whole-life period of building use. The major factor in this estimation is the health and comfort of the users. Comfort has a very important impact on the productivity in office buildings. Since the energy costs represent a small part of the total costs in a tertiary building, the first aim of the ventilation systems is to ensure comfortable conditions.

REFERENCES

europa.eu.int/comm/energy_transport/en/lpi_lv_en1.html

Brightman, H. S. and Moss, N. (2001) 'Sick building syndrome studies and the compilation of normative and comparative values' in Spengler, J. D., Samet J. M. and McCarthy, J. F. (eds) *Indoor Air Quality Handbook*, McGraw-Hill, New York

BS 5760-23 *Reliability of Systems Equipment and Components, Part 23: Whole Life Costing*

BS ISO 15686 *Buildings and Constructed Assets: Service Life Planning*

DeMeo, E. A. and Galdo, J. F. (1997) *Renewable Energy Technologies Characterizations*, US Department of Energy, Washington, D.C.

EC (European Commission) (2001) *Green Paper: Towards a European Strategy for the Security of Energy Supply*, EC, Brussels

Fisk, W. J. (2001) 'Estimates of potential nationwide productivity and health benefits from better indoor environments: an update', in Spengler, J. D., Samet J. M. and McCarthy, J. F. (eds) *Indoor Air Quality Handbook*, McGraw-Hill, New York

Fisk, W. J. and Rosenfeld, A. H. (1997) 'Estimates of improved productivity and health from better indoor environments', *Indoor Air*, vol 7, pp158–172

Hanssen, S. O. (2000) *Evaluation of Association between Indoor Air Climate, Wellbeing and Productivity*, Healthy Buildings 2000, Espoo, Finland

Lee, H., Oliveira-Martins, J. and van der Mensbrugghe, D. (1994) *The OECD Green Model: An Updated Review*. Working Paper no 97. OECD Development Centre, Issy-les-Moulineaux, France

Lomborg, B. (2001) *The Skeptical Environmentalist*, Cambridge University Press, Cambridge

Martin, A. and Fitzsimmons, J. (2000) *Making Natural Ventilation Work*, Guidance Note GN 7/2000, BSRIA

Pr EN (Project of European Norm) 13779 (2003) *Ventilation for Non-residential Buildings: Performance Requirements for Ventilation and Room Conditioning Systems*, ISO, Geneva

Wargocki, P., Krupicz, P., Szczecinsk, A., Fanger, P. O. and Clausen, G. (1999) 'Perceived air quality SBS-like symptoms and productivity in an office at two pollution loads', Proceedings of Indoor Air, June 30–July 5, 2002, Monterey, Canada, pp131–136

Wargocki, P., Wyon, D. P. and Fanger, P. O. (2003) *Productivity is Affected by the Air Quality in Offices*, Fourth International Symposium on HVAC, 9–11 October, Beijing

WHO (World Health Organization) (1997) *Health and Environment in Sustainable Development*, WHO, Geneva

Index